LEAP

Adweek and Brandweek Books are designed to present interesting, insightful books for the general business reader and for professionals in the worlds of media, marketing, and advertising.

These are innovative, creative books that address the challenges and opportunities of these industries, written by leaders in the business. Some of our writers head their own companies, others have worked their way up to the top of their field in large multinationals. But they share a knowledge of their craft and a desire to enlighten others.

We hope readers will find these books as helpful and inspiring as *Adweek, Brandweek,* and *Mediaweek* magazines.

Published

Disruption: Overturning Conventions and Shaking Up the Marketplace, Jean-Marie Dru

Under the Radar: Talking to Today's Cynical Consumer, Jonathan Bond and Richard Kirshenbaum

Truth, Lies and Advertising: The Art of Account Planning, Jon Steel

Hey, Whipple, Squeeze This: A Guide to Creating Great Ads, Luke Sullivan

Eating the Big Fish: How Challenger Brands Can Compete Against Brand Leaders, Adam Morgan

Warp-Speed Branding: The Impact of Technology on Marketing, Agnieszka Winkler

Creative Company: How St. Luke's Became "the Ad Agency to End All Ad Agencies," Andy Law

Another One Bites the Grass: Making Sense of International Advertising, Simon Anholt

Attention! How to Interrupt, Yell, Whisper and Touch Consumers, Ken Sacharin

The Peaceable Kingdom: Building a Company without Factionalism, Fiefdoms, Fear, and Other Staples of Modern Business, Stan Richards

Getting the Bugs Out: The Rise, Fall, and Comeback of Volkswagen in America, David Kiley

The Do-It-Yourself Lobotomy: Open Your Mind to Greater Creative Thinking, Tom Monahan

Beyond Disruption: Changing the Rules in the Marketplace, Jean-Marie Dru

And Now a Few Laughs From Our Sponsor: The Best of Fifty Years of Radio Commercials, Larry Oakner

Sixty Trends in Sixty Minutes, Sam Hill

LEAP

A Revolution in Creative Business Strategy

Bob Schmetterer

AN ADWEEK BOOK

JOHN WILEY & SONS, INC.

For Stacy

Contents

INTRODUCTION   **Why Leap?**   ix

CHAPTER 1   **Tales of a Left-Brain/Right-Brain Thinker**   1

CHAPTER 2   **Creative Business Ideas**   15

CHAPTER 3   **Creativity at the Top**   33

CHAPTER 4   **The Creative Corporate Culture**   49

CHAPTER 5   **Creativity at the Heart of Business Strategy**   71

CHAPTER 6   **Do You Know What Business You Are In?**   91

CHAPTER 7   **The End of Advertising . . .
the Beginning of Something New**   137

CHAPTER 8   **The Entertainment Factor**   159

CHAPTER 9   **A Structure for Creative Thinking**   183

CHAPTER 10   **Make the Leap**   217

Website   222

Acknowledgments   223

Notes   226

Credits   231

Index   234

About the Author   242

INTRODUCTION: WHY LEAP?

This is a book about Creative Business Ideas™.

These words do not necessarily trip off the tongue. And there are those who might suggest that "creative" and "business" are as unnatural a combination as "business" and "ideas." I can understand that. Most often, business thinking is based only in numbers, research, analysis, and logic. These are comfortable staples of predictability for business-trained minds and corporate decision makers. And for risk avoidance in general. Creativity is for the artists and dreamers, poets and ad people. It is fine to support business decisions with creative advertising, but not to have creativity be core to business thinking and business strategy.

This book is going to show you that there is another way. Before you have turned the last page, I think you will not only be surprised by the excitement and potential of creative thinking about business strategy, you will also be determined to borrow some of the solutions we have developed and learned from others and try them within your own organization.

These may sound like the words of a proverbial ad man. They are not. They are not because I am not.

What I may be is a 1960s idealist who found himself in a business—advertising—where outsiders believe ideals do not matter. They could not be more wrong. Over the years, I have found myself surrounded by like-minded people who have a passion for finding out deep truths about superior products and businesses and presenting them to the public in the most creative of ways for the good of all. Our frustrations stemmed not from a disbelief in the worth of our work, but from the limitations of our knowledge. We were like gifted physicians who were hired for our first-aid skills (in our case, making funny or emotional TV commercials). Certainly important, but it did not let us get down to the basics of the problem. Then we had a breakthrough: We needed to become our clients' partners in the deepest sense. We needed to dive into business strategy in the most creative of ways, not simply respond to whatever symptoms were deemed in need of immediate care. Only after we were sure we understood what our clients—not just our clients' consumers—were about would we set off to create solutions.

The difference is enormous. It is like investigative journalism . . . when the subject wants you to know everything. It is like medicine . . . when the patient cooperates completely. It is like detective work . . . when no one is standing in your way.

It is, in short, the most exciting and productive and honorable (and, okay, profitable) way I know to spend my waking hours. It is about wisdom and magic and the leap in between. It engages my left brain, my right brain, and my life experience. It demands that I set aside all the pat answers and approach new problems with humility, an open mind, and an insatiable appetite for knowledge.

And, on a regular basis, it delivers the thrill of discovery. It is about taking research, instinct, and originality and watching them come together with such force that the room practically vibrates. It is about hoping to get from A to B . . . and leaping miles ahead, to M.

If you are up for that kind of challenge, engagement, and achievement, you are in the right place. Because in these pages, I have laid out the practical experience and the tools that we need to transform our businesses and to transform the relationships between ourselves as clients and agencies.

Fifty-three percent of the companies on the Fortune 500 list in 1980 are no longer in business.[1]

Creative business thinking and Creative Business Ideas—let's call them CBIs—might have saved lots of them. Because the whole point of CBIs is to jump-start groundbreaking ideas—ideas that not only sell products and establish brands, but, more important, transform entire companies and categories. It is a tall order. It is not something you see every day—at least not yet. But look hard and you will find CBIs alive and well around the world. For example,

- In Argentina, a real estate developer wanted an ad campaign to promote a new project. Creative thinkers at an ad agency thought it would be a better creative business idea to build a bridge with the millions budgeted for advertising. Not a figurative bridge—a literal one. Imagine the reaction.

- Volvo had built its automobile business on a single idea: safety. How to announce to the world that the carmaker had added new values to its brand and was not the same old boringly safe Volvo? Not an ad campaign. Instead, a "Revolvolution" in its business and marketing strategy.

- Until Frank Perdue came along, the chicken business was a commodity business. Now it's a branded business. His.

- A South American confectioner was watching sales drop. So it launched an ongoing contest that gave children the opportunity to create their own business ideas in the form of candy. Sweet success.

- A Swedish paint consortium wanted to increase sales. It did . . . but not with an ad campaign—with a hit TV show.

- Nokia wanted to broaden its appeal to mobile users in Europe beyond its ad campaign. The answer was the first pan-European interactive multimedia game.

Though some of these CBIs were the work of our global agency, Euro RSCG Worldwide, we are not the only ones focused on creating ideas that take a company's business strategy light-years beyond its CEO's dreams. Some brilliantly led companies have done it.

What makes Euro RSCG different is that CBIs are now our global focus for our clients. They are what we shoot for. And, more often than not, what we deliver.

Some might suggest that writing a book in which I lay bare the essence of my business philosophy is insanely shortsighted. After all, if Creative Business Ideas are my agency's "secret sauce," why am I putting the formula out there for all to see?

Partly because, after more than 30 years in the advertising business, I am convinced that the best ideas in advertising and communication have never been produced—they were killed either internally or externally because they were looked at as mere advertising ideas, not business ideas. I would like to help reduce the number of fatalities. That would be good for us all.

It is also partly because all the clients I have ever known have started by saying they want great creative thinking. If everyone wants creative thinking, why are they not getting it? Within these pages lies the answer.

I also believe that the people in the advertising industry, the people who get paid to think creatively about communications and advertising, are better equipped than anyone else to bring creative thinking to business strategy. Favoritism, yes, but it is based in fact.

Finally, I plead guilty to having a strong vision of where our industry needs to go. Not only do I log a quarter of a million miles annually talking passionately to the people within our network, I went public years ago. I have repeatedly spoken out, pleading with both our clients and others within our industry to ignite a revolution in creative thinking, to find the twenty-first-century version of the creative "book" of ads and "reel" of TV commercials, and to redefine the agency/client relationship for the times in which we live. Connect the creative and business worlds, instill the magic of creativity into the very fabric and nature of business itself, and we can create the future. And what an exciting and rewarding future it will be.

What you are about to read is based in theory—theory that is richly supported by success story after success story. The theory, I promise you, is written in plain English. There will be no business school mumbo jumbo here. The success stories? They are, I think, irresistible. And compelling. Because if there is one thing on which everyone in business can agree, it is that there is nothing quite as satisfying as success and the wonder of creating it.

Chapter 1
Tales of a Left-Brain/Right-Brain Thinker

"Ideas are only the beginning," adults like to tell precocious youngsters. "Ideas are a dime a dozen."

Easy enough for successful adults to say—they've already climbed a mountain or two. But when you're a 19-year-old kid, born in the Bronx and raised in a small New Jersey town, and you're not rich and you're about to be married, good ideas that you can put to practical use are hard to come by.

It wasn't that I lacked imagination. Like many who grew up in the 1960s, I spent a lot of time inside my own head, trying to figure out what was good and true and worthy. In my case, that project was perhaps made more difficult by my awareness, from a very early age, that I had both left-brain and right-brain interests. Part of me was attracted to a creative, aesthetic way of life—to music and art and fashion and design and writing. And another, seemingly equal part craved logic and order and ideas based in reason.

After a very early first marriage, I had less time to ponder anything. And when I became a father, at age 20, I really had to scramble. I worked all day and went to college at night, studying liberal arts and sociology. It was a tough slog; at the rate I was going, I calculated it would take me nine years to get the right degrees.

When I was 22, we had our second child. Reality and practicality loomed even larger. I recalibrated my dreams: Another 14 years of night school and I'll have enough advanced degrees to be a high school guidance counselor. I'll make $12,000 a year.

Enter the wise man.

Well, that's how it works in the myth anyway. In my case, I happened to run into a salesman. As it happened, he sold printer's ink, but he explained that the product really didn't matter—he just loved to sell. "Do something you love," he told me. "The success and money will follow."

Simple enough. But what did I love? I mean, really love? Well, if I cut through intellectual pretension and financial ambition, the answer was cars. Beginning at age 10, I learned everything I could about them. I memorized my father's car magazines. I knew automotive statistics the way some kids know batting averages. And when the new models were about to come out, I would run to the dealerships just to see how the cars looked under their thick canvas covers.

At this point, according to myth, something else is supposed to enter: synchronicity. That is, now that you have taken the first step on the correct path, you get information that supports your choice and takes you to the next level. In my case, it was another random event—a classified ad for a job in the parts department of British Motor Corporation. This was the company that made the MG and Austin-Healey, those beautiful, classic sports cars so beloved by American automobile buffs. Okay, so it was the parts division, working with computer inventory control systems. No matter. It was cars. I went for an interview and got the job.

EUREKA! AN EARLY CBI

A year later, I had a revelation so stunningly obvious you have to wonder why nobody came up with it earlier: Sports cars, in and of themselves, were not enough for those who bought them. They wanted accessories to make them more personal and authentic. And so they ordered wood steering wheels, racing mirrors, chrome luggage racks, and more. We didn't make or sell those accessories; we just let customers order from a bunch of small specialty companies. But as I saw it, we could do more. We could sell those accessories through our dealer organization. And we could do one more thing: We could create a Special Edition MG model that came fully accessorized. We could expand the horizon of our business.

So there we have it: A 22-year-old whose education consists of a continuing bout with night school gets an idea. It's not a trillion-dollar idea, but it does contain an underlying concept that I have returned to over and over again: What business was I in? Specifically, was I in the business of selling parts to car dealers, or was I in the business of discovering what car owners wanted and, whatever it was, getting it for them? If this were a business school case study, the question would be, "Am I in marketing or manufacturing?"

I WARNED YOU . . .

Back in 1965, I was simply in the enthusiasm business. I had an idea I really liked, and I wanted to see if it would work. I told my boss, who liked it enough to ask me to write a proposal. Shortly thereafter, I found myself in the office of Graham Whitehead, head of British Motors in America. He was the classic Brit: dashing, mustache, RAF demeanor. . . .

His office had no papers, only antiques. Naturally, he was neither chatty nor welcoming.

"Tell Graham your idea," my boss said at last.

I blurted it out.

"Very interesting," Graham said. "But I don't see how we could do it."

"The challenge is to coordinate with accessories suppliers," I said. "I think we can do that—we're sort of doing it already."

Graham warmed ever so slightly. "Just remember—I warned you," he said, in the most backhanded way of signaling approval I had ever heard.

Well, the 1966 MGB-GT Special sports cars were a terrific success: We sold every car we built. If we had any problem, it was supply; we had so many orders that the little shops that made wood-rim steering wheels and luggage racks couldn't keep up with demand. We had to go as far as Australia to find a supplier.

If this were a business school case, we'd be looking for the lesson here. And I imagine it would be something about using the logistics competency of a parts department. I see a different lesson. The guy who had the idea (me) loved the product. Knew everything about it. Was buoyed by the support of others, but would have tried to make it happen anyway.

BEFORE YOU LEAP: Understand that passion is the starting point of all great creative ideas. If you are looking to make your mark by creating something new, make sure you are in a field that totally fascinates and captivates you.

Remember, too, success does not mean you become vice president for Great Ideas overnight. In my case, I followed up my triumph by continuing to work on computer-controlled inventory systems. And I kept on going to night school. The big news was that I switched my major from sociology to psychology.

LEFT BRAIN MEETS RIGHT BRAIN

Then something interesting happened. At school, I needed to choose a couple of electives to finish my degree. I chose Life Drawing and started spending an evening a week sketching nude models. My other class that term was Market Research. The conflict? For me, there was none. In what I now regard as an inflection point, I saw that creativity was the connection between art and market research—and between psychology and my job. For the first time, I sensed I could use my left and right brain in a harmonious way to do worthy, useful work.

Around this time, Volvo Cars called me about a job. What did I know about Volvo? Mostly, that my father had recently bought one because "It's the safest car on the road, and it will last forever." I liked that high-minded appeal, so I went there, ostensibly to start a computer inventory system. But my officemate was doing market research—which seemed much more interesting. "Nine of ten Volvos ever sold are still on the road," he mumbled one day. "How do I prove that for our advertising?" I showed him how. Soon enough, I was spotted by a brilliant vice president of marketing named Jim LaMarre, and he asked me to become director of marketing research. It was 1968. I was 24, fearless, and bulletproof.

Part of my job was to update our ad agency on who was buying Volvos and why. Other marketing research directors liked to present decks loaded with numbers; I liked to tell stories. I felt I was the ombudsman for consumers because, after all, the knowledge of what will work resides somewhere in the consumer experience. In the late 1960s and early 1970s, Volvo had a riveting consumer profile: More than 80 percent of its buyers were college graduates. Which put them in an interesting political sphere. If you were a Volvo owner and lived on the East Coast, you were on the left. If you lived on the West Coast, you were on the right. And if you lived in the middle, Volvo was probably the last car you would think of driving.

I found all this customer information fascinating. I talked about it all the time with the agency people. Which leads me to yet another lesson:

> **BEFORE YOU LEAP:** Recognize that sharing information leads to trust. And trust, as we shall soon see, is the first and most necessary building block of creative collaboration and creative thinking.

After taking a course in marketing, I did what I could never have imagined doing a few years before. I signed up for an MBA in it. A child of the '60s turns. But a Young Turk (as they used to call us) with the beginning of a reputation for creative thinking going for an advanced degree is often a hot property. I soon had three job offers—from Volkswagen, from a New York City research firm, and from a very new and small advertising agency, which now had the Volvo account. Marvin Sloves, one of the founders of that agency, was a wonderfully intelligent and persuasive man, and we had come to know each other during a series of Volvo meetings.

ANYTHING BUT AN ACCOUNT EXECUTIVE

I asked myself: All other things being equal, where can I do something that matters, something that suits my '60s sense of social responsibility? And I kept coming back to Volvo, a company with social responsibility in its DNA. Sweden should not be able to support a car company—the entire country has just 8 million people, about the size of New York City. And yet it had two: Volvo and Saab. Both emphasized people values. Volvo cared about saving lives. A lightbulb went on when I realized that if it weren't for advertising, Americans would not know about Volvo. So I told the agency I would take the job I never dreamed I would. . . . I was going to work in an ad agency. An agency called Scali McCabe Sloves.

My first order of business was to impress upon my new boss that I had no intention of continuing with only car companies. "No Volvo," I insisted to Marvin Sloves. "Start me on another client. And please, please don't ever call me an account executive." My perception was that the account guys just carry around the bag with everyone else's ideas in them. Marvin said, "Don't worry, Bob, you can be anything you want and have any title but mine. I'll teach you style and you'll teach me substance, and before long . . . you'll be farting through velvet!"

I realized, more than anything, I wanted to bring the voice of people, of consumers, of real-life experience to this brilliant group of young creative people. I did not want to sell ads to clients, I wanted to sell ideas to creative thinkers who could transform them into something that would Make the World a Better Place. Another generation would call this "account planning," and it would become the center of creativity in London and Los Angeles and New York. But for me, it was just the boy of the '60s still wanting to do social good . . . although it was now 1971.

That is how I found myself standing on a chicken farm in Salisbury, Maryland, listening to a curious-looking man named Frank Perdue tell us about the excellence of his flock. He impressed on us that his chickens were better than all the others, and that meant he could charge a premium—a penny a pound more. He was very credible and his speech tough but polished. It should have been considering how often he had given it. . . . Perdue had talked to every agency in New York in search of one that would take his puny $200,000 ad budget and help him on his way to the poultry—and creative—hall of fame.[1]

Perdue talked nonstop. Very quickly, we learned all about chickens—and all about Frank Perdue. As loving as he was toward his chickens in their brief, nine-week stay on earth, he was just that demanding of his employees. Woe to the truck driver who was 10 minutes late taking Frank's chickens to market. As we watched this remarkable man, an idea began to form—an idea that would eventually make Perdue's fortune. You know it, everyone knows it: "It takes a tough man to make a tender chicken." It was the result of understanding deeply all that Perdue and his company believed in and all that consumers would find good and real. It was brilliantly written by Ed McCabe and art-directed by Sam Scali. It was simply a great advertising idea. It was the beginning of an entirely new way of thinking creatively about even the most mundane of businesses.

Before You Leap:

- Listen, listen, listen, and learn. No advertising executive knows as much about a client's business as the client does. But it is our job to unlock that knowledge and the DNA of the company and discover how it can be used to creatively connect consumers to brands. Become a power listener.
- And know this: There is no such thing as a mundane product or mundane business. Only mundane ideas.

One might marvel at what a clever agency we were to make such groundbreaking advertising for Frank Perdue. And there is no shortage of agency people who will step forward to take credit for building companies like Perdue into giant brands. But who are the real heroes? The clients are! They are the brave ones who create new and better products with no assurance the public will want them. They are the ones who seek great creative partners with whom to make magic. They are the ones who demand courageous creativity from their advertising agencies. And later, they are the ones who never say, "That's good enough."

Before You Leap: Realize that in advertising, as in any good relationship, it always takes two. Clients and agencies. One can't lead, one can't follow. Both have to pull equally and together. Then, magic happens.

A CREATIVE REVOLUTION

For 13 years at Scali, from 1971 to 1984, I worked with a legion of brilliant colleagues and a stream of great clients: Castrol, Conair, Continental Airlines, Data General, Maxell, Nikon, Olivetti, Perdue, Pioneer, Playboy, Sharp, Singer, Sperry Corporation, Texas Air, Volvo, Warner Amex Cable. Creative colleagues included Ray Alban, Lars Anderson, Ron Berger, Larry Cadman, Earl Cavanah, John Danza, George Dusenbury, Mike Drazen, Frank Fleizach, Bruce Fierstein, Geoffrey Frost, Ed McCabe, Scott Miller, Ray Myers, Tom Nathan, Bob Needleman, Joe O'Neill, Jim Peretti, Bob Reitzfield, Sam Scali, Joe Schindelman, Tom Thomas, Rodney Underwood, Bob Wilvers—and many, many more extremely talented associates.

It was a wonderful time to be in advertising. The 1960s and 1970s saw a creative revolution in our business, a shift from the large-scale, quantitatively driven decision-making agencies to advertising that was more human, more real, with more humor. A small number of agencies at the forefront—Doyle Dane Bernbach, Lois Holland Callaway, Papert Koenig Lois, Jack Tinker & Partners—in turn spawned a whole new set of agencies, including Scali, Ally & Gargano, Della Femina, Wells Rich Greene, and Chiat/Day.

The revolution gave us permission to be more creative, and the new agencies helped to shape the future of advertising creativity: DDB's work on Volkswagen; Wells Rich Greene's work for great brands like Alka-Seltzer, American Motors Corporation, and Braniff International Airways; Ally & Gargano's work for MCI, Federal Express, and Dunkin' Donuts. For the first time, clients came to understand and believe that creative thinking could be a superior strategy.

During those years, I also had three different experiences of what agency life is like—working in a small agency, a midsize one, and eventually a big one. They all had the same name: Scali McCabe Sloves. In 1974 *Advertising Age* named Scali Agency of the Year,[2] and I moved from vice president marketing research director to senior vice president client services to executive vice president and managing director. When Ogilvy & Mather bought Scali in 1977 to start a second international network, I was tapped to become COO and to run the entire U.S. agency. My early marriage ended after 13 years, and I was single and successful in New York City. I spent increased time with my two sons and started seeing more of the world and enjoying the energy of New York nightlife in the early 1980s. Studio 54 glowed, and for the next seven years I continued to grow and enjoy the wonder of the creative brilliance of great clients and creative thinkers with great ideas.

Despite changing times and my changing roles, the learning only became clearer.

> **BEFORE YOU LEAP:** Understand these three things:
> - There are great products, made by wonderful people who care deeply, and it is no social sin helping them become better known. It is good and important work.
> - Creative advertising is not made only by famous advertising talents. More often, it is made by a wonderful collaboration of people who deeply understand the client's business and who are passionate about what they do.
> - The legendary film producer Dino De Laurentiis used to say, "America is only 50 percent of the world."[3] Though 50 percent still seems excessive, it is imperative to reach out to the rest of the world.

Suddenly I was 39. Ed Ney, chairman of Young & Rubicam, convinced me I should be running a significant agency, one with global reach. Y&R had a plan to build a second global network by creating a joint venture with French advertising giant Eurocom. They would put together all of the Marsteller agencies Y&R owned with all of the Havas agencies Eurocom owned and call it HCM. It was the beginning of the real globalization of advertising. They wanted a president and CEO worldwide who had come from neither organization. I signed on.

BEYOND MADISON AVENUE

In the fall of 1984 I left Scali McCabe Sloves and began a journey into the "real" world of advertising. It was a wonderful, eye-opening experience. Another inflection point. The realization that the world of creativity is really that—and that what was happening in London and Paris and Brazil was a whole lot more exciting than what was happening in New York. It was exciting to work with international clients like Danone, Peugeot, and Air France.

A couple years and one merger later, I realized I had had a great and transforming short-term experience, but that the situation had the potential to be very unrewarding over the long term. The experience also helped to crystallize something for me: I knew that I wanted to start my own agency, but I wanted to do it right. I resigned and, after 10 years of New York bachelorhood, proposed to a young producer named Stacy Chiarello, the love of my life. I took my first summer off since high school to spend at our home on Martha's Vineyard and hoped the phone wouldn't ring. But it did.

FIVE PRINCIPALS, NO CLIENTS

The man on the phone was Ron Berger. In 1986, Ron and two of his colleagues from Ally & Gargano, Tom Messner and Barry Vetere, had joined with Wally Carey Jr. to found Messner Vetere Berger Carey. Ron, Tom, and Barry had not only shared responsibility for creative direction at Ally & Gargano, they were also central members of the landmark Tuesday Team, the marketing and advertising engine behind Ronald Reagan's 1984 reelection campaign.

Soon enough, we agreed I would join as president and my name would be added to the banner after some months. So there I was, in a new agency with five principals and no major clients and no immediate prospects of generating any major income—all five of us had agreed to draw no salary for the first two years. What was so enticing? A flat organization, with no CEO. An entirely new business model, more like a law firm than a boutique, where we could add partners as we wished. A principal on every account. No media-buying department—we would subcontract that. Strategic planning was more important; we'd burrow into each client's business so deeply that we could be strategic partners in the truest sense.

All was not right with the industry in the later 1980s, and my partners and I represented an alternative. It was a time of acquisitions and mergers for big agencies, and the astronomical prices being paid for agencies had completely disintegrated whatever trust clients and agencies once shared. The commissions agencies made on media buys only fueled the perception of greed. And clients hated it when consolidation led to turnover and people on their account left. There was an interest in agencies that offered something different. We would show them we were different by putting a partner on every account and making clients part of the strategic process. Above all, we would always do what was right for the client.

Being different came naturally to us. There was no other agency we really wanted to model ourselves after. In our view, those agencies that did truly groundbreaking creative work—and were rewarded for it—had a tendency to look to the past when trying to get new work. They wanted to see what they had done and then try to replicate it. To us, that kind of thinking represented a step backward. We wanted to look forward to where we might go and take our clients with us, not back to where we had been.

NEW TIMES, NEW TOOLS

As we grew, our offices even looked different from those of our competitors. We had a computer on every desk. We were, I think, the first agency to use e-mail. We certainly didn't have to; there were only 10 of us—we could have yelled across the room! And we were the first to insist that our clients get wired, too. Our mantra was communication, lots of it. And speed. We liked research, but we didn't live and die by it; our goal was to help clients move their businesses forward.

The first major client that gave us the chance to show our stuff was MCI. Tom Messner had helped create its original and brilliant position at Ally & Gargano. But times had changed. Whereas long-distance phone service had been a commodity, MCI wanted to be a brand.[4] We came to the strategic conclusion that choosing a long-distance provider is a lot closer to voting in an election than it is to making an outright purchase. In this case, the candidates were three phone carriers, and the incumbent was AT&T.

We created advertising for MCI as if it were a candidate for office, tailoring our commercials to respond to each new spot from AT&T. We hired a political strategist and a pollster to work with us: Roger Ailes, the famed Republican strategist, and Peter Hart, the exceptional Democratic pollster. We conducted monthly polls, and we shifted our creative based on the findings. But things really didn't start to heat up until we shifted the discussion to savings, with advertising like the electronic board in Times Square that ticked away, showing the billions of dollars Americans were saving with MCI. That really blew the client away—it was an entirely different way of looking at its business.

Soon MCI had such a solid relationship with its customers that it could offer what I would consider the first long-distance brand ever: Friends & Family. That invocation of intimacy was possible for MCI. For AT&T? No way.

This account was significant for another reason: It defined the way we work best. That is, in rooms totally dedicated to the single problem of the particular client. I am talking war rooms. Lots of "windows" of research and information on the walls. Lots of oversized blank paper on stands. And then lots of scribbled notes, odd facts, and first-draft perceptions filling those pages. It is an exciting environment: a literal storehouse of knowledge, with a concentration of energy that feeds on itself. Very much what you would expect to find in a political campaign. Not something you would imagine seeing in an ad agency—at least not then.

Winning the MCI account was a long shot. We couldn't compete on size; we had to be smarter. Winning the account gave us our first major client. We had competed with intelligence and with courage. Some part of that courage came from a sense of financial security. Even before the MCI win, we had said yes to a suitor that had approached us. The French company RSCG wanted us to sell them an interest in the agency. For five fortysomething ad execs, the idea of financial stability was a no-brainer. Not for ourselves . . . for the idea of the agency. We would have the freedom to invest in new technology and pursue new ways of pitching business. The larger benefit was that, right from the start, we could be an international player. It was time to play ball on a global scale.

THE BIG LEAGUES

A few years passed. We were reunited with clients from our former lives (yes, including Volvo). We connected with new ones, among them Nasdaq and New Balance. By age nine, we had grown to 16 partners and 350 other really talented people, and a lot of people had written about us. *Fortune* called us the new breed of agency, lean and fast . . . with partners focused on clients' businesses.[5] We had built the agency on a different platform, and that was enabling us to do better work. It was a platform in which everything and everyone is accessible, everyone has access to the same information, and everyone is empowered to make things happen.

> **BEFORE YOU LEAP:** Level the place. If you knock down walls (literally) and do away with doors and traditional hierarchies, you will foster an environment and a culture that promotes creative collaboration on the highest level—and allows for greater and more courageous thinking.

Our nontraditional structure meant we had more insights about our clients' businesses and opportunities. We had more insightful strategies. And we had more clients who had come to believe that as their partners, we could play a deep and meaningful role in their future success.

CARTE BLANCHE

We merged once more, this time with Eurocom (the other France-based agency group from my HCM days) and its New York agency Della Femina McNamee, and became Messner Vetere Berger McNamee Schmetterer (MVBMS) Euro RSCG. A couple of years later I was asked to become chairman and CEO of Euro RSCG

Worldwide. It hadn't been on my list of things to do, but it was 1997 and I had this passionate belief that we were living in an incredibly interesting and exciting time. How could anyone deny that? The explosion of the Internet, the impact of the digital revolution, globalization (and the idea that we are all living within one degree of separation), the deregulation and privatization of state-owned media and industries, consolidation in virtually every industry . . . all of it spelled enormous opportunity. I guess I'm still in the enthusiasm business.

My French partner, chairman and CEO of Havas Alain de Pouzilhac, told me, "Bob, we need you to lead Euro RSCG and make it a truly global network . . . and you have a white card." I thought for a moment and understood: *carte blanche.* I played that card early and often in an attempt to communicate better, faster. We were now a broad-based global services company of more than 10,000 people worldwide, with divisions for advertising, direct marketing, interactive, public relations, and promotions. This platform of agencies could become the launching pad in a major way for what we had been experimenting with at MVBMS years earlier. On a much broader scale, we could make clients part of the strategic process. And we had the resources to execute creative ideas in any form, in any media, anywhere in the world.

We began to hold managers' meetings every 100 days to get people talking and to reinforce that vision. We invited creative thinkers to join us. One was Thomas Krens, director of the Guggenheim Museum. He had a completely radical concept of museums and had brilliantly applied breakthrough creative thinking to that world. It added fuel to a concept that was beginning to gel in my own left-brain/right-brain mind: that of harnessing creativity to direct business strategy, not just communication strategy.

"Creative Business Ideas" were just a few meetings away. The penny was about to drop.

Chapter 2
Creative Business Ideas

Franklin Delano Roosevelt is said to have remarked that if he could put just one book in every Russian home, it would be the Sears, Roebuck catalog.[1] He had the right idea. American products have universal appeal. And in countries where people are said to hate the United States, they have even greater power. Black-market Levi's, Elvis recordings, and other iconic products of American pop culture probably had as much to do with the fall of communism as Ronald Reagan's willingness to outspend the USSR's military budget. Even now in Afghanistan we see the markets flooded with American goods—or knockoffs with quaint misspellings.

But it's not generic products that people crave. It's brands.

"Brand! Brand!! Brand!!! That's the message . . . for the late '90s and beyond," says Tom Peters, the social thinker who has been studying business trends for decades.[2]

Also obsessed with brands is Tom Wolfe, the journalist turned novelist, who still uses the tools of journalism in his writing: "Brand names, tastes in clothes and furniture, manners, the way people treat children, servants, or their superiors, are important clues to an individual's expectations. This is something else that I am criticized for, mocked for, ridiculed for. I take some solace in the fact that the leading critic of Balzac's day used to say the same about Balzac's fixation on furniture. You can learn the name of more arcane pieces of furniture reading Balzac than you can reading a Sotheby's catalogue."[3]

How is it that brand names have become so important?

Well, it certainly didn't happen by accident. Every day we are bombarded by messages telling us that our lives will be lesser if we don't run out and buy Brand X. (In the case of our clients' brands, of course, it's true!)

Television viewers must sit (or click) through so many commercials that they might well think TV was invented primarily to sell products—and they would be mostly right. Magazine readers are confronted by so many ads that they might conclude that the articles are only there to keep the advertisements from fighting. On the

The problem is too many of us follow the structures, the disciplines that have worked before. We play it safe. Our clients give us new products to sell. New cars with incredible innovations. New drugs that will change our lives and the lives of our loved ones. So why do so many of us take the "new" and drop it into an "old" structure? Let's do a 30-second TV spot! Let's do some outdoor!
—Israel Garber, Euro RSCG MVBMS, New York

names of theaters and stadiums, on scoreboards and sidelines, on T-shirts and shoes and hotel keys—just about everywhere one looks, some giant corporation is pushing its name.

The reality is that advertising is ubiquitous, insistent, insidious; its music is the soundtrack of our lives, its tag lines are fodder for our daily conversation.

And we have worked hard to make it that way.

In our fervent desire to connect with the consumer, all marketers have a common goal: Find a competitive advantage. We are all on a quest to uncover what we used to call a *unique selling proposition*—a fact about the product or a way of communicating its virtues that is drop-dead compelling. When an agency discovers that idiosyncratic fact, the executives behind the genius commercials are lauded as marketing gurus, philosophers, or seers. Their tenets become magazine think pieces—or even books. Clients sell more products.

And now that the noise level in our brand-name culture has risen to deafening levels, we have all taken to chanting the same brand-value mantra.

IF ONLY WE COULD BUILD SOLID AND LASTING BRAND VALUE, WE SAY TO OURSELVES, IF ONLY WE COULD JOIN THE RANKS OF THE WORLD'S MOST VALUABLE GLOBAL BRANDS OR MAKE ONE OF THE TOP 100 OR TOP 500 LISTS, LIKE MICROSOFT AND INTEL AND CISCO HAVE, THEN EVERYTHING WOULD BE OKAY.

But wait a minute: An Apple campaign brilliantly uses real people to discredit Microsoft's superiority. A rival manufacturer has a chip that it claims may even outperform the Intel microprocessor. And although Cisco was once the darling of high-tech analysts, its three-year price chart looks like the electrocardiogram of someone who has settled into deep unconsciousness.

How do brands rise? Why do they tumble?

From my seat in an ad agency, I would say: Look first to the product itself. Is it endlessly being improved—or is innovation a low priority?

From seats in other offices (in the executive suites of American companies) you might get a different answer. And it would, I'd bet, be a one-word response: *advertising.*

And both the advertising exec and the corporate CEO would be right.

CHASING CREATIVITY

In my more than 30 years in advertising across hundreds of companies and brands, every single client I have ever met has expressed a desire for "great creative thinking," "great creative campaigns," and "great creative ideas." No one has ever said, "Hey, Bob, let's skip the creative stuff and get right to some straightforward ads and media plans." No one. Ever. They want creativity in all its forms: in data-based direct marketing, interactive marketing, and sales promotion as well as advertising. They want it in all communications and in their overall business. They want it in their own businesses and in their own lives.

If everyone wants great creative thinking, why are we not seeing more of it? Why is branding so very, very difficult?

In the advertising industry, the road to brilliance traditionally passed through a room in which a handful of creative people brainstormed until they came up with a "great" campaign. That path may have worked in the early days of advertising, when products did not have to fight for shelf space—or our attention—but now agencies must come up with ideas that go beyond advertising to add value to the client's business. At Euro RSCG Worldwide, we call those Creative Business Ideas (CBIs).

Why are CBIs so important that we are building the agency around them? Well, for one thing, because advertising agencies are no longer in the business of advertising.

The theory will come later. First, let me introduce you to Creative Business Ideas at work in the real world.

PROFITABLE INNOVATION: SIX TO LEARN FROM

Some of the following Creative Business Ideas come from my own personal experience, from agencies with which I have worked and people I have been fortunate enough to know; others are drawn from more general business knowledge. What these examples all have in common is a basis in nonlinear thinking. Without it, none of these ideas would ever have seen the light of day. . . .

A BRIDGE IN BUENOS AIRES

A few years ago, I met a couple of brilliant young partners of a small agency in Buenos Aires, Heymann/Bengoa/Berbari, who tried to create a commercial for a riverfront real estate development. They were talented and innovative, but no matter how hard they tried, they just could not convince themselves that an ad campaign would cut through the clutter and generate enough noise in the marketplace.

But while they were searching for alternatives, the creative team made an insightful, ingenious observation: They recognized that, unlike many of the world's major capitals, Buenos Aires had few landmarks. In fact, there was only one—this in a city of nearly 3 million people that covers some 77 square miles.

Instead of building an ad campaign, they decided to tell the client to build an instant landmark. The real estate development—which included offices, apartment buildings, shops, restaurants, and a hotel—was not located in a high-traffic area of town. It was out of the way, not so easy to get to. So the agency conceived the idea of building a footbridge so pedestrians would have easy access to the area. A bridge. Literally, a bridge across the river.

That is nonlinear creative thinking that goes from A to B to M. That is a huge creative leap.

So far, this is great creative thinking.

BUT IMPLICIT IN EVERY CREATIVE BUSINESS IDEA IS A QUESTION: HAVE YOU GONE AS FAR AS YOU CAN? CAN THIS BIG IDEA BE EVEN BIGGER?

In Buenos Aires, as it happened, the idea had one more leap: The bridge could be designed by a world-renowned architect. What did that mean? That it would become a focal point for tourists and residents alike. A must-see attraction. A destination in and of itself. It would be a tribute to the city's culture and people and pride. And, of course, this bridge would be a magnet, attracting people to the riverfront—and to the real estate development. The idea generated an enormous amount of free PR, airtime, and media attention. More than any ad campaign.

Building a city landmark instead of creating a bunch of ads and putting together a media buy? That is creative business thinking at a higher strategic level than simply executing an advertising campaign. It is a true Creative Business Idea.

SAFETY SELLS

Another example: Volvo Cars. The reason I am in advertising.

Quick quiz: Ask an American to describe, in one word, what he or she most associates with Volvo.

Donald Sutherland? (The veteran actor does the voice-overs for our Volvo commercials, which is a good thing to know if you're playing Trivial Pursuit, but it's not the answer most people would give.)

The answer is *safety*—a value that has become synonymous with the brand. Because of that association, Volvo has attained a position as one of the most potent brands in the world.

Today, safety is more than ever a primary consideration when buying a car. Checking out crash-test ratings is de rigueur for most buyers. But back in the late 1950s, when the first Volvo touched American soil, selling cars based on safety was considered a highly unmarketable idea.

Ford knew that. It had tried using safety features—padded dashboards and recessed steering wheels—as a selling point. The result? In 1956, Chevrolet outsold Ford by a wide margin. The experiment was a colossal failure. Hey, it was America in the 1950s—who cared about safety?

Enter Gunnar Engellau, the CEO of Volvo Cars at the time. In 1957, outside of the United States, Volvo was already considered a leader in safety innovations. Back in 1944, it had begun installing laminated windshields in all its vehicles to prevent flying shards of glass in the event of an accident. Some 15 years later, this became a legal requirement in the United States. Volvo also was already boasting a two-point diagonal safety belt. But that safety belt proved to have serious shortcomings. A colleague of Gunnar Engellau had been in an accident and was thrown from his car and seriously injured, despite the fact that he had been wearing the diagonal belt. That accident ignited a passion in Engellau that would ultimately shape the future of Volvo. As the man recruited to solve the problem remembers it, "Engellau called me up to his office and demanded a better solution. He was not the sort of person you say no to."[4]

That man was a brilliant engineer by the name of Nils Bohlin, who was then working in the Swedish aviation industry and would go on to become Volvo's head of safety engineering. By 1959, because of Engellau's passion for safety and his willingness to take a risk and make a leap that flew in the face of U.S. marketplace trends, Volvo became

the first car company anywhere to offer three-point seatbelts. Engellau's decision to build a car brand on safety is a Creative Business Idea that is still influencing Volvo's business strategy more than four decades later. And it proved the naysayers wrong: Safety does sell.

The three-point seat belt

EXPERIENCE BRANDING

Next case: theme parks. Imagine you are Walt Disney. How does a creator of animated characters come up with the idea to create a theme park? How does one make the mental leap from Snow White to roller coasters?

Disney was not obsessed with theme parks. He was obsessed with the idea of building the Disney brand. And a theme park was a way to create a brand experience. An amazing leap? A huge gamble? Absolutely.

Back then, Americans viewed amusement parks as seedy and low class. "Why do you want to build an amusement park?" Disney's wife asked. "They're so dirty." Walt replied, "[That's] just the point—mine won't be." His vision: "What I want Disneyland to be most of all is a happy place, a place where adults and children can experience together some of the wonders of life, of adventure, and feel better because of it."[5]

For nearly half a century now, that creative leap has been the driving force behind every extension of the Disney brand. Disney is not in the movie business or the theme park business or even the entertainment business. Disney is in the business of making people happy.

A Tough Act to Follow

And what about the Chicken Man? The first client I ever had in advertising.

Up until the early 1970s, if you walked into a market and wanted to buy a chicken, that is exactly what you got. Frank Perdue changed that with what people in my agency would call a world-class Creative Business Idea. His breakthrough idea: Take a commodity— chicken—and brand it.

This was not a marketing scheme. Perdue sincerely and passionately believed that his chickens were of a higher quality than others, and for that reason he believed he was entitled to charge a bit more per pound than everyone else in the business. But first he had to convince Americans of a radical proposition: Something you used to buy by the pound you would now buy by the brand. This was a radical, monumental creative leap. And with that leap, Frank Perdue did something that had never even occurred to anyone else: He created a marketplace in which all chickens are not created equal. It was not an advertising idea. It was a big Creative Business Idea.

It's Inside . . .

Another example, this time for the largest client I've ever worked with.

You know the Intel slogan? Look at your computer. Odds are it is right there: "Intel Inside®."

Talk about a difficult proposition! With chickens, at least you can see what you are buying. But imagine coming up with the idea to brand a tiny piece of technology—microprocessors—so deep inside the computer that the consumer never sees it. That is a big leap.

Like Perdue, Intel had a strong, even urgent, need to create desire in the hearts and minds of consumers for its product. MIS managers knew what microprocessors were; the average consumer didn't have a clue. The company had its work cut out for it: first to explain what its product line was all about and then to convince consumers that Intel microprocessors were the best available.

ULTIMATELY, WHAT INTEL ACHIEVED WAS EVEN MORE POWERFUL THAN JUST DIFFERENTIATING ITSELF FROM ITS COMPETITORS: IT CONVINCED CONSUMERS THAT WHAT WAS INSIDE THE COMPUTER WAS AS IMPORTANT AS, IF NOT MORE IMPORTANT THAN, THE BRAND NAME ON THE OUTSIDE. IT TURNED A COMMODITY INTO A BRAND.

Perdue branded chicken

That creative leap catapulted Intel from a little-known engineering company to one of the most recognized and valuable brand names in the world today. Not an advertising idea. A big Creative Business Idea.

MOBILE ENTERTAINMENT

In 1977 I took a ski trip with my boys to Courchevel in the French Alps. They brought along two fairly small, blue metal boxes with headphones. "Listen to this, Dad," they said. I did, and I couldn't believe what I was hearing. These small boxes would change music and define a generation. Consider the Walkman in the days before music started being burned on CDs and the portable tape player gave way to the CD Walkman. Notice the ubiquity of the name: No one calls this device "a portable stereo cassette player with miniature headphones." We call it a Walkman.

How did that happen? Again, through a brilliant piece of nonlinear thinking and a great creative leap. Many know the name Akio Morita, the founder of Sony. Lesser known is his cofounder, Masura Ibuka, the engineering counterpart to Morita's marketing genius. In 1979, in one part of the company, people were developing a new technology for portable cassette drives; in another, they were working on lightweight headphones for outdoor use. This was not proprietary technology—other companies were working on smaller headphones and portable cassette drives. However, only Sony had Masura Ibuka, the guy who made the creative leap and put the two together.[6]

When Ibuka approached Morita with the idea, it was in the form of a personal request—he wanted to put headphones on a portable stereo tape player so that he could listen to music without bothering people around him. Morita immediately saw something Ibuka had not: the potential for a new product that would change the way people consume music. He had long ago made the observation that young people loved music so much they would go to great lengths to take it with them, even to the point of lugging cumbersome portable stereos around. Now he would give them the ability to listen to that music anywhere and everywhere. This breakthrough solution, an industry first, would transform the marketplace. And it all came from the leap of putting together headphones and a portable tape player.

What these examples have in common is that they are all great creative leaps leading to business strategy. And they are all rooted in nonlinear thinking. One could not have arrived at any of these breakthrough ideas by following a strictly linear thought process.

BEFORE YOU LEAP:

- Toss out all your preconceptions and prejudices. Creative Business Ideas know no limits. They need not be connected to any traditional discipline within advertising or marketing. They could be as unusual as . . . building a bridge.
- Invent desire and be steadfast in your focus. Half a century ago, drivers were looking for sex appeal, not safety. What might consumers value tomorrow?
- Build "sense-ational" experiences. Create a world in which consumers can see, touch, smell, and taste your brand. Provide them with conversational currency in the form of new adventures and exposure to new ways of living and thinking.
- Color outside the lines. Turn a commodity into a brand. A brand into an experience. An experience into a connection.
- Let them know you are there. Not every brand can be seen, but they all can be heard.
- Pay attention to your own needs and desires and to those of people you know. If you would buy it, chances are lots of other people would, too.

BARRED FROM THE BOARDROOM

Today's world is not lacking in people really good at developing business strategy. There are plenty of smart people out there—solid strategic thinkers, even brilliant ones, with smart mechanisms for evolving business. The caliber of management consulting firms and strategic planning experts has probably never been higher.

But the difference between great strategic thinking and great creative thinking is linearity. In the business world, we define a good business strategy as one that is scientific, consultative, analytical, quantifiable, and measurable—the more measurable the better. And the way we develop those business strategies is through a very linear and logical process. A leads to B leads to C.

What is lacking in that process is the *leap:* the creative idea that enables you to start at point A, move to B, and then leap all the way to M . . . or maybe even Q. The leap puts you in a place you might otherwise never have reached. It is all about using creative thought to build a business strategy in ways that never would have occurred to you if you had followed a linear thought process.

Where has that creative thinking been all these years? Probably neatly tucked away on another floor, in another department, or in another office. Nonlinear thinking—creative thinking—has been relegated to the communications arena. Rather than a business fundamental, creative thinking has been considered the domain of advertising people, of creative types. It is okay to be creative with an ad campaign, a PR push, or some terrific idea for event marketing. The more creative, the better—anything to cut through the clutter. But, for the most part, creativity has been barred from the corporate boardroom—with the Do Not Disturb sign out. There has been no room for creative thinking in the development of core business strategy—or in defining corporate goals—because it is not typically seen as having any real corporate value.

THE REALITY IS THAT THE VAST MAJORITY OF COMPANIES ARE NOT STRUCTURED IN A WAY THAT ALLOWS NONLINEAR THINKING TO BE A PART OF THE BUSINESS STRATEGY DECISION-MAKING PROCESS.

How many CEOs do you know who are intimately involved in creative thinking? That is not what they are paid to do. They are paid to be involved in linear thinking, to deliver the highest bottom-line results with the least risk.

Business ideas are tangible. Creative thinking has a tendency to deal with intangibles. Business ideas lead to measurable results. Creative ideas can be hard to measure. Business ideas are safe. Creative ideas carry risk. Business ideas are indispensable. Creative ideas are considered nice to have, but not considered integral to the essence of the business.

Creative Business Ideas are not always easy. You try convincing a CEO to approach the market in a completely new way. Where are the numbers? It has never been done before!
—Matt Donovan, Euro RSCG Partnership, Sydney

That way of thinking needs to change. Now.

In today's volatile business environment, creativity has to be invited into the boardroom. *Demanded* in the boardroom. If we want to grow and flourish and prosper, to move our businesses forward, we need creative ideas that transcend advertising. We need Creative Business Ideas.

And to get there, we should *not* be asking how we can formulate an advertising campaign, be it traditional or interactive. We all need to start by asking, "How do we, together, define a Creative Business Idea?" By *together,* I mean clients and agencies. Not management consulting firms. Agencies. Creative idea companies.

Why? Because creative advertising thinkers are not just well equipped to think about business in creative ways, they are the best equipped. Whether they are advertising agencies, direct marketers, PR firms, Internet companies, promotions companies, or interactive companies . . . creative communication companies are filled with people who are paid to think creatively and to make leaps on a daily basis. Well over half of our employees are paid to think creatively. That is how they make their living. In a business context, it is their fundamental reason for being.

No one is better qualified to put creative thinking to use at a higher level than the creative people of advertising.

THE PENNY DROPS

How and when did the penny actually drop?

I had taken part in a lot of creative leaps over the years, but it was not until 1999, nearly two years after I became chairman and CEO of Euro RSCG Worldwide, that I resolved to drive CBI thinking throughout our global agency. In New York and Chicago, in Paris and Buenos Aires, in Amsterdam and Sydney, I had seen evidence of great CBIs springing up all across the network. In fact, the successes of many of our agencies around the globe were a direct result of unorthodox thinking—creative thinking that got to the core of business strategy.

I wanted more.

We started to experiment with a number of our key creative agencies. The premise was to figure out how we could use this resource more effectively, how we could use what is one of the few reasons that advertising and marketing communications agencies exist—in other words, creative thinking—in a more effective way. As is so often the case, one of the first places the experiment manifested itself was not in the laboratory, but in the real world.

THE VERY BEST

Enter another wise man.

This one was a visionary CEO. He asked us to do what most clients ask: help him build his business. But then he told us to do something no client had ever requested: *Do not do any advertising.* The agency happened to be Euro RSCG MVBMS in New York. The CEO was Irv Hockaday. The company was one that consumers had turned to for generations: Hallmark Cards, "When You Care Enough to Send the Very Best."

How the agency responded is a subject I will come back to. What was so revolutionary to me was the idea that this CEO would turn to this densely populated group of creative people—of really talented art directors, creative directors, copywriters, production people, planners, interactive people, strategists, people whose fundamental reason for being is to think creatively—and give them the assignment to think creatively about his business. It was a breakthrough, another inflection point. A client asking for what we already had been doing—disguised as advertising.

BEYOND ADVERTISING

I asked Ron Berger, CEO of Euro RSCG MVBMS, to share the Hallmark story with our entire management team at our next 100-Day Meeting (meetings we have every 100 days with our top 100 executives.) The Hallmark case became a way of articulating and demonstrating what was already beginning to be done in a number of

No other industry is composed of the eclectic talent one finds in our business: Former architects become creative directors, lawyers become producers, and a commercial fisherman can become a successful writer. It's an industry that attracts people with passion about a lot of things in life—and, unlike most businesses, those passions are not reserved for one's "outside life," they are part of what contributes to new and interesting thinking every day.
—Trish O'Reilly, Euro RSCG MVBMS, New York

our agencies, but it enabled us to focus on it in a different way. Just saying those five words—*Do not do any advertising*—instantly brought a laser-sharp focus to the idea. I shared several other examples of Creative Business Ideas, the bridge in Buenos Aires among them, and then gave the group their own assignment: Submit creative ideas based on business thinking.

When the ideas were submitted, you could feel the buzz in the room, a buzz that happens only when you have truly captured the imaginations of people. *Do not do any advertising* had unleashed a torrent of creative thinking that was coming from a whole new place. The shackles had been removed.

And then came the inevitable: What to do with all that energy—an energy level that, when combined with the staggering executional potential of all the different agencies and disciplines in our network, became explosive.

We had put together a group of people to do what they always do, what they get paid to do, which is to think creatively—but this time we asked them to focus on how we could put that creative thinking to use at a higher level than simply executing marketing or communication strategy. The name may not have been a stroke of genius, but the thinking behind it was. We christened our new way of working the Creative Business Idea.

The next step, I knew, was to have all our offices adopt CBIs as their way of doing business, on a daily basis, across the entire agency. If we were able to do that, we would have reshaped our business—and our industry.

I wanted everyone throughout the agency to understand that we were no longer in the ad business.

Did the business model have to change? The advertising model did.

THE BEGINNING OF SOMETHING NEW

Traditional advertising starts with market research . . . which in turn leads to the strategy . . . which in turn leads to the media and to the advertising itself.

But between the strategy and the advertising is a gap: the gap between the wisdom of strategy and the effectiveness of advertising.

What happens in that gap is magic.

Magic is a forbidden topic in business. CEOs routinely consult psychics and astrologers, but they do it covertly, as if public knowledge of their interest would tank their stock price and force their resignation. In fact, a passion for alternative knowledge has always gone hand in hand with rigorous rationality. "Even the greatest figures of the scientific revolution dabbled in the mystical arts," writes Langdon Winner in *Autonomous Technology*. "Kepler was a confirmed astrologer; Newton tried his hand at alchemy."[7]

THE FORBIDDEN MAGIC IN OUR AGE IS CREATIVITY, WHICH IS STILL RESERVED FOR ARTISTS AND BOHEMIANS. BUT THIS KIND OF MAGIC IS COMPLETELY CAPABLE OF CARRYING A STRATEGY THAT'S INTERESTING AND RELEVANT AND MEMORABLE TO PEOPLE.

Leaping the gap in that systematic way is what great creative thinking is all about. It is what separates advertising from all other businesses.

Leaping the gap is what enabled Nike to tell the world "Just Do It." It is what enabled Volkswagen to tell people to "Think Small" and Apple to tell them to "Think Different." It is what enabled De Beers to make the claim that "A Diamond Is Forever."

In today's business world, that kind of creative thinking is needed not only to leap the gap in the middle of the journey as the advertising strategy . . . the magic of creativity is needed at the very beginning of the process. We need it where it can help to define the journey and define the primary strategic business idea, where it can be used to invent and define both brands and businesses.

Branding is no longer about communication strategy. It is about business strategy.

DECODING CBIs

How to accomplish that? First, we had to clearly communicate just what a Creative Business Idea is. No easy feat. Over the years, we have continued to revise and refine the definition of the Creative Business Idea. Right now we say it is this: an idea that combines creativity and strategy in new ways and results in breakthrough solutions and industry firsts. It arises from and influences business strategy, not just communication strategy, and it leads to innovative execution across traditional and new media—brilliant execution *beyond* traditional and new media. This results in business solutions that influence the nature of business itself: profitable innovation, transformed marketplaces/marketspaces, and new ways to maximize relationships between consumers and brands.

THE THREE COMPONENTS

We have also discovered that, when you break it down, a CBI is typically made up of three components: a strong product component, a strong communication component, and a powerful brand experience. That is the essence of twenty-first-century business strategy: the product, the communication, and the brand experience.

1. *The product component.* The idea is rooted in the product, grows from it, is almost an organic extension of it. In some cases, the product is even created or transformed as a result of the creative idea. Perdue's branded chicken, Hallmark's Flowers, Sony's Walkman—all are rooted in creative business strategy.

2. *The communication component.* The communication of the idea must demonstrate a deep understanding of the essence of the brand and must be fiercely protective of the brand's integrity. One cannot arrive at a Creative Business Idea for Volvo, for example, without first understanding the DNA of safety and what safety symbolizes to Volvo and Volvo's brand history. Likewise, you won't get to a Creative Business Idea for Disney without understanding what the brand means to people personally, that it's not about rides and cartoon characters, it's about happiness and joy.

3. *The brand experience.* It's a bigger idea than just advertising. For Perdue, the brand experience extends to having yellow dividers

in the cases so that shoppers can instantly identify where the Perdue chickens are, using pop-up thermometers that indicate when the bird is done, and printing recipes on the package. Walkman delivered the brand experience of bringing music into people's everyday lives and everyday activities—you could suddenly take your music with you anywhere and everywhere. The bridge in Buenos Aires not only delivered a wonderful new outdoor space for the city's residents—to gather with friends and families, to meet, or just to go and be alone—it gave the beleaguered residents of the city a majestic land-mark and reignited pride in their hometown.

Greatness never occurs within the context of safety and comfort.
—Don Hogle, Euro RSCG MVBMS, New York

Again, the baseline is the idea. The bigger the better. And there are extra points for nonlinear, "irrational" leaps.

No Fear

Forget the solitary genius in a garret.

CREATIVE BUSINESS IDEAS ARE THE RESULT OF A REMARKABLE BLEND OF TEAMWORK AND DISCIPLINE.

The first step in this process is exhaustive research. Then the client and agency have to look to the innate creativity of their employees, not just in the so-called creative departments, but throughout both organizations. All preconceived notions and all plans for the future must be set aside, as the client, with the agency's help, considers all possibilities. Then everyone in the process needs to be fearless about embracing ideas that are considerably bigger than the creation of advertisements.

It is a daunting process and a tough discipline. At various points along the way, there are plenty of opportunities to cut corners, edit ideas, and play it safe. This is not for the faint of heart. Creative Business Ideas, on every level, take courage. It takes courage to develop a CBI, to propose it to one's colleagues and clients, to fight to see it accepted, and to push it through to fruition.

It also takes courage to embrace the very concept of Creative Business Ideas. It means being open to creative thinking and will-ing to apply it to business strategy, not just advertising. It means resolutely making the leap to transform your business in ways you never imagined. It often means being the minority voice and having to stand your ground against the Lilliputians' pull toward mediocrity. You have to be fearless.

Above all, Creative Business Ideas mean change. Get ready to break down the walls within your organizations and between agency and client. Get ready to be courageous enough to step outside your traditional role as marketers and advertisers, clients and agencies, to embrace all communication channels and use them to connect to consumers in new ways. In a changed world, we all need to play by new rules.

YOUR REWARD

There is a payoff. A big one. For those businesses and agencies that can instill the magic of creativity into the very fabric and nature of business itself, the rewards are there, and the rewards are great.

But how does one get there? How does one foster an environment conducive to Creative Business Ideas, a place that not only gives rise to great ideas but actually welcomes them, accepts them, and implements them?

In my experience, it always starts—or, in some cases, ends—at the top.

Chapter 3
Creativity at the Top

Robert De Niro acted in *Awakenings,* a film about a brilliant neurologist and his comatose patients. What did De Niro, who is famed for his intensity, do between takes? According to the film's director, Penny Marshall, De Niro spent a lot of time on the phone talking about napkins—he was opening yet another restaurant.[1]

The legendary acting teacher Konstantin Stanislavsky was a great fan of pianist and composer Sergey Rachmaninoff and asked him the secret of his piano technique. Rachmaninoff's reply: "Not touching the neighboring key."[2]

So much for the myth of the tortured genius.

When we think about creative CEOs, our mental picture is just as out of focus. An executive who paints on weekends? No problem. Someone who is creative in the office? Much harder to imagine. And if you want to know why corporate jobs are still considered duller than other kinds of work, there's the start of your answer.

How many truly creative CEOs do you know? Not many, I would venture to guess. Yet in the absence of creative leadership, what are the odds that you will ever come face-to-face with a bona fide Creative Business Idea? Or, if you do hit upon such an idea, that you will have the support necessary to see it implemented?

Fear not. In the words of author Warren G. Bennis: "There are two ways of being creative. One can sing and dance. Or one can create an environment in which singers and dancers flourish."[3]

The singers and dancers are those blessed CEOs who think creatively about their businesses and have no problem generating sharp, relevant business ideas. They do not need others to make their leaps for them. They soar just fine on their own.

Then there are the CEOs—a far larger group—who recognize full well that they are not singers and dancers, but who understand and have embraced the power of creative thinking as it applies to their businesses. Instead of making the leap themselves, they work with their agency partners to get there. Let others sing and dance; these CEOs can produce the show.

In my experience, the key to creativity is not simply hiring bright, creative people. You also must hire bright leaders who recognize the power of creative thinking—because the one common thread through every Creative Business Idea that I have ever encountered is a high-level executive who relishes and embraces new ideas. That executive sees the adoption of new ideas as a key part of his or her job and is prepared to defend those ideas from the naysayers who will take any measures to try to block them.

HIGH-LEVEL CORPORATE ACCEPTANCE OF CREATIVE THINKING IS A PRE-REQUISITE FOR CREATIVE BUSINESS IDEAS.

Without it, a CBI will not survive. It is that simple. Unless creativity starts at the top, you can be damn sure it will eventually get stopped there.

BEDTIME FOR BOZO

Case in point. We met with a CEO to show him the finished work for a new campaign that was about to air. The work was thoughtful. It was on target. It was on strategy. How do I know that? Because it was the result of a true partnership between the singers and dancers in our organization and the ones in his. It was the culmination of countless hours spent together in the war room.

But there was a problem.

In one of the spots, there were clowns. Not just one clown, but four clowns. They were not old, has-been, veteran circus clowns. They were a group of twentysomething, clean-cut aspiring actors, running late for a gig, all trying to pile into their car, in costume. "What do clowns have to do with my company?" the CEO asked us. "There will be no clowns in these commercials. They are not in keeping with the brand image." This was despite the fact that the clowns were doing volunteer work and were on their way to perform at a children's hospital . . . which perfectly achieved our objective of evolving the brand image by showing that the employees of the client company actively participated in their communities and cared about people.

The clowns were out . . . and so was a great idea.

BECOME A CHAMPION

"A man's mind stretched to a new idea," Oliver Wendell Holmes Sr. noted, "never goes back to its original dimension."[4] So the trick is to stretch minds—from the top of an organization to the bottom. That way, creative ideas have a chance. But a chance is only a start. Ultimately, creative ideas must be accepted (or rejected) by executives at the highest levels. And there the issue is no longer the idea itself. It's the leadership. Without a chance of acceptance at the highest level, ideas die. It is why most great ideas have never even been presented, let alone produced. If they are not killed externally, they are killed internally. But when CEOs embrace an idea, they can become its biggest champion. They do not need to sing or dance; they simply need to support the performance.

The stories that follow spotlight three CEOs who *can* sing and dance—people who have made tremendous leaps on their own. Significantly, all have become their own best brand champions.

BUCKING THE CROWD

For starters, consider a great idea that would never have become reality if a CEO had not been its sole champion: the Sony Walkman. In Chapter 2, we discussed the nonlinear thinking—the

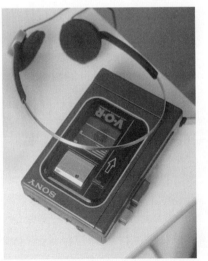

Sony Walkman

Our industry is best suited to see CBIs come to life. However, it will only come into being if the clients have equal passion and courage to bring forth brave new paths, new routes to new flow of ideas.
—KuanKuan Ong, Euro RSCG Partnership, Beijing

leap—that led to this revolutionary personal technology. In this chapter, we consider the man behind the brand—and how his unrelenting enthusiasm was essential to the product's success. If Akio Morita had not pushed it, our streets and beaches might still be clogged with boom boxes. . . .

Years after the Walkman had become a phenomenal success, Norio Ohga (successor to Akio Morita) had this to say about its development: "When they showed it to me . . . I was preoccupied with CDs and optical laser technology, which was much more difficult and more interesting. Frankly, I couldn't see why Sony should make a product that was boring technically. And that is the major difference between me and Mr. Morita. He had the merchant's intuition that allowed him to see what it would become. If it had been up to me, it never would have happened."[5] Ohga didn't understand at that time how this seemingly boring piece of creative thinking could be applied to his business.

So convinced was Morita that putting together a portable tape player with miniature headphones had huge potential as a Sony product that he adopted the idea as a kind of personal crusade. He instructed Sony technicians to strip the company's compact tape recorder of its recording capabilities and speaker, replace them with a stereo amplifier, design lightweight headphones that would still maintain high-quality sound—and do all that so cheaply that teenagers could afford the product.

Throughout the process, Morita came up against strong opposition from his technicians and his marketers, all of whom argued that the product was not viable and would not sell. They questioned why someone would buy a tape recorder that did not record. "[I]t embarrassed me," Morita wrote in his memoir, *Made in Japan,* "to be so excited about a product most others thought would be a dud. But I was so confident the product was viable that I said I would take personal responsibility for the project."[6] In fact, in order to price the Walkman where he wanted it, Sony had to produce 30,000 units for the Japanese launch—twice the number of units its highest-selling tape recorder was selling per month. When the sales force flat-out objected, Morita pledged to do something that few CEOs would do today: He said he would resign if they could not sell them. All 30,000 units were sold within two months. Profitable innovation was a hallmark of this Creative Business Idea from the start.

> **BEFORE YOU LEAP:** If you are passionate about your idea, and you believe that what you are doing is right—right for the business and for the brand—do not be afraid to put yourself on the line. Fight for it. Fight the tug toward mediocrity. And if you happen to work for a CEO who is fighting for a creative idea that seems insane, give him time. He might be one of those CEOs who can sing and dance.

The Sony Walkman was such a brilliant idea because it combined creativity and strategy in new ways. It was an industry first. It was a breakthrough solution that transformed the marketplace and, in fact, spawned a whole new industry. It is a powerful example of a new way to maximize relationships between consumers and brands.

WHO IS AGAINST CREATIVE THINKING?

In 1995, when *Fast Company* first appeared on the newsstands, I gave everyone at our next 100-Day Meeting a copy. I wanted them to learn from the magazine's insights into change—and from the companies that react swiftly to the changes around them.

Later, I invited Bill Taylor, *Fast Company* cofounder, to address one of those senior management meetings. Taylor and I had an instant connection. It was as if he knew all about us, even though he knew nothing about us.

In Taylor's view, if one asks, "Who is against creative thinking?" not a single hand will be raised. Of course everyone is for creativity; in the abstract, it is right up there with motherhood and the flag. On the other hand, Taylor points out, if you look at 90 percent of the companies in the world, and particularly the senior executives of those companies, everything they do sends precisely that message: "I hate innovation; creativity is my enemy." Why? Because we are against mistakes, we are against failure, and it is hard to have creativity and innovation without mistakes and failure.

NO GUTS, NO GLORY

Morita did not always win. Think of Betamax, Sony's videotape player. If you are young, you have never heard of it—the industry standard is VHS. That is because Sony developed a technology using a tape size that few other makers adopted. Sony got crushed. But here, too, there is much to be learned from Morita and his successors in the way they were able to take risks, make mistakes, accept defeat. They were passionate.

It was passion for their ideas—from the Walkman to the first videocassette recorder to the compact disc—that gave them the courage to fearlessly bring these products forward, against all odds. It was passion that led Gunnar Engellau to defy every automotive trend in the marketplace in pursuit of his belief that safe can be sexy. Passion was also the trademark of that "tough man" in the poultry industry, Frank Perdue.

BE A RENEGADE

When people talk about leaders who have a passion for ideas, one cannot get too deep into the conversation without mention of one of the true renegades of the business world: Richard Branson, chairman of the Virgin Group. Not only does Branson love to challenge the status quo, most of the time he is remarkably successful at it. He's had not just one, but multiple industry firsts. He's been remarkably successful at profitable innovation. And in the process he has reinvented entire categories of business.

I asked a group at the agency to look more deeply into Branson's empire for two reasons: First, because we felt he could be a potential client (he hasn't become one yet). And, second, because I felt there was a lot we could learn from Virgin. As it happened, I had a small revelation as we studied the brand: Branson and his enterprise were a wonderful example of a truly great Creative Business Idea. This guy does not just leap, he *jetés.*

What is Virgin? Is it a music company? An international airline? A cola? An online bank? A bridal shop? All of the above . . . and more. So, what is the Virgin brand? At first glance, the company looks like an array of wildly divergent products and services with little in common. What connects them all—what is at the core of the Virgin brand—is a lifestyle, a mind-set, and a perspective on the world. Virgin is the little guy against the Establishment. And Branson is David taking on a long line of Goliaths: British Airways, Coke and Pepsi, the British upper class.

In his autobiography, *Losing My Virginity: How I've Survived, Had Fun, and Made a Fortune Doing Business My Way,* Branson tells of how he always had trouble in school, in part as a result of his dyslexia.[7] But he also had issues with many of the traditions of the boarding school he attended. He was looking for a vehicle with which to voice his feelings of rebellion; he found it in his first major business venture, *Student* magazine. Though essentially the business consisted of a child making calls from a phone booth, Branson managed to procure advertisers and went on to publish interviews with such figures as Vanessa Redgrave, Mick Jagger, and John Lennon. He wanted *Student* to offer a new and better, antiestablishment lifestyle—the rebellious attitude that would eventually define the Virgin brand.

HIRE A DYSLEXIC

How do you go from being a rebellious kid who always had trouble in school to an entrepreneur with one of the most recognizable brands in the world? I am going to take a leap of my own here and suggest an unlikely answer: Maybe Branson's dyslexia helped him. Dyslexia is a huge liability when it comes to what you are supposed to learn in school: reading, writing, and arithmetic. But it is a major asset when it comes to what most schools (or corporations, for that matter) do not value highly: creative thinking. Dyslexics have a tendency to excel at such things as art, architecture, drama, and music. Tell them to sit down and read a 500-page novel cover to cover, out loud—and they will cringe. Ask them to express themselves creatively—and they may soar.

Although the stereotyped perception is that dyslexia is a matter of reversing numbers and letters, the reality is far more complex and far more interesting. Dyslexia is deeply rooted in the actual way the brain functions, in the way one processes information. Scientists now believe that the disorder is characterized by out-of-place neurons wandering around the brain, causing a "cascade of connectional differences," wiring regions of the brain not normally connected.[8] Most of us think in a linear fashion. A leads to B leads to C. The way dyslexics think, A leads to M or R or Z. They are practically incapable of linear thinking, unless they really work at it. It does not come naturally.

Leonardo da Vinci. Albert Einstein. Rodin. Agatha Christie. W. B. Yeats. Winston Churchill. Nelson Rockefeller. All are now thought to have had dyslexia. So do Charles Schwab, John Chambers (president and CEO of Cisco Systems), Paul Orfalea (founder of Kinko's), and Craig McCaw (the cellular industry pioneer). And on and on.

A disproportionate number of CEOs? In a recent cover story in *Fortune* magazine, Sally Shaywitz, a leading dyslexia neuroscientist at Yale University, put it this way: "Dyslexics are over-represented in the top ranks of people who are unusually insightful, who bring a new perspective, who think out of the box" (see Note 8).

Bill Dreyer, a dyslexic inventor and biologist at Caltech, says he thinks in 3-D Technicolor pictures rather than words. In his mind, that is the very thing that has enabled him to come up with breakthrough theories about antibodies and to invent one of the first protein-sequencing machines, which has in turn helped to launch the human genome revolution. "I don't think of dyslexia as a deficiency," he told *Fortune.* "It's like having CAD [computer-aided design] in your head" (see Note 8).

Cisco's John Chambers says, "I can't explain why, but I just approach problems differently. It's very easy for me to jump conceptually from A to Z. I picture a chess game on a multiple-layer dimensional cycle and almost play it out in my mind. But it's not a chess game. It's business. I don't make moves one at a time. I can usually anticipate the potential outcome and where the Y's in the road will occur" (see Note 8).

NONLINEAR THINKING. LEFT-BRAIN/RIGHT-BRAIN THINKING. FROM A TO B TO M.

These are people whose brains are wired to make leaps. Suddenly, the idea of bringing more dyslexics into our organizations seems not quite so far-fetched. Dyslexia could be the perfect predisposition for the generation of Creative Business Ideas.

MAKING THE LEAP

So how did Branson make his leap?

Virgin Records was born out of an idea Branson had for selling discounted mail-order albums through *Student.* He and his team settled on the brand name Virgin because they were virgins in the business world and got a kick out of the irony of the word in relation to their lifestyle. The idea took off. Then, in 1971, when he was just 20, Branson suffered his first setback—a postal strike was seriously threatening his small mail-order business. This was when Branson had the insight to see the need for a product that did not yet exist.

In the 1970s in England, records were sold in stores that typically had drab, sterile environments. Branson saw the opportunity to capitalize on the social aspect of music. He wanted to open a record shop that would be "an extension of *Student,* a place where people could meet and listen to records together." Like Sony's Morita, he was keenly aware that young people spend more time listening to music than doing almost anything else. Branson's goal was to provide a less expensive product in an atmosphere designed around a customer experience. "In exploring how to do this," Branson writes, "I think we created the conceptual framework for what Virgin would later become."[9]

That is creative thinking applied to business strategy. And it is a solid illustration of another key aspect of CBIs: Don't just offer a product. Create a customer experience. Branson's Creative Business Idea wasn't just to open a record store—that would have been going from A to B. It was his decision to open a retail store designed around a customer experience that took him from A to B to M. And it was that idea—the idea of retail entertainment—that would eventually give birth to the Virgin Megastore. Sofas, earphones for private listening, tables stocked with music magazines, and free coffee . . . that's a Creative Business Idea.

Almost immediately, Virgin had a loyal following and a distinct brand image. But Branson already had his sights set on reinventing another category of the music business. Just as he had seen a disconnect between music retailing and youth culture, he saw a disconnect between the way music was recorded and the culture of the musicians. Music studios were run as traditional businesses, but musicians were antitraditional. Branson envisioned musicians recording in an unstructured atmosphere, so he purchased an old country manor and turned it into a studio with a relaxed, alternative ambience.

Once again, creativity was applied to the fundamentals of business itself. Both of these leaps arose from and influenced business strategy, not just communication strategy. They eventually led to innovative execution across and beyond traditional and new media. The result was a business solution that transformed marketplaces and resulted in new ways to maximize the relationship between consumer and brand.

A SKY-HIGH LEAP

Leaping from a record store to a record label makes some sort of sense. But to go from a record label to an airline? That is a stretch even for a nonlinear thinker. The impetus for this leap came from an American lawyer looking for someone to invest in a Gatwick–New York airline. This man approached Branson, whose partners at Virgin thought he was crazy to even consider it. Understandably, they saw no connection between their company and the airline industry. What does the record industry have to do with aviation? In his book, Branson described his strategy: "I rely far more on gut instinct than researching huge amounts of statistics. This might be because, perhaps due to my dyslexia, I distrust numbers, which I feel can be twisted to prove anything. The idea of operating a Virgin airline grabbed my imagination, but I had to work out in my own mind what the potential risks were."[10]

As it turned out, the potential risks were enormous—as were the obstacles before him. Branson was going to challenge the giant British Airways. And with that challenge, he would put into place a philosophy that would allow him to take the Virgin brand from one industry to another. "Typically, we review the industry and put ourselves in the customer's shoes to see what could make it better. We ask fundamental questions: Is this an opportunity for restructuring a market and creating competitive advantage?"[11] Branson's creative leap was not just to start a new airline. That would be linear thinking, from A to B. The leap from the record business to the airline business happened because Branson thought he could do it better. And that's how he got from A to B to M.

Here was a little company, taking on a giant airline and promising to do it better. Was it hype—or was there something there? I went out of my way to find out, promptly booking a flight to London. The first difference I noticed was at Newark airport. Right after checking in, I was asked whether I wanted to eat before boarding. No one had ever given that option before, ever. Then I was asked whether I wanted to be awakened for breakfast prior to landing. Again, this was before even boarding the plane. Unheard of. I was offered pajamas. Free transportation, in a luxury car, to my London hotel. A manicure or backrub en route. What's not to like?

Once I boarded, I could see a great difference in the attitude of the flight attendants. They actually seemed to enjoy what they were doing. The finishing touch was an announcement made just before landing, inviting passengers to donate their pocket change—which no one ever knows what to do with anyway, because you do not exchange coins in foreign countries—to one of Virgin's charity efforts.

Put it all together, and it is not so much that Virgin was giving customers what they had always wanted—because I was not looking for all those things. What Virgin did was make the experience more interesting. It was no longer just a transatlantic flight that would get you to and from your destination. It was way more. It was a transatlantic experience. Like Morita giving people the opportunity to experience music wherever they went with the Walkman, this was a great brand experience. And it has absolutely nothing to do with advertising. In fact, everything about Virgin Atlantic Airways provides almost a textbook definition of a CBI. It's applying creative thinking to business strategy in a way that results in breakthrough solutions and industry firsts. It's brilliant execution *beyond* traditional and new media. It's profitable innovation, transformed marketplaces, and new ways to maximize relationships between consumers and brands. It also has a strong product component, a strong communication component, and a powerful brand experience.

BEFORE YOU LEAP:
- Prepare to ignore industry borders.
- Be willing to take risks. Even when someone else seems to have locked up the market.
- Be willing to make mistakes. Big ones.
- If you passionately believe in an idea, pay no heed to the naysayers. It is their job to squelch the song and dance. Do not let them.

SELLING A PERSONA

And what about the use of traditional media? To promote Virgin, Branson has relied very little on traditional advertising. Rather than purchase airtime and print pages, Branson has used his outsized personality to sell and publicize the airline (as well as his other brands). For the first flight of Virgin Atlantic Airways, Branson filled the plane with Virgin employees, friends, and journalists. It was a huge publicity spectacle, complete with the irreverent stunt of a false video of the pilots lighting up a joint after takeoff. Since that time, Branson has continued to fuel the hype by putting himself out there in the public eye—whether by trying to set a speed record across the Atlantic in a racing boat, by attempting to be first to fly a hot air balloon across the same ocean, or by donning a bridal gown to open his shop in downtown London. Subtle, he is not.

Branson's decision to take on the "upper classes"—that is, British Airways—paid great dividends. Not only did he gain a big slice of BA's business, he built himself as a brand. In 1994, a BBC poll asked 1,200 British respondents ages 15 to 35 who should be charged with the task of rewriting the Ten Commandments. Branson was the fourth most popular answer, tied with Oprah, after Mother Teresa, the Pope, and the Archbishop of Canterbury.[12]

Do You Sing and Dance?

Richard Branson, Akio Morita, Walt Disney, Gunnar Engellau—all are individuals who had really big visions, really big ideas. They are among that rare breed of visionary CEO entrepreneurs who have the ability to invent or reinvent a category of business, start a company, and, because they are such charismatic leaders, mobilize throngs of people around them. They have the ability to make great leaps, to think creatively about their businesses, and to come up with CBIs that transform entire industries.

Virgin Atlantic Airways

It is about the right group of talent, including the leadership. Leadership in a CBI-focused environment is about coaching. It is not about the dictatorial style of an orchestra conductor producing his or her desired version of a set written piece, but about the qualities of a great jazz musician guiding a jam session, where harmony and structure have to be there, but the brilliancy of everybody has to come through for a result that is new and unique.
—Juan Rocamora, Euro RSCG Southern Europe, Madrid

They are effective, but theirs is not the only way to be effective. There are also leaders who get to the top and find themselves not just reinventing categories, but reinventing an entire company. They are not visionary entrepreneurs. They do not sing. They do not dance. They are the visionary catalysts, the ones with the ability to transform an organization—oftentimes by breaking down the walls of bureaucracy and tradition. It is their job to create an environment in which singers and dancers—and ideas—can flourish. It's their job to get others to think creatively about their business and to help them make the leaps they can't make on their own.

What is the role of a leader in instigating or enabling creative thinking?

Fast Company's Bill Taylor has some interesting insights into the question. In his experience, the senior executives who create a positive and welcoming environment for innovation share a number of attributes. The most significant is enough self-confidence and security to admit to the rank and file, "I do not have all the answers. It is not my job to think for this company."[13]

As Taylor sees it, the mythology at so many companies is that the big boss does the strategizing and the heavy thinking, and it is the job of the troops to execute the ideas. But at really innovative companies, senior executives get up all the time and say, "The world is way too complicated; it is changing too fast for me as an individual or for this small number of people around me to come up with all of the answers." The group brain triumphs over the individual brain all the time.

This argument flies in the face of CEO mythology. For most CEOs, the assumption is that they are, by definition, the smartest people in the room. It makes sense, then, that they be the thinkers, the men and women who make decisions across the board.

At innovative companies, however, that is not how it works. The CEOs are smart, all right. Smart enough to know that they must focus their thinking on very particular aspects of the company, not on the minutiae of everyday business. As Bill Taylor puts it, "CEOs are responsible for painting a compelling picture or portrait of the future. They are the ones who must determine, in general terms, where the organization is going. They are responsible for creating an environment where they can honestly say, 'We have the best talent in the world in our industry working here.' But then it is up to everybody else to do the thinking. And what the leader is responsible for is to create the conditions whereby the best creative thinking can happen."

Easier said than done.

Chapter 4
The Creative Corporate Culture

Who among us would step away from a big decision and say, as if looking heavenward, "It's out of my hands"?

Well, that has happened.

Consider: Millions of dollars are being spent on new commercials. Hundreds of millions more are on the line. You are the head of marketing. Unlike most marketing czars—men and women who are inclined to push themselves into every creative meeting, every commercial shoot, every editing session and focus group—you say, "I do not need to approve the commercials. I will watch them on TV when everyone else does."

How long do you think you would keep your job if you said that?

And, digging deeper, why would you say that?

Let Jerry Taylor, former president and CEO of MCI, explain why he declined to be involved in the approval process. In his view, he had total confidence in his advertising staff, so why preview the commercials? "There's nothing I could offer—other than approval."[1]

There are some companies that seem to perpetuate a culture of creativity within their organizations—companies where creativity is not just a lofty intellectual goal or part of a mission statement, but is genuinely embedded in the culture. These companies recognize that their best path to creativity is to establish an environment in which those singers and dancers can flourish. They're the companies where it's not necessarily the CEO who makes the leap, but where the CEO embraces creative thinking and provides an environment that fosters CBIs by encouraging people to think creatively about the business. In my mind, MCI is one of them.

TEAR DOWN THE WALLS, DITCH THE DOORS

I first began working with MCI back in 1990, when it was a client of ours at Messner Vetere Berger Carey Schmetterer/RSCG. Tom Messner, who had a long history with MCI from its very beginning, knew Bill McGowan and Bert Roberts and Jerry Taylor and many of the other top executives. It was exhilarating to be along for the ride in the 1990s as MCI revolutionized marketing in the telecommunications industry with one breakthrough campaign after another: Friends & Family, the first branded long-distance calling plan; the Anna Paquin campaign, the first advertising to talk about the Internet and its incredible future; the Gramercy Press Campaign, the first to launch simultaneously on TV and the Internet; 1-800-COLLECT, the first brand for collect calling.

And one other first: MCI was the first telephony company to approach the business market as a mass market—and reach business customers as it would any other consumer, through mass media.

FROM COMMODITY TO BRAND

With Friends & Family, MCI was also the first to move long-distance calling from a price-oriented commodity to a brand. We may take it for granted now, but if we do, it's because of MCI. Branding long-distance calling was a huge creative leap; it was like Intel's leap to brand a microprocessor or Perdue's to brand a commodity that was publicly traded (chicken). Before this branded product, there were company names (AT&T, MCI, Sprint), but never a brand name that meant something unto itself. After the program was launched, that changed. If you asked anybody in the early to mid-1990s to tell you about Friends & Family, they might have said bad things about it or they might have said great things about it, but they knew what it was. In fact, a survey conducted by MCI at the time showed that more Americans knew about Friends & Family than knew that Hawaii is a state or that our vice president was Al Gore. Those years—1990 through 1996—were the most creative, explosive, unbelievable time in the company's advertising history.

In transferring our partners' experience from political campaigns to product campaigns, we were mavericks, nonconformists, throwing out all the old assumptions. We loved the urgency, the immediacy, of turning around spots on a dime, shifting our advertising from negative to positive, from attacking to defending, creating biographical spots just as candidates do. We broke all the rules.

My partners Tom Messner and Barry Vetere led the creative way, and brilliant contributions were made by other very talented creative people. I led the strategic thinking and account management. But we could not have done it without the client. Once again, the client was the real hero.

NURTURE CREATIVITY FROM THE TOP DOWN

MCI, in the early 1990s, was one of those companies with a CEO who embraced and understood the power of creative thinking as it applies to business. In fact, the entire senior management understood the power of creativity and the value of creative thinking. It made our jobs easy; it was an environment in which we could flourish. But MCI also created an environment internally in which the singers and dancers within that organization could flourish. It did not matter who you were or what your job was—the best idea won.

Creativity was ingrained in the MCI culture. It made the client a joy to work with and it was a huge factor in enabling the company to achieve so many industry breakthroughs. And I think one of the things that made MCI so open to creativity was that its own reason for being actually came out of one highly creative thought: Monopolies, in the end, are not the best solution.

Here was this little company that thought it should be in the telecommunications business for the corniest of reasons: It believed it could provide better service. (Sound familiar, Richard Branson?) After taking its case all the way through the courts, and ultimately to the Department of Justice, eventually MCI's efforts did lead to the breakup of AT&T, and MCI was officially in the telecommunications business.

REWARD YOUR CREATIVE THINKERS

Throughout its history, what the company has valued most highly is . . . ideas. And the people who have those great ideas and who make those ideas happen are the people most frequently rewarded. MCI has lots of employee recognition programs. One of them is the Spirit of MCI Award, which is given to those who most exemplify the spirit of the company: employees who are proactive, entrepreneurial, make-it-happen types. You can win the award for coming up with a great idea for a new product, securing a big contract, excelling at customer service—and it doesn't matter what your level in the company.

Ask any of MCI's senior management and I think they would agree: The delegation of power to the very lowest levels of the organization was perhaps the largest contributor to MCI's success. Just to work at MCI, you had to be a self-starter who thrived when given the chance to be individually responsible—a prerequisite for survival in a nonhierarchical, entrepreneurial, unstructured environment.

In some ways, MCI's experience paralleled our own in those days at MVBMS. As I noted earlier, the absence of walls and doors fosters an environment and a culture that promotes—indeed demands—individual contributions, courageous contributions built on great insights and creative thinking. MCI was one of the first major companies to use e-mail. In fact, it invented and marketed MCI mail as one of the first platforms. It was our early adoption of MCI mail—even before we had won the account—that changed the nature of how we worked as an agency, bringing the notion and benefits of connectivity into our practice as it grew and allowing everyone to contribute. As business guru Warren G. Bennis puts it, "Good leaders make people feel that they are at the very heart of things, not at the periphery."[2]

> **BEFORE YOU LEAP:** Tear down the walls and get rid of the doors. And recognize that one's title or level within a company has nothing to do with one's ability to think creatively.

BECOME A SOLICITOR

There are many ways to be a gifted employer, but one infallible way is not to pull rank. Somerset Maugham, the English novelist, "made it a rule that his house staff should eat the same meals as his guests. They stayed."[3]

Maugham was considerate of his employees not only because it was his nature to be kind, but because it was good business. He observed everyone he met and considered everything as material for his writing. That is the interior process of the novelist. Walt Disney had to be more direct—so he openly solicited ideas from his employees. When Disneyland was near completion, for example, Disney asked everyone working on the park, from construction workers to top executives, to test each ride as it was finished.

He also welcomed visits to his office from employees who had new creative ideas. When he became CEO of Disney, Michael Eisner carried over that tradition in a regular Animation Department event called "The Gong Show," in which employees could make formal pitches to Eisner and other top leaders.[4]

> **BEFORE YOU LEAP:** It is not enough to encourage employees to think creatively. You must provide a mechanism or structure that allows their ideas to be heard.

DO NOT CREATE A GENETIC REPLICA

It may sound obvious to say that you cannot have a company filled with smart ideas unless you have a company filled with smart people. But it really is that simple—and it really does involve employees from the executive suites to the custodial staff. As Bill Taylor puts it, the problem with so many companies is that they are, by and large, unwilling to bring into the organization—and unwilling to bring into positions of authority—people who make the leaders uncomfortable. Yet that is precisely the way to constantly renew and refresh a company; it's critical to developing Creative Business Ideas.

In my sociology classes, professors referred to the tendency to hire people from a similar background as "homosexual reproduction." The theory goes that executives who want an employee who will make decisions the way they do should hire someone from the same socioeconomic stratum, with a similar educational background, and so on. The problem is that this is the quickest route to stultifying conformity. There is no voice in the distance encouraging the pursuit of a different path.

"A lot of this comes down to, are you a secure person?" Taylor

Any individual can have a flash of brilliance that leads to a great CBI, whether they ever repeat it or not. Enough flashes can shed a lot of light.
—Rich Roth, Euro RSCG MVBMS, New York

Take a simple problem: 1 + 1. Consider the answer you would get from different people. The bean counters will tell you the answer is 2, the strategists that you could make it 3. Toss it over to some creatives and you might get 11 or even L. And the answers are all correct but somehow expected. Now consider if you put those left-brain people and right-brain people together, let them work with problems together— all of the time. Create a world where you do not just have left-brain thinking or right-brain thinking anymore, but whole-brain thinking. Think then how powerful your solutions could be and how often you could achieve once-in-a-lifetime thinking.
—Fergus McCallum, KLP Euro RSCG, London

says. "Are you confident enough to be willing to bring into your organization and put into positions of power people who are very, very different, who bring a different history, a different perspective, a different thought? Because otherwise, what you do is you create a genetic replica of you, and then the minute the world moves in a different direction, your organization is incapable of evolving."[5]

Writer and political commentator Walter Lippmann agrees. "Where all men think alike, no one thinks very much."[6]

WANT TO HAVE A REALLY CREATIVE COMPANY? RECRUIT PEOPLE IN UNUSUAL WAYS AND RECRUIT THEM FROM UNUSUAL PLACES.

To make his point, Taylor tells the story of a couple of companies on Wall Street that were recruiting for their bond trading departments and decided to hire chess enthusiasts. Granted, chess freaks likely would not know anything about bonds, but they have immense powers of concentration, and Wall Street companies can never have enough talent with that ability. So the Wall Streeters did not go to the best business schools and try to recruit the top 5 percent of the class; they recruited at chess tournaments and placed advertisements in chess magazines.

WELCOME DIVERSE THINKING

Once an organization has brought in people with different perspectives, Taylor cautions, it needs to let those people continue to be who they are. What, after all, is the point of drumming out of them the very stuff that attracted you to them in the first place?

BENETTON: BUILT ON DIVERSITY

United Colors of Benetton has taken that "all ideas welcome here" approach to the nth degree. It helps that Benetton is a family-run business that built its brand on the authenticity of its product. It is also one that values the power of true creative talent.

Benetton is a global company, but it is also decidedly local. Other companies in its category have central design offices and factories around the world. Benetton, in contrast, manufactures clothes only in Europe, with a core, high-tech facility at Castrette (Treviso) in Italy. It is one of the most advanced clothing complexes in the world, capable of turning out more than 110 million garments a year. The products reflect the brand's focus on authenticity. The clothes are made of 100 percent wool or 100 percent cotton; they are 100 percent colorful, an absolute value for the money, simple and unsophisticated.[7]

Since the mid-1980s, the Benetton brand has been associated with youth and cultural diversity. It broadcasts its identification among that audience by offering bold messages about race relations and international human rights issues. In the mid-1980s, the United Colors of Benetton campaign was particularly irreverent and evocative—basically asserting that Benetton respects all people but has no respect for social conventions.

These messages were communicated mostly by Oliviero Toscani's powerful imagery—in the company's ad campaigns, in-store visuals, and its magazine, *Colors*. Whether it was the images of death row inmates, the bloody uniform of a dead Bosnian soldier, or a priest kissing a nun, it was impossible for consumers not to have a reaction.

AN R&D CENTER . . . DEVOTED TO COMMUNICATION

In 1994, Benetton created Fabrica, its artistic laboratory. The company describes Fabrica (the Latin word for *workshop*) as its communication research and development center, a concept that I find fascinating when I think of the idea being applied to corporations at

I firmly believe that the soundest ideas emerge from a conversation between creative thinkers who are committed to finding a solution to an issue; and they are often ideas that no individual who is part of the conversation would have come to on his or her own.
—Don Hogle, Euro RSCG MVBMS, New York

Benetton Fabrica Features

large. Fabrica is housed in a large complex designed by the Japanese architect Tadao Ando. Located outside Treviso, the more than 11,000 square meters of space contain a cinema, a library, an auditorium, laboratories, and photographic studios. Young artists studying a wide range of media come from all over the world to collaborate on communications projects.

Benetton promotes Fabrica as "a way of marrying culture and industry, using communications which no longer rely on the usual forms of advertising, but transmit 'industrial culture' and the company's 'intelligence' through other means: design, music, cinema, photography, editorial and Internet."[8] What Benetton has clearly realized is that branding is no longer about communications strategy. It is about business strategy. And while Fabrica may be innovative, it is also deeply consistent with the company's heritage of innovation, particularly in addressing important social and political issues and refusing to rein in creative talent. In a media interview, Toscani talks about the importance of giving strategic freedom to creatives: "Agencies get huge budgets, but the money is wasted because strategies are decided upon by managers, economists, focus groups—not the artists. In the past, patrons had the sense to tell Michelangelo what they wanted and to let him decide how to do it, but it does not work that way anymore" (see Note 8).

Benetton found itself mired in controversy when its 2000 ad campaign featured death row inmates from the United States. The media debacle included a lawsuit from the state of Missouri and the loss of a new deal with Sears, Roebuck and Co. The controversy may or may not have caused Toscani to leave Benetton, but it did not stop the company from keeping creativity at the heart of business strategy. With the departure of Toscani, Benetton put its communications strategy into the hands of his creative legacy, Fabrica.

In a June 2001 interview, Luciano Benetton spoke about his company's close working relationships with advertising talent: "Since its beginning, the company has had just two relationships regarding advertising, first with a local advertising agency for 18 years. Then we had a relationship with Oliviero Toscani for 18 years. So we are quite faithful. Now we have invested in Fabrica, and we hope this will be useful for more than 18 years."[9] Luciano Benetton has invested in creating an environment in which singers and dancers can flourish. Which makes him, in my view, a very smart CEO.

For me, Benetton reinforces so many of the same lessons to be learned from MCI. Create a culture that invites and rewards creativity. Empower employees to take the initiative and pursue new ideas. Give people autonomy and, as a result, a sense of worth.

BEFORE YOU LEAP:

- To communicate a brand's DNA, go beyond traditional communication vehicles and use other strategic weapons—design, music, cinema, photography, editorial, the Internet, whatever it takes. What Benetton has done, particularly evidenced in its store in Bologna, is to create a brilliant and innovative brand experience. In the future, for every brand, that will not be an option. It will be an imperative. (More on that later.)
- The other wildly innovative initiative, in my mind, is Benetton's communication research and development center, Fabrica. Virtually every corporation has centers devoted to research and development and coming up with new products. Why is it that more companies do not have R&D centers devoted to communication? Perhaps an idea worth borrowing.

THE CREATIVE BUSINESS IDEA AWARDS

My experiences with MCI taught me not just about the value of fostering a culture in which creativity can flourish, but also about the importance of rewarding people for their ideas. And did MCI ever reward! I saw firsthand the kind of spirit that is ignited with that sort of recognition and reward; it is something you cannot buy at any price.

It was shortly after the 100-Day Meeting in which we christened our new way of thinking "Creative Business Ideas," that I decided it was time to institute a similar reward mechanism within our network.

Even before we had formally adopted the CBI name, I had talked extensively both inside and outside the network about the need for a revolution in creativity. I used examples of numerous companies (some clients, some not) to communicate the concept. These were teaching stories—a dramatic, shorthand way to signal to my colleagues my belief that branding is no longer about communication strategy, it is about business strategy, that as a young network we had the opportunity to redefine what creativity means in our new age. In communication after communication, my message was that we have to help our clients build their businesses in new and creative ways.

In June 2000, I introduced the concept of CBIs at the International Advertising Festival in Cannes. I also decided it was time to integrate the concept formally into our agency offices around the world. If Euro RSCG Worldwide really believes that our industry should be valuing creativity based not on reels of work but on the brilliance of Creative Business Ideas, then we should lead by example—by rewarding that kind of high-level creative and strategic thinking within our own organization.

On a hot summer day in New York, a small group of us sat down for what we thought would be a short meeting. Essentially we were there to discuss what kind of contest it should be. What were the rules? The prizes? Who should be the judges? And by what criteria should they judge?

Seven hours later, we had made a few critical decisions. We refined the definition of Creative Business Ideas and established the criteria for judging them. We decided that the jury should consist of top creative people within the global agency, as well as one or two outsiders. Instead of printing a traditional entry brochure, we would announce the contest online. And we decided that the prizes would take the form of money—and that they would be substantial. By doing so, we were not only guaranteeing that agencies would enter the contest, but also reinforcing our commitment to rewarding big, brilliant, industry-changing ideas.

The official kickoff was in September 2000, when I sent a message to more than 7,000 people in the agency and invited them to visit the contest's website. I urged every individual in every office throughout the agency to enter this new contest. I encouraged people to submit their best work; to dazzle us with their ideas; to present examples of creative thinking that go far beyond all traditional means of communication.

The response was overwhelming. On an average day prior to the announcement of the contest, there were 7,500 hits on our agency's intranet site. On the day we announced the contest, that number doubled to more than 15,000. When we distributed an HTML-animated e-mail card to the network, another record was set: more than 20,000 hits. Most impressive, though, was the number of responses we received: more than 90 submissions from offices all over the globe.

We narrowed the submissions to 14. The day the shortlist was posted on our intranet site, there were some 32,000 hits.

If an office made the shortlist, we asked it to submit creative material. The jury was made up of some of the most creative minds in our network, from five cities on four continents and from all disciplines. Our outside judge was Romain Hatchuel, CEO of the Cannes Lion International Advertising Festival. In January, the jury of nine met for two days to select the winners. The judging process was similar to that of the major international festivals.

Here's what I said in a welcome message to the jurors: "Just a year ago, I could count on one hand every example of a true Creative Business Idea. And only one of them was ours. Now we are presented with the rare opportunity to evaluate not just one or two of these ideas, but fourteen. Fourteen examples of exceptional thinking and creativity—and all of them are ours. From our own network. From our own people and agencies around the world."

By the end of the two days, we had our winners. One was clearly in first place. The other two were tied for second. Ironically for me, one of them was Volvo.

VOLVO: DRIVE SAFELY

When I first began working with Volvo Cars again at MVBMS, more than 20 years after I had left the company and 5 years after leaving Scali McCabe Sloves, the people at Volvo were not particularly happy. A misguided ad campaign had threatened to undermine the brand's essential message, *safety*. Their concern: Could Volvo reclaim the safety positioning?

Our response was that Volvo not only could, it had to. Safety was tied to the fundamental idea of the brand. Safety was the soul of Volvo.

But one cannot step in the same stream twice—we knew we needed to stake that claim in a different way. We needed to explain that safety was the soul of Volvo because it connected with what people cherish: their families, their children, their friends. We would ultimately talk about that in a way that only Volvo could: "Drive Safely."

Drive Safely became more than a tag line. It captured the essence of the brand. It enabled us to say that, while we are selling cars, we are also selling something much bigger: the idea of families and loved ones, the idea that people who care deeply about life can take steps to protect their closest relatives, friends, and themselves. We told Volvo to sign their letters and answer their phones with "Drive Safely"—and they did.

With the Survivors campaign, we showed people from all walks of life who shared a common belief that they would not have survived a particular car crash if they had not been riding in a Volvo. At the same time, veteran actor Donald Sutherland became the new voice of Volvo, a voice that distinctly embodied the set of values and

Volvo for life ad

sensitivity and intimacy we were trying to create. Over time, we felt, we could take this simple idea of Drive Safely and make it much bigger than just an ad campaign. Drive Safely not only allowed us to reclaim Volvo's preeminence in safety, it was a way for us to take Volvo to a new level.

VOLVO FOR LIFE

By the mid- to late 1990s, Volvo had begun to introduce a series of new products that would literally change its image: the S80 luxury sedan, the C70 coupe and convertible, the V70 T5 turbocharged high-performance sportswagon, the S&V40 (the new smaller Volvos) and the SUV-like Cross Country all-wheel-drive wagon.

These were not the old boxy Volvos that had been on America's highways since the mid-1950s. They did not look at all like the old Volvos. They were beautifully styled cars. As the head designer of Volvo, Peter Horbury, once said, "We have kept the toy and thrown away the box!"[10] With these new product introductions, we were able for the first time to talk about performance and design and styling within the context of Volvo's core values. We could talk about not just why you might need a Volvo, but why you might actually want to own one.

It was an exciting time at Volvo. The new product introductions enabled us to communicate the passion behind the brand. Volvo now began to stand for more than just protecting life; it began to stand for celebrating all that life has to offer. We said that in an emotionally potent phrase and, again, in a way that only Volvo could say it: Volvo for Life.

We had gone from a phrase said to departing friends, Drive Safely, to a more celebratory statement, a toast: for Life. We were not leaving behind what we stood for; we were broadening the meaning of what we stood for.

MAKING THE LEAP TO REVOLVOLUTION

By the end of the decade, Volvo as a company had been through radical changes. With the launch of the S60 in October 2000, it had, in a matter of just a few years, revamped its entire product line. It had also expanded its offering exponentially: from a two-model company to a nine-model company. It had been purchased by Ford and had become a part of the Premier Automotive Group (PAG). Volvo Cars of North America was also about to move from its longtime headquarters in Rockleigh, New Jersey, to new headquarters in Irvine, California—a move prompted by Ford's belief that Southern California is where car trends start and where its luxury brands needed to be in order to monitor the pulse of those trendsetting consumers. And, of course, Volvo had gone from saving lives to celebrating life.

In that 18-month period, Volvo probably went through more changes than it had in its entire prior history. By Volvo standards, it had been through a revolution. And that was the springboard for a concept that would become a rallying cry for everyone within the company and a proclamation to the outside world that this was not the same old Volvo. With Drive Safely and Volvo for Life, we had gone from A to B. This time we made the leap from A to B to M. The leap was Revolvolution.

The work on Revolvolution initially focused on the launch of the S60, which was slated to hit the market a year later. But it was clear from the start that this was no ordinary car launch. The S60 represented an entirely new and expanded product line. It offered the most exciting Volvo driving experience ever, with superior performance and styling.

The S60 was also a very different vehicle than the model it replaced—so we needed to appeal not only to Volvo's current customers, but also to consumers who had never previously considered the brand. These consumers in particular were the ones who needed to be made aware of the "new Volvo." The S60 was more than just a car; it was the banner of the revolution, an icon that symbolized all that the company had become.

Gradually, Revolvolution—as with all CBIs—became a much bigger idea. Revolvolution was a concept that conveyed the breadth of the changes at Volvo. It represented the culmination of the direction in which the brand had been moving for the past several years. Ultimately, it would serve not only as the mantra of the S60 launch campaign, but as a rallying cry for the company. Because it forced everyone to look at the business in nontraditional ways, Revolvolution became the business strategy.

The agency was convinced it had brought great creative thinking to Volvo's business. And how did top management react? When the idea was presented to Hans-Olov Olsson, president and CEO of Volvo Cars of North America, he immediately bought into the concept. One of his objectives was to double Volvo sales in North America, a truly revolutionary move for the company. Revolvolution fit right in with that. Olsson also saw Revolvolution as a way to convey the message internally to his organization . . . that everyone, throughout the company, needed to work differently and think differently. He wanted to look at everything, across the board, and evaluate it against a new criterion: Is it revolvolutionary? Everything from the structure of the used-car program to the use of media to event marketing, PR programs, and so on. He did not want Revolvolution to be just a slogan while everything else in the company kept to business as usual. He wanted it to be a benchmark against which everything was measured.

But as much as the president and CEO of Volvo Cars of North America liked the idea of Revolvolution, the president and CEO of Volvo Car Corporation in Gothenburg, Sweden, did not. He had major concerns about the phrase. He thought it was a misuse of the Volvo logo—very understandable, given that tampering with logos has been a long-standing taboo in most corporations, and particularly given the recent purchase of Volvo by Ford.

What happened next reminded me of my early days with Perdue, when Frank rejected the idea of being the company spokesperson and we went to the number two guy and said, "Hey, you have got to help us out here." As Jay Durante, the partner on the Volvo account and global brand director remembers it, he, too, had gone to the number two guy, in this case the vice president of global marketing, and asked what the agency needed to do to get approval for

Revolvolution. Whom did we need to convince? The agency passionately believed in its thinking—it was ready to fight for it. Durante was told it was an internal issue and to be patient.

Not being a patient person, Durante saw an opportunity to speed up the process one evening when several members of the agency team and Volvo senior management were attending the same benefit dinner. At that dinner, Durante approached Olsson—literally on the dance floor! The next day, Olsson would be attending meetings in Gothenburg. Durante asked whether he thought there was any possibility of Revolvolution being kept alive there. As Durante tells the story, Olsson grabbed him by the shoulders and said, "Revolvolution, Revolvolution"—as if to chant, "This is what we are doing." He also said it with a kind of knowing confidence.

What we did not know was that Hans-Olov Olsson was on his way to Gothenburg to become president and CEO of Volvo Car Corporation. Revolvolution was a go.

At the very first board meeting, Olsson made the announcement, "We are about to start a Revolvolution." As the story goes, he then made all of the board members stand up and chant "Revolvolution!" three times. From then on, Revolvolution became a global rallying cry that symbolized the company's forward focus and the need to reexamine everything about the way Volvo does business.

We created a CD-ROM about Revolvolution that announced to the outside world and the internal organization that Volvo had changed. Revolvolution became the theme of the annual Retailer Conference, promoting the message that change is here and everyone is a part of it. We also created a "Manifesto," which we distributed via companywide e-mail, as screen savers, and also used at point-of-sale and in print ads. It went like this . . .

THE MANIFESTO

Forward.
It's a Direction.
It's a Promise.
It's a Passion.

It's Revolvolution.

It's a commitment to moving the automobile forward.

It's moving from helping save lives to helping people feel more alive.

It's building a magnificent machine. Not for the sake of a machine. But for the joy of human beings.

It's moving from a car you need to a car you desire.

It's moving pleasure from a solitary pursuit to one that is shared.

It's moving beauty from something shallow to something deeper.

It's moving performance from something reckless to something sublime.

It's moving safety from the sedate to the sleek.

It's Revolvolution.

And today you can see it and feel it in the new Volvo S60.

Forward.

It's where the automobile is going.

THE S60 LAUNCH

Revolvolution was a Creative Business Idea that ignited a revolution in every part of the company, from corporate headquarters to Volvo's design studio to dealerships across America. It announced that, from this day forward, Volvo was doing things differently.

In turn, the launch of the S60 needed to be symbolic of that, which meant changing both the message and the way it was delivered.

Revolvolution ad

In short, a concept as big as Revolvolution demanded that we look at every aspect of the S60 launch differently. In essence, we took the opportunity to relaunch a company.

By the time of the S60's debut, Volvo had already rolled out two new vehicles in the year 2000 alone. The company was moving forward—fast. But there was a caveat: Volvo needed to launch the S60 with relatively minimal marketing expenditure. That meant the traditional media vehicles, used by virtually every car company for every car launch, were essentially unaffordable.

That was just fine. Revolvolution demanded a revolutionary approach to media. It would come in the form of using the Internet as the only national medium for the launch—a first for the automotive industry. Some time before, America Online had pitched the idea of an online launch directly to Volvo. Volvo turned to us for our recommendation. As Sean McCarthy, account director at Euro RSCG MVBMS, explains it, the idea of an online launch in and of itself was initially unappealing. Traditionally, everyone used television as the primary vehicle with which to build awareness and interest—if you had the resources, you probably would not choose online as your sole form of media. But what if you could bring creative thinking to the concept of an online launch? Then you might have something extraordinary, something with which to challenge the conventional methods of launching a car.

Volvo knew that 80 percent of people looking for a car and considering Volvo would research it on the Internet. So the company made a bold—and what many viewed as a risky—move: It formed a partnership with AOL to launch the S60 exclusively online. That partnership, in turn, enabled Volvo to incorporate innovative promotions into the Revolvolution launch. The S60 was promoted through welcome-screen placements, banners, and special-content areas. A special options package was offered exclusively to AOL subscribers, giving them up to $2,100 in complimentary Volvo accessories when they purchased an S60. A direct-mail piece with a CD-ROM offered an instant connection to the Revolvolution.com website, where consumers could configure their new S60 online and request a price quote directly from a Volvo retailer.

Consumers who conduct online research are more informed—and that is good for Volvo. Nevertheless, Volvo retailers were skeptical. Revolvolution necessitated a revolution in the mind-set of retailers with regard to the sales process. Volvo had to convince them that it is good for consumers to start the buying process online.

There is a happy ending here. Part of the original plan was that a world-first idea like this would garner significant press. Which would mean that the launch of Revolvolution and the S60 itself would be featured in mass media—at no additional cost. Indeed, it was viewed as so innovative that it was covered in the *Wall Street Journal* and was picked up by more than 60 mass-media outlets—in just the first week of the campaign. That is significant exposure. And significant value.

The campaign also generated 2 million visitors to Revolvolution .com, 300,000 opt-ins for future Volvo communications, and 45,000 online sales leads. The retailers needed no more convincing.

The objectives of the Revolvolution launch had been to communicate changes at Volvo in a new way; to build awareness and interest in the new S60 sports sedan, positioning it as an emblem of change; to support Volvo's aggressive sales goals within the first three months after launch; and to illustrate how the S60 overcomes historic barriers to purchasing Volvos. In the end it accomplished all of these, but it did much more. The exclusive use of online media saved Volvo money, but more important, it added credibility to the claim that Volvo was changing the way it did business. It was a big, bold public statement that clearly said, "This is not the same Volvo."

That's why Revolvolution was recognized and rewarded as one of the top three CBIs within our network during the past year. It's an idea that combined creativity and strategy in new ways, resulting in breakthrough solutions and industry firsts. It arose from and influenced business strategy, not just communications strategy, and it led to innovative execution across traditional and new media. It transformed

I think technology and new media have been monumentally instrumental in helping to drive CBIs into our culture. Look at the launch of the S60 . . . Revolvolution . . . for Volvo. An unbelievable example of how the Internet launched a car model, a first in the category. We can look to that effort and apply all that was good about it to many other categories.
—Daniel McLoughlin, Euro RSCG MVBMS Partners, New York

marketplaces/marketspaces and created new ways to maximize relationships between consumers and brands.

DO YOU NEED A REVOLUTION?

THERE IS NO WAY REVOLVOLUTION EVER WOULD HAVE HAPPENED WITHOUT THE COMMITMENT OF THE PRESIDENT AND CEO, HANS-OLOV OLSSON.

Olsson and I have known each other for almost 30 years. He is a remarkable leader. Which gets back to what is probably the most important prerequisite for CBIs: There can be no Creative Business Idea without corporate acceptance of creative thinking at the highest levels. It is imperative that there be high-level executives who relish new ideas. Hans-Olov Olsson was as passionate as one can get. And, yes, Swedes can be very passionate.

> **BEFORE YOU LEAP:** Know that sometimes incremental change is not enough. For a company in need of a new direction, everything must be shaken up—from the corporate mission to brand communications. Monumental change requires high levels of energy, which cannot be attained when everyone at the company remains seated.

Volvo had to start a revolution in order to encourage people at the company to think in new ways. What do you have to do?

THE REVOLVOLUTION CONTINUES

Let's say you have just implemented an incredible CBI, as brilliant as they come. It directly influenced your business strategy. It led to innovative execution not just across traditional and new media, but beyond it. It was a breakthrough solution, an industry first. Okay, let's go all out: It transformed your business, and even the category in which you compete. Are you done?

Hardly.

CBIS ARE NOT ONE-TIME-ONLY EVENTS. IT IS NOT AS IF THE PERFORMANCE IS OVER, THE CURTAIN COMES DOWN, EVERYBODY APPLAUDS AND CONGRATULATES YOU FOR YOUR BRILLIANT IDEA, AND THEN YOU GO HOME.

CBIs are part of an ongoing process that requires you to constantly build on what you have accomplished. We are talking multiple encores here.

What's next for Volvo? Launching the S60 online became an expression of how the company intended to do business in a new and different way. Just a few months after the launch, Volvo continued its innovative efforts in new media with a fully integrated promotion built around the NCAA Final Four college basketball tournament. The promotion, which launched on March 15, 2001, was designed to drive people to Volvo's Revolvolution.com website by reaching them at every touch point: television, interactive TV, the Internet, PDAs, and WAP-enabled cellphones. You could run, but you could not hide! The sweepstakes culminated in a live webcast, on the day of the championship game, during which a Volvo S60 T5 was given away.

Once on the website, signing up for the S60 promotion was only a click away. Visitors could also sign up for free tickets to the Final Four and Championship games—as long as they filled out an online questionnaire. As Phil Bienert, manager of CRM, e-business, and future product strategy for Volvo Cars of North America, said in the March 16, 2001, issue of the *Wall Street Journal,* "We know convergence is coming. We need to try these things out now and be prepared for it."

Through its tracking mechanisms, Volvo could determine which form of media was most effective in driving people to the website. It also gained a qualified-lead database of potential customers who agreed to receive future online promotions from the company. In a two-week period, the Revolvolution message was exposed more than a quarter of a million times. There were more than 62,000 entries in the contest, more than 20,000 opt-ins who were willing to enter into a dialogue with Volvo, and more than 10,000 consumers who filled out the questionnaire.

The NCAA sweepstakes is something that, even a few years ago, would not have been Volvo's style. Revolvolution changed that. This was not your same old Volvo. And in the fall of 2001, Volvo further demonstrated its commitment to new and innovative ways of marketing by teaming up with the Bravo cable television network to create the first synchronized interactive program of its kind. The program is the network's popular interview show, *Inside the Actors Studio,* which spotlights actors, writers, directors, and composers. Volvo has been sponsoring the creation of content linked to each episode, calling the interactive experience, "Interact with Inside the Actors Studio."

Volvo has a presence throughout the program, and during the "classroom" discussion that takes place online immediately prior to and following the show it offers additional content and gives users the opportunity to get exclusive information about Volvo products. There are also links to the Volvo website and opportunities to explore in-depth information on purchasing or leasing a car, car safety, automotive design, and so on.

Today, as Volvo continues to think differently about how it brings cars to market, the Revolvolution continues. The company is still looking for the Revolvolutionary in everything it does.

How about you? Is it time for you to start a revolution?

Chapter 5
Creativity at the Heart of Business Strategy

The Power of Two (or More)

"No man is an island" may be half of all we need to know to get by in life, but it's been repeated so often over the past four centuries that many of us have become numb to its truth. Talking about clichés, "We're all connected" is a corporate slogan. Just lose your job and your money, cynics would say—then see how connected you are. We are born alone, we die alone, and if we are part of a social unit that's bigger than our immediate family, we can count ourselves among the lucky.

Our understanding of the arts, which glorify individual achievement, reinforces this sense that this is a world of sole proprietors. Bach, Mozart, Beethoven—we see them alone at their pianos, composing in a solitary reverie. But that's not quite accurate. After Bach, all composers stood on the shoulders of their predecessors or had the support, if not the outright inspiration, of others. Beethoven was overt about it; he kept a picture of Bach on his desk. And for all Mozart's genius, we might not have the overture to *Don Giovanni* if his wife had not sat up all night with him, feeding him delicacies and telling him stories to keep him awake as he wrote.

Or consider the ultimate solo performer of our time, Bob Dylan. He's written hundreds of classic songs, all of which he's capable of performing alone. But if you read the biographies, you see that Dylan—particularly in the early days—has been the ultimate creative "blotter," absorbing influences, musical themes, and lyrics from everyone and everything around him. And not to denigrate Dylan's brilliance, but his career moved to a much higher level when The Byrds began recording his songs (and turning them into hits) and, later, when he started performing with The Band.

The theologian Pierre Teilhard de Chardin had it right: When minds rub together, the mental temperature increases. New ideas emerge. And they're stronger.[1]

We actually learned this in the eighth grade. Remember Gregor Mendel and the breeding of hybrid peas? Capital and lowercase As and

Truly great advertising people are those who think not of clever advertising ideas, but of clever business ideas that fundamentally change the way in which customers think of a product, brand, or company. If one approaches a problem by trying to find a real Creative Business Idea, it allows everyone to focus on big business solutions rather than one-off communications ideas.
—Chris Pinnington, Euro RSCG Wnek Gosper, London

Bs were matched to form a telling little square of possibilities. The moral: When varieties with various dominant genes get together, a better, stronger strain of pea emerges. That's called *hybrid vigor.*

Or look at any university graduate-degree program or corporate training program. There's a senior figure, with a distinguished career. And then there's a Young Turk, bursting with ambition and energy. One mentors the other. But don't both benefit?

It was into this tradition that I arrived at Scali McCabe Sloves, eager to learn and make my name. As luck would have it, I ran almost immediately into one of those protean figures who really was a one-man show—he'd made his fortune his own way, he'd defined his product according to his own priorities. An island? Too small. Frank Perdue was a continent.

And how do you move a continent?

Fight for What You Believe In

The year 1971 was the first time I presented a strategy and advertising campaign to a client. It was—Ed McCabe, Sam Scali, Marvin Sloves, partner Alain Pesky, and I immodestly thought—a brilliant campaign. And it was an incredibly exciting moment for me, personally. Mind you, I was still in the enthusiasm business more than I was in the advertising business. I had just made a cosmic personal leap of my own and was now in an industry I never imagined I would be in. I had also abandoned my lofty perception that all the account guys do is carry the bag around with everyone else's ideas in it. Once I hit the real world, it did not take me long to figure out that the way you get things done in the ad business is to work directly with the client—which is exactly what those account people do. So here I was, one of "those guys." This was my first account. I could not wait to help make the pitch.

It was an utter failure—at least initially. The client hated it.

The client was Frank Perdue.

At Scali McCabe Sloves, as a small, creative, up-and-coming agency, we had been thrilled to win the Perdue account. We also thought we had the creative nailed. "It takes a tough man to make a tender chicken" and "How to tell my chickens from the rest of the flock" seemed perfect ideas for starting to transform what was just a commodity into a real brand. Perdue chickens *did* stand out from the rest. They were yellow in color rather than white. The coloring came from the feed, which included corn gluten and marigold petals. They *looked* like higher-quality chickens, and they were.

It was not the concept to which Perdue objected, it was the execution. But his rejection revealed a quality I came to admire about Perdue: his openness to creative thinking.

WHICH CAME FIRST? THE EGG!

Perdue's father had started the business in 1920, the year Frank was born. Frank joined the business in 1939, at age 19 and took it over in the early 1950s. The family initially sold eggs, then moved into the business of raising live chickens to sell to processors. It was not until 1968, in a down market, that Perdue decided to get into the processing end of the business. Perdue saw that as a way to get around the processors, who were squeezing profits. But that would also catapult him into a new business arena: differentiating his product from the competition.[2]

Frank Perdue's chickens were better chickens for a host of other reasons—which we realized on our first visit to Salisbury, Maryland. And, as Perdue recognized, that meant he could charge a premium for them. But how would consumers distinguish Perdue chickens from the other guy's? They wouldn't have . . . if Frank Perdue hadn't come up with a brilliant creative idea.

He would put a tag on his chickens so that everyone would know they were his. He would brand his chickens with his own name.

Does Frank Perdue fit into the category of visionary entrepreneurs, those CEOs who in and of themselves think creatively about their businesses and have the ability to single-handedly make leaps that take them to new places? Frankly, Perdue does not fit into any category. He is a wild, unique individual. But he sure knows how to make a leap. Whose idea was it to turn the commodity of chicken into a brand? It was Perdue's. But his motivation was not to get his name in lights—which is probably why he initially rejected our first ad campaign. Ego-driven he is not. He simply believed that he had a better product and that he should be paid more for it. That is what drove him. Frank Perdue is a great example of a really driven CEO who understands that to be successful requires thinking outside the traditional boundaries of business. And doing things that extend way beyond traditional advertising.

Getting the Word Out

Soon after he established his plant, Perdue began doing some advertising, mostly radio, on a small budget. As his business grew, he set his sights on Madison Avenue. A lightbulb had gone on, which I have always thought must have been similar to the one that went on when I realized that if it were not for advertising, Americans would not know about Volvo. Perdue, too, was beginning to see the impact of advertising. But, as with Volvo, Perdue did not decide to seek out a Madison Avenue agency just because he wanted to build brand awareness and get his name on the public radar screen so he could sell a lot of chicken. Advertising was a way to build his business, to become known as the premium producer of chickens. Advertising would help create demand that exceeded supply, thereby giving him permission to charge a higher price per pound.

I think that is why Frank Perdue's quest to find an ad agency was, like Perdue himself, anything but traditional. It took an enormous amount of time. After extensively researching the advertising industry (he became an amateur expert in it) Perdue holed up in a hotel room in New York and interviewed agency after agency. He finally selected Scali McCabe Sloves.

Part of the reason he chose us is that we were a young firm, and a small one—there were only 15 of us. Perdue was a hands-on guy, and our size would give him the opportunity to be involved directly in the advertising. We had the Volvo account, which I am sure helped. But I think the deciding factor was probably Ed McCabe, who was one of the true creative geniuses in the business. When Perdue hired Scali, he did not just get advertising, he got large-scale creative thinking about his business, based on a deep understanding of what his business was—namely, one of creating demand that exceeded supply and affected pricing.

Our work on the account was about a whole lot more than just pushing chicken. For instance, when trying to find a way to maintain premium pricing for chicken parts—FDA regulations dictate that if there is a tear on the skin, it cannot be considered Grade A and must be cut up and sold as parts—the biggest challenge was the physical branding itself. On whole chickens, you could tie a string with a tag onto the wing. How do you put a tag on other parts? Someone in the agency came up with the idea of a pincher tag, which could be easily applied to every piece. As a result, Perdue could charge the same premium pricing for his parts.

We also helped move Perdue into the hot dog business very early on—chicken hot dogs, of course. The point is, Perdue got more than advertising, he got great creative thinking about his business. And, eventually, together, we built a brand whose substance and depth reflected the soul of the company.

Perdue was a visionary who made an incredible leap of his own when he decided to brand chickens with the Perdue name. But he also knew that to make the additional leaps to take his business where he wanted it to go, he could not go it alone. He needed a strong agency partner. And McCabe was a critical element in that partnership.

That said, the relationship was tested almost from the start. Once we had been awarded the account, the phone calls started coming—nonstop. Some clients leave you alone and let you do what you do. Perdue was the opposite. At one point, McCabe told Perdue, "You know, Frank, I'm not even sure I want your account anymore because you're such a pain in the ass." Perdue's response was typically Perdue. Instead of being insulted or pulling the account—a likely response if it had been any other client—he told McCabe he agreed with him. And then continued the conversation where they had left off.[3]

PUTTING A FACE ON THE BRAND

The first campaign that we created was based on an approach that, though commonplace today, was fairly revolutionary at the time—we decided to put Frank Perdue on the air. To us, it made total sense. Perdue was animated, credible, and totally passionate about the quality of Perdue chickens. He would be the ideal spokesperson.

But when Perdue saw the campaign, he flat-out rejected it. Our thinking was that this man's passion would be great—how could it not be contagious? His thinking was that it was way too egocentric, that the public would not respond, and that his employees would not, either. There was no way he was going to be in the commercial. Remember, this was way before CEOs took to the airwaves in droves. He told us to get rid of the campaign and opined that maybe he had picked the wrong agency.

If we had not been such a young agency, I suppose we might have killed the idea right there and gone back to the drawing board. But we could not. We were just as passionate in our belief that he was the ideal spokesperson because he was passionate about the quality of his chickens. We went back to the number two guy at Perdue and said, "You have got to help us."

> **BEFORE YOU LEAP:** Take a lesson from Perdue. And Volvo. Do not underestimate the value of maintaining a good working relationship with your client's second in command!

I don't remember how long it took, but eventually Perdue came around. The commercial went on to become that year's best TV commercial under 60 seconds, according to the Copy Club of New York. *Advertising Age* ranked it "the best trade campaign of the year" (see Note 3). Demand soared. Sales skyrocketed. And Perdue was on his way to transforming his commodity—into a brand.

BEFORE YOU LEAP: Know that if you believe in an idea—if you really feel passionate about it—you have to be willing to pursue it relentlessly and to fight for it. Even if it is initially rejected, you cannot give up. Sometimes even truly great CEOs who are genuinely open to creative thinking do not embrace an idea immediately. But that doesn't necessarily mean they've closed the door forever. Some have the courage to admit they have changed their thinking. And once an idea is proven to be successful, they may even be grateful.

BREAKTHROUGH SOLUTIONS, INDUSTRY FIRSTS

Frank Perdue's is a classic Creative Business Idea. It revolutionized the poultry industry. And likely many others. Years later when I was to meet Dennis Carter—the man who led Intel to the Intel Inside® idea—he would tell me that his primary influence was learning about a man and a company named Perdue.

Like all great Creative Business Ideas, Perdue's idea also led to numerous industry innovations and breakthroughs. And those firsts go way beyond being the first to brand chicken successfully and being one of the first to have the CEO serve as the company spokesperson in advertising. According to the Perdue website, Perdue was the first, in 1974, to develop a new product: the Perdue Oven Stuffer Roasters, which are bigger birds weighing around five to seven pounds. It was the first poultry company to provide nutritional labeling on packages. The first to offer a money-back customer satisfaction guarantee and a toll-free consumer hotline. The first to use special packaging to ensure freshness. The first to offer fully cooked chicken in microwaveable containers. This first to have pop-up thermometers in the chicken to ensure they would be cooked perfectly. And on and on.

INNOVATION HAS BEEN AND CONTINUES TO BE A CORNERSTONE OF THE COMPANY'S SUCCESS.

Today, Perdue is among the largest poultry producers in the United States, with revenues of $2.7 billion. Still privately held, Perdue is ranked by *Forbes* as one of the 100 largest private U.S. businesses.[4]

From the day the very first advertisement was scratched on the wall of a cave, true creative thinking has remained the domain of clients. In the products and services they create, in the creative ways they market those products and services. Historically, agencies have merely spread the word, pushing their clients' wares. Yet somehow agencies garnered the lion's share of creative credit. Through the CBI, agencies now have the opportunity to earn their creative keep . . . working with clients to enlarge their visions, embark on more-profitable missions.
—Jim Durfee, Euro RSCG MVBMS, New York

INTEL: THE POWER OF BELIEF

A month after I was named chairman and CEO of Euro RSCG Worldwide, I had my first meeting with our clients at Intel. Our group had handled the Intel business in Asia for some years, had recently won it in Europe, and had also acquired the U.S. agency that had the business. So Intel had become a global client. In June 1997, I met Andy Grove for the first time. Grove is another leader whose openness to creative ideas is legendary. It began with his eagerness to brand the computer inside the computer—and invest enormous resources in building that brand. That required tremendous leaps of faith in the power of marketing and communications—and a very high level of trust in his agency partner. He had to believe in the magic of connecting people with something they cannot see.

RED X

Intel's first venture into marketing directly to consumers—now known as the Red X campaign—began back in 1989, coinciding with a general market shift toward the home PC user. The goal was to get consumers to upgrade from the 286 chip to the new state-of-the-art 386 SX microprocessor, which needed a boost in sales. The campaign was simple, but bold—the visual was the number 286 with a huge graffiti-style red X spray-painted over it. What was even bolder was that Intel had intentionally set out to cannibalize its own product line.

Dennis Carter, then the marketing director, was given an advertising budget of $5 million—a turning point in the brand's development. "We were changing people's buying behaviors," said Carter. "We proved to ourselves that we could communicate technical information in a basic way, and I concluded that we should do this more. Inadvertently, we had created a brand for processors."[5]

THE COMPUTER INSIDE™

Intel had always been a leader in technology—consistently the first to market with new generations of product. With the 286 and earlier generations of microprocessors, Intel had also licensed its technology to other companies, which manufactured the chips under their own names but to Intel's architectural standards. With the introduction of the 386 that changed: Intel did not license its 386 technology.

But that didn't stop competitors from marketing their microprocessors under the number 386 and, later, the 486. Intel knew its microprocessors were not the same as everyone else's. But the consumer didn't know that. Suddenly, Intel was confronting the same challenge that Frank Perdue had faced 20 years earlier: how to demonstrate the superiority of its brand. Because most consumers never see it, Intel needed to make the microprocessor "visible." It needed to convince people that it isn't just the name on the outside that counts—Dell, Compaq, IBM, whatever—what is inside the computer is equally important. Then it needed to get the word out that Intel technology is the best you can buy.

The idea of turning the microprocessor into a brand was a brilliant creative leap. From the start, Intel understood the critical role of communications in building that brand. And it put the same demands on its agency partners as it did internally—it expected nothing less than large-scale creative thinking. Not just about the advertising, but about the business.

It was in 1990, while working with a new agency, Dahlin Smith White (now Euro RSCG Tatham Partners) out of Salt Lake City, that Intel unveiled a new ad in the Red X campaign. Partner Jon White had worked directly with Dennis Carter to do something great. The ad continued with the graffiti-style imagery, with the numbers 386, 386SX, and 486 spray-painted on an image of a brick wall. But no red X this time. Instead, the text read, "The numbers outside." That was on the first page. By turning the page readers discovered the word *Intel* spray-painted on that same wall and, underneath, the phrase, "the computer inside."

The copy read: "Since buying a computer today is such a numbers game, here is a simple rule of thumb. Look for i386™ SX, i386™

DX, or i486™ on the outside to be certain that you have Intel technology on the inside . . ." (see Note 4).

Was it an advertising idea? Its execution was advertising. But it was part of a much bigger idea, and the result of much larger creative business thinking: to begin to change the consumers' mind-set—the way they think about computers—and convince them that the name on a component within the computer was far more important than the name of the computer's manufacturer. The CBI was not the advertising, it was the creative business strategy leap of branding the microprocessor. The advertising was creative thinking applied to that business proposition . . . which expressed to consumers in a meaningful way that the brains of the computer are what counts.

INTEL INSIDE®

The Computer Inside™ campaign was so successful that Dennis Carter decided to apply it globally. All went well until it hit Japan, where the Japanese agency deemed the slogan too complex and not readily translatable. Instead, it adopted the phrase, "Intel In It." The U.S. group liked what the Japanese had done with the phrase graphically. It even considered adopting the slogan as part of the companywide branding strategy. It was while brainstorming ways to adapt the slogan to a broader audience that the team came up with the tag line it uses to this day, Intel Inside®.

> INTEL INSIDE® CONVEYED, IN NO UNCERTAIN TERMS, THAT WHAT WAS INSIDE THE COMPUTER WAS AN INTEL MICROPROCESSOR. A SWIRL WITH "INTEL INSIDE®" WAS ADOPTED AS THE NEW LOGO—AND INTEL WAS SUDDENLY FRONT AND CENTER WITH THE GLOBAL CONSUMER.

BRANDING FIRSTS

Is it possible to turn a commodity into a brand? Today, we do not question it. But at the time, critics had a field day—especially with the company's plan to create a co-op advertising fund.

Dennis Carter called it a win-win situation. Any computer manufacturer that used the "Intel Inside®" logo in its advertising was eligible to participate in a market development fund. Though some manufacturers were reluctant to sign on for fear it would minimize their own brands, others applauded the idea—it reduced their advertising costs. For Intel, the exposure would be invaluable. The ad agencies felt otherwise. As Carter put it, they "hated it because they created these beautiful ads and they're told they have to stick the logo in the lower right corner."[6]

Carter's initial instincts proved right. The program was started in July 1991. By the end of 1999, Intel's expenditures on co-op advertising reached $800 million. A brilliant marketing move.

The co-op program gave tremendous exposure to the Intel name. Simultaneously, the company worked to make the name more meaningful to consumers. In the fall of 1991, it turned to television as a vehicle to do that, with the launch of the now legendary Power Source commercial.

In the spot, the agency used an innovative fly-through camera technique to take viewers on a visual journey inside the computer— to show in a hip, exciting way that the microprocessor is the brains of the computer, that it is what makes all those software programs run. And that the best microprocessor is Intel. The ad was an industry first. No one had ever advertised microprocessors on television before. It was the start of a decade-long period of breakthrough advertising.

DEMAND A CREATIVE RELATIONSHIP

I think what enabled Intel to create so many advertising firsts is that the relationship between agency and client has been truly collaborative. Euro RSCG Worldwide has been Intel's global agency since 1996, and our partnership has the ingredient that is essential above all else when aiming for great creative thinking and nothing less: a high level of trust at every level. As our global brand director for Intel, George Gallate, puts it, "Intel's culture is one of empowerment. Efficiency. It is highly organized. Highly aggressive. It is also highly passionate. Discourse is welcome, even encouraged. But when you disagree, you disagree and commit to the decided course of action." Intel expects the same passion and openness to new thinking from its agency.

And then there is Intel leadership. Without these executives' willingness to embrace creative ideas, none of the breakthroughs would have happened.

THE BUNNYPEOPLE

It is 1996. Imagine being pitched an ad campaign designed to show that Intel puts the fun into computing. You listen to the rationale: With the Intel Pentium® processor, consumers will have a better multimedia experience at home—they will even have fun. Then you see the execution: a bunch of BunnyPeople dressed in neon-colored bunny suits, dancing around a factory as they assemble Intel microprocessors. Yes, these BunnyPeople are supposed to represent your valued employees.

Be honest. How many CEOs do you know who would say, "Hey, that is a great idea, it is really creative. I really want to have my product associated with . . . BunnyPeople!" Fortunately, Andy Grove understood the power of the idea. The BunnyPeople were clearly having fun. So much fun, in fact, that you wanted to have something made by these fun-loving people, because then you could have fun, too. After all, home computing is supposed to be fun. That just somehow gets lost in a lot of the high-tech messaging.

The ad was launched during the Super Bowl in January 1997. The brand icon was so popular that it became a mascot. There were BunnyPeople toys for kids—even BunnyPeople keychains. More than 1 million dolls were sold.

ONCE AGAIN, EVERY CREATIVE BUSINESS IDEA THAT I HAVE EVER ENCOUNTERED INVOLVED A HIGH-LEVEL EXECUTIVE WHO RELISHES NEW IDEAS.

Intel: BunnyPeople ad

One cannot have a CBI in the absence of corporate acceptance of creative thinking at the highest levels. And Andy Grove has a tremendous openness to creative thinking.

ANOTHER INDUSTRY FIRST . . .

Intel was one of the first movers on the Internet. The company uses the Web for customer service, marketing, advertising, and developing relationships with end users. In fact, it uses the Web as a facilitator for all of its business transactions with its immediate customers, the PC makers. So it should come as no surprise that Intel would be the company to create another world first: the first-ever interactive TV commercial.

The commercial ran just a year after the debut of the Bunny-People. Same time: January. Same place: the Super Bowl. In the first part of the commercial, which ran early in the game, someone who looks like one of the BunnyPeople steals one of the Intel microprocessors. Who is this? And what is the motive? In this whodunit, that was left to the viewer to decide. Viewers were invited to log on to the Intel website and vote for one of a number of endings to the mystery. A staggering 2 million people logged on. Some 400,000 votes were cast. It was the world's first interactive commercial.

> **BEFORE YOU LEAP:** Understand that consumers are looking for a way to connect to and experience your brand. Give it to them.

BEYOND TRADITIONAL OR NEW MEDIA

Intel understands very well that it is a global company, and it acts like one. It uses the Internet to customize information for its customers, channels, and end users in 50 countries and in 15 languages. China is a key market for the brand, and Intel has invested extensively there. In fact, Andy Grove was the first CEO ever to do a webcast in China and the first to use webcasting to address a global audience from China. Exploring how to develop the Chinese market would also lead Intel to another great Creative Business Idea—an idea that has nothing to do with the Internet or mass media.

When Intel first entered China, back in 1994, it was still very much a developing market—nowhere near as mature as in the United States or Western Europe. In Western markets, Intel was making inroads into raising consumer awareness of the microprocessor and its importance. In China, most consumers had no idea what a processor was. Many did not even know what a PC was.

As with the Japanese market, attempting to translate The Computer Inside™ advertising campaign into Chinese was proving difficult. The Power Source ads were very successful in China because they were so novel and revolutionary for the marketplace. They helped create incredibly strong brand awareness. But the fact remained that most Chinese did not understand what a computer was, much less what a microprocessor did. So the agency in China decided to create a complementary campaign that would educate the consumer about what a CPU is and how important it is to the computer. As Mason Lin, group account director for Intel eight years ago and CEO of Euro RSCG China Group today, puts it, "With the messaging in the U.S., they were able to skip the fundamental message. There was no need to educate consumers on what a computer was. Here, if we had used that same messaging, it would have been like teaching the kindergarten student using a college textbook. If they do not know their ABCs, how can they be expected to read a novel?"

In developing that complementary campaign, the agency also faced another challenge. Because the country is so vast, using traditional mass media can become very expensive. And since Intel didn't need to reach the entire population of China (many residents, especially in the smaller cities and more rural areas, couldn't afford a PC even if they knew what one was), it wouldn't have been terribly cost-effective. So the agency turned to a very nontraditional means of building brand awareness: the bicycle.

THE BICYCLE AS MEDIA

The bicycle is still the most widely used form of transportation in China. What Intel decided to do was create bicycle reflectors, which would be distributed free of charge. The reflectors took the form of stickers to be placed on the backs of bikes. At night, the stickers reflected light—a safety feature for the rider. On the front of the sticker was the Intel logo and the slogan, "Intel Inside®." On the back were instructions on how to use the reflector and information on the importance of the CPU. And while the objective of the campaign was to expand brand awareness and educate consumers on the importance of the CPU, it also produced another major benefit: free advertising for Intel. The campaign ran until 1998 and was hugely successful, once again demonstrating the power of great creative thinking that transcends both traditional and new media.

> **BEFORE YOU LEAP:** Don't ever forget that consumers are your most powerful brand ambassadors! (And if the message happens to glow in the dark, all the better. . . .)

THE FIVE NOTES

Intel's willingness to invest enormous resources in building the brand has paid off. The "Intel Inside®" logo is recognized all over the world. So are the five musical notes that accompany that logo whenever it is broadcast.

In his book *Only the Paranoid Survive,* Andy Grove says, "If competition is chasing you (and they always are—this is why 'only the

Intel: Bicycle reflector

paranoid survive'), you only get out of the valley of death by out-running the people who are after you. And you can only outrun them if you commit yourself to a particular direction and go as fast as you can."[7] Andy Grove has demonstrated incredible leadership and courage. He has also exhibited another quality that goes a long way in learning to live with fear: optimism.

BE AN OPTIMIST!

There is a great quote in the lobby at Intel headquarters from one of the Intel founders, Robert Noyce, that says that "optimism is an essential ingredient for innovation."[8] It has to do with the notion that anything is possible, an idea most people do not grow up with. Yet optimism, I think, has been a major factor in allowing Intel to be so innovative and so successful in what it does. Ironically, that success takes place in an environment that is all about standardization: making millions of chips that are exactly the same and constantly raising levels of productivity at an exacting level.

You might not think there would be much room for creativity and innovation in such a structured environment. Intel has proved otherwise.

THE CHICKEN CONNECTION

Some months after becoming CEO of Euro RSCG Worldwide, I wound up having dinner with Dennis Carter at the "21" club in New York City. Carter was then vice president of corporate market-ing for Intel. By this time, Intel was our global client. Over dinner, I asked him, "How did our agency and your people get to the idea of 'Intel Inside®'?"

Carter told me that though his background was in engineering, he had switched gears and entered the MBA program at Harvard. While there, he happened upon a case study about a chicken com-pany—and learned a valuable lesson about turning a commodity into a brand. A lesson that would later be applied to Intel's microprocessors.

I simply could not speak. I could not say, "Dennis, you're not going to believe this, but Perdue Chicken (the case study that so profoundly affected you and Intel) was my first account in advertising. My training ground for understanding the power of branding." It was one of those moments of serendipity that is almost too good to believe. I feared it would sound false in some way and lose meaning. So I said nothing. It wasn't until much later that I finally told Carter and we both laughed.

Branding a chicken: clever. Branding something hidden, like a computer chip: also clever . . . but a lot harder. Then Nasdaq came to us with an even steeper challenge. How do you brand something as intangible as a virtual stock market?

Until 1990, no one had ever even considered advertising a stock market. There was no need. Most Americans thought of the New York Stock Exchange as *the* stock exchange—a monolith of a financial institution if ever there was one.

And then along came Nasdaq.

In 1961, an act of Congress authorized the Securities and Exchange Commission (SEC) to conduct a study of fragmentation in the over-the-counter market. The SEC proposed automation as a possible solution and charged the National Association of Securities Dealers (NASD) with its implementation. The Nasdaq was founded in 1971 as the first electronic stock market.

Nasdaq's vision was ambitious, to say the least: "to build the world's first truly global securities market . . . a worldwide market of markets built on a worldwide network of networks. By continuing to shape the new world of investing, Nasdaq is challenging the very definition of what a stock market is . . . and what it can be. Today, Nasdaq lists the securities of nearly forty-one hundred of the world's leading companies." Its open-architecture structure allows an unlimited number of participants to trade in a company's stock. Nasdaq transmits real-time quotes and trading data to more than 1.3 million users in 83 countries.[9]

It is especially important to have people open to new ideas. CBI thinking can stop dead in its tracks if the status quo rules. Part of the reason is just laziness; it is always easier to do what was already done than to come up with something new.
—Joanne Tilove, Euro RSCG MVBMS, New York

But being virtual has its challenges. Nasdaq was so virtual that it didn't physically exist anywhere. No monolithic building on Wall Street. No TV images of people making trades on the floor. No photo opportunities for the press.

Mind you, there was no disputing the performance of Nasdaq-listed stocks. In 1994, Nasdaq actually surpassed the New York Stock Exchange in annual share volume. But with success would come a new set of challenges. As the once-small technology stocks listed on the Nasdaq began to skyrocket, the exchange found itself confronted with an interesting dilemma: keeping those high-performing stocks from migrating to the NYSE. The NYSE had a strong and appealing image; the Nasdaq had none.

BRINGING CREATIVE THINKING TO THE BUSINESS

When the Nasdaq executives came to us, it was with a total openness to creative thinking. In fact, that is *why* they came to us.

The strength of the relationship we established with Nasdaq enabled the company to understand what its core business issue was: Most people didn't see Nasdaq as a stock market. To most investors, Nasdaq was a listing of over-the-counter stocks—a page of numbers in a newspaper. They didn't think of it as a stock market alongside the NYSE or the American Stock Exchange.

The initial business thinking on the part of the agency and Nasdaq—and a great deal of the credit—belongs to Brian Holland, formerly at Nasdaq, as well as to my partner Ron Berger.

Holland and Berger and I had all worked together for a time at Scali McCabe Sloves, and Holland had great respect for Berger's creative thinking and for my strategic thinking. Together we set a path for Nasdaq that would take it well into the future. The creative leap? To brand a stock market in the first place . . . starting with the positioning of Nasdaq as the stock market for the twenty-first century, "The Stock Market for the Next 100 Years." It was a brilliant Creative Business Idea.

REMEMBER: I WARNED YOU

To get the campaign approved we had to present it to the Nasdaq board. Holland did an introduction that included some research insights. Ron Berger and I presented the strategic thinking and the advertising and the overall idea: "The Stock Market for the Next 100 Years." The board liked it. One member stood up and said, "I am sure this is a good idea and will work, and for what it's worth Bob showed me how to make ideas happen many years ago with some wood-rimmed steering wheels." It was Graham Whitehead, now the head of Jaguar Cars and a member of Nasdaq's board of directors.

ONCE YOU HAVE SET A CLEAR PATH, AND IT IS THE RIGHT PATH, IT CAN TAKE YOU TO PLACES YOU NEVER BEFORE IMAGINED.

Out of that creative thinking would eventually emerge another big idea: the idea to somehow create a brand experience around Nasdaq. A tangible brand experience that took Nasdaq out of the virtual and anchored it in reality. Ultimately, we made another big creative leap. We decided to create an actual physical location for Nasdaq, a market site—to physically anchor it in a geographic place.

The goal was to provide Nasdaq with a visible and high-profile presence in New York City, the world's financial capital. But not on Wall Street—that would be way too twentieth century. We located it in a seven-story tower in the heart of the rejuvenated Times Square.

The Nasdaq tower—called MarketSite—was designed to dominate the neon landscape, with up-to-the-minute market information displayed 24/7 on the world's largest video screen. The high-tech

Nasdaq building in Times Square

CEOs take note: Those analyst meetings would go a lot better armed with consumer-spend reaction to your new CBI. CBIs breathe the life back into the role of the ad agency. Not the twentieth-century agency. It is dying. But the role of the twenty-first-century agency. The agency of the future. The agency I want to work for. For too long companies have downgraded the importance of their agency's role as a contributor of business advice. With CBIs, we are back. It is time to reclaim the streets. CBI development delivers new and exciting briefs for creatives to work on. Great for our clients' businesses and great for ours.
—Matt Donovan, Euro RSCG Partnership, Sydney

screen literally wraps around the cylindrical Nasdaq building, providing a panorama of financial news, market highlights, and advertising. The bottom three stories house the broadcast studio, with multiple satellite uplinks and live data feeds for TV networks. And, of course, the studio gives the press a place from which to report.

> **BEFORE YOU LEAP:** Understand that in any industry—but particularly in an industry that involves finance—consumers need the reassurance that brick and mortar provides. From Gateway to E★Trade, more and more companies are recognizing that truth.

As with Intel, Nasdaq has succeeded in turning an invisible technology into a powerful brand. It all began with the creative leap of deciding to brand a stock market in the first place. It is another textbook definition of what CBIs should be: It arose from and influenced business strategy. It led to brilliant execution *beyond* traditional and new media. It was a powerful new way to maximize relationships between the consumer and the brand. This kind of thinking never would have come about without the strong relationship that existed between agency and client and without the senior management at both companies leading the ideation process.

Chapter 6
Do You Know What Business You Are In?

Very often, when I give speeches or talk to our agencies about Creative Business Ideas, I reference Theodore Levitt's famous *Harvard Business Review* article on "Marketing Myopia."[1] Levitt very persuasively uses the example of railroads to emphasize the importance of figuring out what business one is really in. Until you truly and deeply explore and understand the definition of your business, you cannot possibly begin to take advantage of the opportunities before you.

From 1850 to 2000—in the industrial and information ages—the railroads believed they were in the railroad business. Those that became great at the railroad business learned to dominate that business. But in their apparent clarity of understanding about what business they were in, they missed an enormous opportunity. Imagine what might have happened if they had realized that they were not in the railroad business, but in the transportation business. They could have leveraged all their unique competencies in logistics and control systems and dominated the growth of transportation in the twentieth century. They would have seen the massive opportunities in trucking and containerized shipping and overnight delivery and maybe even the airlines. They would have seen how the innovation and technology of the twentieth century was reshaping what they could be—and should become. Their destiny would have been profoundly altered, to say nothing of their success. Had they had the kind of breakthrough that leads to a Creative Business Idea, they might have been bigger than Microsoft, Intel, and General Motors combined.

Does anyone remember Wang Laboratories? It was the Dell of the early 1980s, having moved from producing desktop calculators to pioneering word processing systems. Then the PC revolution hit. Wang should have been leading that revolution; instead, it was filing for Chapter 11. What went wrong? Wang failed to realize that it wasn't just in the word processing business, it was in the computing business.[2]

DISCOVER YOUR DNA

The lesson is simple, but critical to creative business thinking. Start every project by asking what business you are really in. If you understand that, you also begin to understand the essence of your brand and the DNA of your company.

Why is that inquiry so vital?

UNLESS YOU KNOW WHO YOU ARE, THERE IS NO WAY YOU WILL EVER BE ABLE TO COME UP WITH A CREATIVE BUSINESS IDEA. IT IS IMPOSSIBLE TO ARRIVE AT SUCH AN IDEA WITHOUT FIRST UNDERSTANDING THE FUNDAMENTAL ESSENCE OF THE BRAND AND THE BUSINESS IN WHICH YOU OPERATE.

Whether you get there on your own or partner with an agency that can think creatively about your business does not matter. What counts is that you get there. Because once you understand the business you're really in, you have the potential to transform your brand, your category, your company, and even your industry.

RATP: PROVIDING SERVICES TO MOBILE PEOPLE

One of our Creative Business Idea Award winners is a striking example of understanding the business you're in (or that your client is in). It's a brilliant piece of creative thinking that is revolutionizing the way people in one city are looking at public transportation. As luck would have it, that city is one that is held dear even by people who have never been there—Paris.

THE PROBLEM

If you rode the Paris subway system (Regie Autonome des Transports Parisiens, or RATP) in the mid-1990s, your experience was not particularly pleasant. And you weren't alone in that feeling; many riders complained that the metro was smelly, noisy, dirty, and dark. Robberies were not infrequent. And a series of subway bombings only exacerbated the problem. People used the metro not because they wanted to, but because they had to.

WE NEED AN AD CAMPAIGN

Faced with a serious image problem, RATP turned to our brilliant Paris office, BETC Euro RSCG. It requested the agency to create an ad campaign that would improve the metro's image. Short term, RATP needed to win back the riders who had defected. Long term, it hoped to increase ridership by making the metro an attractive and satisfying alternative to its main competitor: cars.

Agency planners began their research by going underground and riding the subway system. It didn't take them long to realize that dirt, overcrowding, and a persistent sense of unease added up to a fairly degrading experience. It also didn't take them long to realize that this dismal situation could not be reversed with advertising alone. What was needed was a bigger idea. So big, they sensed, that they decided to draw on the expertise of two of our other business units: design and interactive communications company Absolut Reality, to help define the idea, and Euro RSCG Corporate, which specializes in integrated corporate communications and consulting.

THE LEAP

How many agencies, when asked by a client to create an ad campaign, would come back and say, "Sorry, you don't need an ad campaign?" It goes against the grain of everything that we have been taught, and it's in complete opposition to the business model that has been gospel for the past half century. But that is exactly what BETC did: It said no.

During the research phase, BETC conducted consumer surveys. It even provided metro users with cameras and asked them to take snapshots of their underground experiences. The photos that came back focused on details such as gloomy lighting and dirty seating areas; they helped the agency to articulate the key elements of the consumer underground experience. And those insights helped the account team to make a creative leap that would end up influencing RATP's business strategy for years to come: The team asked themselves the key

Being so intimate with our clients' businesses, but not in our clients' businesses, gives us permission to have ideas that are more radical and provocative than ones clients are normally comfortable generating. There may be a sensational business idea but its implementation is blocked because of the perception of it violating some "sacred cow" within the client's organization. As outsiders advocating a bold move, we enjoy the status of disinterestedness and don't fall prey to politics and special interests.

—Marcus Kemp, Euro RSCG MVBMS, New York

question: What business is RATP really in? They realized that RATP should not really be in the transportation business—or at least not *just* in that business. It should be in the larger business of providing services to customers who just happened to be extremely mobile.

After winning the account, the first thing RATP and BETC Euro RSCG did was to form a "brand team." On the client side were experts in design, communications, and marketing—anything and everything that impacts the consumer experience. On the agency side were strategic planners, media experts, creatives, and the account manager. Together, the brand team set out to become a provider of services dedicated to mobile people.

This new vision, client and agency agreed, should not only transform the underground experience by making the space cleaner, more secure, and more beautiful, it should transform the behavior of the people who spend time there. Why should life stop when you enter the subway? In today's fast-paced world, you want to stay active and connected even while you're being transported.

The team envisioned RATP as a company that would fulfill the underground rider's needs. It would deliver goods and services that people consume while going from place to place. And it would provide instantaneous, customized information that would add value to customers' lives. The vision, in short, was "anytime, anyplace mobility services."

From Users to Customers

The first step was to define the target audience. Research revealed that 5 million people spent, on average, an hour a day in the metro. Research also revealed that they were in transit more often than the average urban consumer, for more purposes, at more times of the day and night. Rather than using the subway just for commuting to and from work, they were also likely to use it for getting to and from shopping, entertainment, and socializing. These 5 million Parisians were defined as the key stakeholders, contributing some 80 percent of RATP's revenues.

Were these 5 million people merely bodies that needed to be transported from one point to another? Or were they valuable consumers who just happened to be nomadic? As a first step, the brand team recommended that these Parisians no longer be called *users*. From that point on, they would be called *customers,* in the hope that, one day, they would be proud to ride the metro.

A company changing a point of view is one thing. It's much harder to change the attitudes of people on the front lines. So the agency created an extensive internal communications effort designed to motivate RATP employees to take pride in delivering a quality experience to the customer. To symbolize the transformation of their role, they would now be called *facilitators.*

THE TRANSFORMATION BEGINS . . .

Changing the Paris underground from a transportation company into a provider of mobile services required a complete shift in business strategy, a new competitive positioning, a new business model, and a long-term commitment to the work. The collaboration between agency and client began in 1995 and is still ongoing—some eight years later. In that time, RATP has accomplished the following:

- A complete renovation of the underground, which is now considered by designers and experts to be the most advanced in the world. It is the only metro, for instance, where scents are permanently diffused in the space. The lighting has been dramatically improved; the stations are clean; security cameras have been installed; and in keeping with the tradition of the metro's stunning art deco entrances, numerous other entrances have been redesigned to look like works of art.
- A changed perception about the metro's efficiency. Before the transformation began in 1995, subway riders felt that traveling by metro was slower than traveling by car. In fact, it was faster. Why did they get it wrong? Because they spent so much time on a metro platform, waiting. RATP responded

by installing monitors above the platforms that announced the wait until the next train's arrival.

A NEW BUSINESS MODEL

Five million customers. Five million customers who spend an hour a day on the metro. That's 5 million hours of captive audience. That's a huge business opportunity.

The brand team helped RATP develop a new "partnership" business model, which took the form of new services that could be financed by partners, with royalties paid to RATP. The result: Today, the metro is home to Internet terminals and ATMs, some 300 shops, 1,500 vending machines, and 100 newspaper distributors. Works of art are on display in many stations. In newly created theatrical spaces, performers give concerts. A customer website, launched in 2001, provides traffic information, customized itineraries, and a guide to what's going on in Paris.

Five million people on a moving conveyance can easily become 5 million readers. Recognizing that Paris had no newspaper like New York's *Village Voice* or Stockholm's *Metro* (now in numerous cities), the agency recommended that RATP start one of its own. *A Nous Paris,* a free weekly newspaper, now has a quarter of a million readers and is completely financed by advertising.

Another creative leap!

In a brainstorming session, the brand team made another creative leap. On the weekends, a good portion of the metro ridership was

RATP ad: Provider of mobile services

made up of people who had come in from the suburbs to spend the day in the city. They would require local transportation to areas not served by the metro. Also on the weekends, cycling was popular—on Sundays, some streets were blocked off just for cyclists. Why not put the two together? RATP liked the idea and decided to start renting bicycles. The bikes are painted RATP green, and the company now runs the number one bicycle-rental business in Paris.

RATP is a great example of a Creative Business Idea because the breakthroughs that the agency and client reached have dramatically influenced the nature of the business. In this case study, we see profitable innovation, transformed marketplaces and marketspaces, and new ways to maximize relationships between consumers and brands. And not just on a mildly successful level—RATP's growth was huge. Between 1996 and 2001, ridership rose 16 percent. Customer satisfaction has also dramatically increased. In 1995, the goal was to sell 100,000 annual passes each year, reaching 1 million passes a year in 2005; by 2001, RATP was already selling three quarters of a million passes annually.

And this all happened because RATP made the leap: It redefined the business it was in, from transportation company to provider of services for mobile people. That new mind-set changed everything, from the way the company thought about its opportunities and challenges to the products and services it provided its customers to the messages it communicated to the consuming public. Now, RATP was truly ready to meet the future.

> **BEFORE YOU LEAP:** Collaborate. Collaborate. Collaborate. As Jérôme Guilbert, strategic planning director at BETC Euro RSCG, put it, "It's the work done by the brand team that has completely transformed RATP. We work together, and it's that ongoing relationship that leads to creative thinking."

WHY ISN'T STARBUCKS CALLED MAXWELL HOUSE?

Remember the coffee wars? A decade or so ago, coffee brands Maxwell House and Folgers were fighting for supremacy in U.S.

supermarkets. Their weapons: promotion and price cutting. Their method: substituting poorer-quality beans to cut costs.[3]

Meanwhile, Howard Schultz was planning to reinvent the coffee business.

Coffee was then a commodity (as chicken was before Frank Perdue came along). Schultz wanted to inspire Americans to drink more—and better—coffee. His plan was simple and straightforward: He would offer a premium drink. Clearly, Schultz was in the throes of a Creative Business Idea, for he realized he wasn't just in the coffee business, he was in the business of creating a new-generation café culture.

How did a small specialty coffee store grow into an international business with more than 4,700 retail locations across the globe? How did the Starbucks brand dramatically change consumer behavior and become a part of the American lexicon? What did Starbucks have that Maxwell House didn't?

For starters, Maxwell House lacked a CEO who was a visionary entrepreneur like Howard Schultz.

The Leap

Howard Schultz paid no attention to skeptics who said that consumers would never pay $1.50 for a cup of coffee, let alone twice that for a latte. He never followed conventional business wisdom. Rather, he was driven by an intense, almost obsessive passion for his product and, by extension, for the business and its employees. Starbucks' creative leap was to take the commodity of coffee, produce a superior product, and turn that product into a brand experience that would become a social phenomenon. Starbucks Coffee Company did not invent gourmet international coffees or the concept of a café. But it did build on the history or, to use Schultz's word, "romance" of coffee and café society to make a creative leap that no one had ever made before.

The brand Shultz was determined to build began life in 1971 as Starbucks Coffee, Tea, and Spice in the Pike Place Market in Seattle. It was a small, quirky shop dedicated to selling high-quality, imported whole-bean coffee. Ten years later, it caught the interest of Schultz, at the time a salesperson in New York for a Swedish housewares company. The Starbucks store was selling an inordinate number of specially designed drip coffeemakers for such a small operation, so he went out to Seattle to investigate.

Schultz wasn't born with a discriminating taste for coffee—he acquired it from Starbucks. In his book about the rise of Starbucks, *Pour Your Heart into It,* Schultz describes his first visit to Starbucks as an eye-opening experience. On his plane trip back to New York, Schultz was unable to drink the airline coffee—he was already a convert. From then on, he could easily see himself as a brand champion who would re-create his eureka experience for millions of other Americans—and create a national appetite for good coffee.

After a year of courtship, Schultz joined the company and moved to Seattle. Then, in 1983, he had another eye-opening experience.

THE INSPIRATION

On a business trip to Milan, Schultz was captivated by the espresso bar culture: the many ways to prepare coffee, the skilled baristas, and the community experience of the café. He realized that Starbucks was missing out on what he now saw as the social aspect of coffee. And he was convinced Starbucks could bring this same experience to the United States. Management didn't agree. It saw Starbucks as a retailer, not a restaurant. The owners didn't want to risk diluting or damaging the brand they had worked so hard to build.

THE POWER OF PASSION

Schultz kept trying to convince his superiors that the espresso bar experiment was a good idea. He finally succeeded. In 1984, when Starbucks opened its sixth store in downtown Seattle, it had an espresso bar. On the first day, the store had 400 customers; other Starbucks had about 250. But upper management still wasn't buying it. With Starbucks' support, Schultz left the company and set out on his own to open a chain of cafés. He wanted both to re-create the Italian espresso café culture and to serve what he saw as a growing need for high-quality, quick-service "espresso to go" in urban areas.

He was quickly successful. Soon enough, he acquired Starbucks' six Seattle stores, its roasting plant, and its name. His goal was to open 125 stores in five years.

The true creative leap—and what ultimately distinguishes Starbucks—was Schultz's ambition to create a culture around Starbucks coffee, to reinvent the commodity by translating his "discoveries" into a national and, ultimately, international brand experience. Like Richard Branson and his Virgin empire, Schultz built the Starbucks brand with very little traditional advertising. From 1987 to 1997, the company spent less than $10 million on advertising. How did Schultz do it?

BRANDING THE COMPANY

Communicating a brand experience starts within the company. In the late 1980s, the concept of *shareholder value* dominated business decision making. Schultz wanted Starbucks to stand for higher ideals,

Starbucks store

and the first place to start was with his own employees, to whom he refers as *partners*. By 1988, Starbucks was offering health care benefits to all its employees—including part-time workers, which at the time was all but unheard of in the retail business. The payoff? Dramatically reduced employee turnover rates. And these satisfied, loyal, and enthusiastic employees turned out to be the best ambassadors for the Starbucks experience.

Shultz's second major employee initiative was the Bean Stock. In 1991, he offered stock options to every employee—a highly unusual step for a private company. Employees received 12 percent of their base pay in stock, at the time worth $6 a share. By 1996, an employee who had earned $20,000 in 1991 could cash in his or her stock from that year for in excess of $50,000. "One of the greatest responsibilities for an entrepreneur," Schultz says in his book, "is to imprint his or her values on the organization."[4] This philosophy also translated into a wide array of community-impact programs.

The culture of Starbucks—a dedication to the highest-quality product and respect for its employees—contributed to the success of a word-of-mouth campaign. Soon, with little traditional advertising and with Starbucks employees and the stores themselves serving as communications vehicles, Starbucks was in urban markets across the country. When entering a new market, Starbucks was careful to place stores in highly visible, high-traffic locations. Flagship locations, such as Astor Place in New York City and Dupont Circle in Washington, D.C., were selected to convey a certain style. For each new market, Starbucks hosted one big community event, with proceeds going to a local charity. It became very hard not to think well of Starbucks.

THE BRAND EXPERIENCE

Schultz saw his cafés as safe havens of "affordable luxury." But for luxury environments, the cafés were nearly as uniform as McDonald's. Each store was carefully designed to create the same sensory response—from the smell of fresh-ground coffee to the hiss of foaming milk to artwork and color schemes. In 1994, the number of new Starbucks began growing exponentially. Starbucks hired architect and painter Wright Massey to assemble a creative team of artists, architects, and designers to conceptualize the "store of the future." They cut costs by buying and designing in bulk. But they also drew on mythology, art, and literature to conceptualize and design four models for stores that would communicate the Starbucks brand and respond to both economic demands and the need for flexibility in

Technology is really just another medium. One of the most successful brands in recent years is among the lowest of low tech— namely, Starbucks, that little luxury that you permit yourself to indulge in perhaps multiple times a day, a little jolt of pleasure that punctuates your day.
—Sander Flaum, Robert A. Becker Euro RSCG, New York

appealing to customers' changing demographics. With Massey's team, Starbucks was making an investment in creative thinking at the heart of its business strategy.

Today, Starbucks has a presence in such diverse locations as Austria, Israel, Oman, Dubai, Hong Kong, and Shanghai. In order to reinforce the idea that this is a quality brand, it has introduced new products, including bottled Frappuccino® and DoubleShot, joint ventures with PepsiCo, and Starbucks Ice Cream (with Dreyer's Grand Ice Cream), which became the number one brand of premium coffee ice cream in the United States prior to completion of the rollout. The company also continues to grow its philanthropic pursuits.

Starbucks has succeeded for one overarching reason: It chose not to be a purveyor of coffee, but a purveyor of an experience centered on coffee and café culture. And that understanding permeates every move it makes, every shop it designs, every product it sells.

> **BEFORE YOU LEAP:** Understand that it doesn't matter what the other guys are doing. A single-minded focus on a great idea, pursued with passion, is virtually unstoppable. Another lesson to be drawn from the Starbucks case: Mantras and directives don't make a corporate culture, actions and attitudes do. Starbucks gained the loyalty of its employees by making them—and treating them as—valued partners.

FINDING THE SPACE WHERE CREATIVE BUSINESS IDEAS ARE BORN

In developing marketing communications, strategists and planners and advertisers have traditionally devoted a lot of time to understanding the consumer. The whole business model of building meaningful brands has been rooted in this. That's what creates brand loyalty. But to think in Creative Business Idea terms, all of us in the advertising business—whether CEO or head of planning or creative director—need to go beyond that and deeply explore and understand the nature of our clients' businesses, their companies and brand DNA, just as deeply as we understand the consumer. Then we can begin to see how these two areas of deep understanding can work together.

I think of this approach to ideation as two cells: one representing an in-depth understanding of the consumer and the other representing a deep understanding of the client's business and its brand DNA. Creative Business Ideas exist somewhere in the synapse between the two, in that place where we understand the possibilities of the business and make the link to the consumer.

How do you get to that place? Planners—and all team members—need to realize that we must spend just as much time understanding our clients' businesses as we do understanding our clients' consumers. Does that mean we need to redefine the agency-client relationship? Absolutely. In order for creative thinking to take place at the very beginning of the process rather than in the middle, we need to be there at the beginning, when the business strategy is being developed or reexamined. Often this means an agency must proactively demand a creative relationship from its client—which we'll discuss in more depth later. Creative Business Ideas are dependent on using our best creative people, our best creative thinkers, to think about our clients' businesses as well as their consumers. But our efforts will be well rewarded:

ONCE YOU UNDERSTAND THE BRAND HISTORY AND DNA, YOU CAN EXTEND THE BRAND, EXPAND THE CATEGORY, EVEN CREATE A NEW CATEGORY.

YAHOO!® — IN THE BUSINESS OF CREATING CATEGORIES

Yahoo!® was founded on an idea so obvious that others had already thought of it. It's just this: Organize websites into coherent categories, and suddenly you will be able to navigate the complex Internet. Pretty simple stuff.

So what helped Yahoo!® jump ahead of the other search engines and go on to own the category? Yahoo!®'s creative leap emerged out of one key realization: It wasn't just about the technology. It was about people and helping them find solutions—something that had universal appeal. Ultimately, Yahoo!®'s Creative Business Idea was to

When we speak about creativity, we are not only speaking about advertising creativity. . . . A CBI is an idea that makes you look at a product or a company in a completely different way. When we told Danone that they should say that their business is based on health, it completely changed Danone.
—Mercedes Erra, BETC Euro RSCG, Paris

make Yahoo!® a friendly presence online—not just your basic search engine, but a personally edited directory, a portal, and much more.

YAHOO!®—THE NAME THAT STARTED IT ALL

Back in the distant days of 1994, the two founders of Yahoo!®—David Filo and Jerry Yang—were Ph.D. candidates in electrical engineering at Stanford University. They started an Internet guide in a campus trailer as a way to keep track of their personal interests online. Before long, they were spending more time on their home-brewed lists of favorite links than on their doctoral dissertations. Eventually, their lists became too long and unwieldy, and they broke them into categories. When the categories became too full, they developed subcategories . . . and the core concept behind Yahoo!® was born.[5]

What started out as "Jerry's Guide to the World Wide Web" and then "Jerry and David's Guide to the World Wide Web" eventually received a new moniker. Yahoo!® is an acronym for "Yet Another Hierarchical Officious Oracle," but Filo and Yang insist they selected the name because they liked the general definition of a *yahoo:* "rude, unsophisticated, uncouth." The success of the brand was rooted in this impish attitude. Let others dub their portals with such exalted names as Alta Vista, Galaxy, and Lycos—Jerry and David went in the opposite direction.

But a great name was just the beginning. . . .

YAHOO!® DEFINES THE "MAGIC MOMENT"

In March 1995, Filo and Yang incorporated the business and met with dozens of Silicon Valley venture capitalists. The company went public a year later, with 49 employees and an advertising budget of just $500,000. Then Yahoo!® went in search of a communications agency and found that most agencies simply weren't interested in such a tiny budget. But one was. It was a small agency in San Francisco, Black Rocket, so newly minted that it was waiting for its new computers to be delivered and consequently had to present its ideas as pencil sketches. Only an instinct for self-preservation kept the partners at Black Rocket from telling Yahoo!® they had very little idea what one did on the Internet.

This ignorance was a blessing in disguise. Because the way Black Rocket (now Black Rocket Euro RSCG) began to use the Internet would reflect what millions of consumers were about to discover: "the magic moment," that definitive session online when you find a solution to a problem and get an emotional high. With that revelation, it was only natural that the agency would see that Yahoo!®'s business wasn't about the science of search. Its real business was delivering the eureka moment—"I can find anything!"—to consumers.

Yahoo!® was one of the first Internet businesses to advertise on TV. It was surely the only one to feature a 70-year-old fisherman who isn't having much luck with his bait until he goes online to Yahoo!®. Wham, he is suddenly catching the big ones. At the time, there probably weren't many septuagenarians online, but Yahoo!® never pigeonholed the Internet as it was then; it showed what the Internet would become. By combining somewhat loopy ads with an invitational slogan—"Do You . . . Yahoo!®?"—and a catchy yodel, it was soon on the way to becoming everyone's Internet friend.

YAHOOOOOOO! THE FUN OF DISCOVERY

As Yahoo!® grew, so did its content, its services, and the creative way it promoted the brand. Yahoo!® went on to provide the following:

- A comprehensive news service
- A full financial-information service with data on any company, including a share-price monitor
- Access to more than 10,000 online retailers
- An auction service
- E-mail and instant messaging
- Everything from sports to games to personals to photos to horoscopes . . .

Yahoo!®'s methods of promotion have been innovative from the start. The Yahoo!® name appears on seemingly every available surface:

on Zamboni ice machines at hockey rinks, on wraps on Amtrak trains, and wrapped around taxis (a medium that Yahoo!® invented). Yahoo!® even recently placed product tags around a few cities (including Sale City in Georgia) with an invitation to join in the world's biggest Internet sale.

In less than a decade, Yahoo!® has built a brand equity that is now ranked in the world's top 50. It accomplished this by figuring out very early on what businesses it is and is not in. It is not in the business of technology. It is in the business of people. Yahoo!® is a friend on the Internet, a portal that safely guides visitors to places of interest. It is a safe and welcoming haven in a high-tech world, a world that can oftentimes be intimidating and uncertain.

> **BEFORE YOU LEAP:** When working in a high-tech industry, it is essential to remember that it's never about the technology. It's about the people who use the technology. And never, ever underestimate the value of a great brand name.

MTV: REINVENTING THE MUSIC EXPERIENCE

If you're going to talk about companies that are synonyms for fun and innovation, you have got to look back to the 1980s and consider the early days of MTV. The idea of creating a TV channel of free advertising for music groups was a huge creative leap in and of itself. It forever changed the music industry and the way music is marketed. It forever changed the way music is thought of and experienced and consumed. It played a pivotal social role. It turned a brand into a global phenomenon.

Yahoo!® branded taxi

Marshall McLuhan once said, "You can't see around corners, but you can hear around them."[6] That puts music in a place where it automatically is on a cultural edge, just ahead of mass awareness. What MTV did was to make that edge as visual as it was aural; for the first time, you could see the music that you used to envision in your head.

At the close of the 1980s, the *Washington Post* described MTV as "perhaps the most influential single cultural product of the decade."[7] But 10 years prior, the cable music channel was considered improbable, even contemptible. The reason: It featured rock music. And, since Elvis, rock had been the soundtrack of the counterculture, social protest, and bad taste.[8]

How do you bring music that invites censorship to television? In a way that changes television entirely.

LOOK AT OLD IDEAS WITH FRESH EYES . . .

The idea of music on television, even of music videos, was not a new one. Nor did it have a happy history. Network TV didn't want to show Elvis below the belt, it didn't want to let The Rolling Stones sing "Let's Spend the Night Together" or let Jim Morrison sing about getting high. As a result, the combination of rock music and television was a doomed proposition. The very nature of this music and the musicians' identities conflicted with television executives' idea of what Middle America wanted to see on TV. As a result, popular music on network television was generally designated to family-style programming. We're talking Donny and Marie and Sonny and Cher . . . really cutting-edge stuff.

> *"New" doesn't mean taking the latest technological advances and shoe-horning your product pitch into it. Some of the most innovative ideas come from combining two ordinary things you never thought would fit together. It's as simple as the Reese's peanut butter cup. You got your chocolate in my peanut butter. You got your peanut butter in my chocolate. Success. Every opportunity to create should be fearless.*
> —Israel Garber, Euro RSCG MVBMS, New York

Music videos, in their rough form, had already existed for decades. They just weren't on TV—at least not in the United States. In the 1940s, Mills Panoram Soundies were jukeboxes into which you could deposit a dime in order to watch a short clip of someone such as Nat King Cole or Louis Armstrong lip-synching a song while being projected onto a small plastic screen by a lens and a mirror with closed-loop film. In the 1960s, the European version of the video jukebox, the French Scopitone, was popular. In the 1970s, on the heels of Beatlemania, record companies began producing promotional clips—visual interpretations of songs—to help sell albums. Bands like The Rolling Stones, The Beatles and The Who could be seen on European TV programs such as the British *Top of the Pops.* Michael Nesmith—a former member of the made-for-TV band, the Monkees—turned his attention to producing music video clips for television in Europe. He also had an idea for a music video show in America. John Lack, one of MTV's early crusaders, heard about it. The stage for MTV was now set. . . .

THE ORIGINS OF THE IDEA

In 1979, American Express bought 50 percent of the Warner Cable Company. It formed Warner Amex Satellite Entertainment Company to pursue specialized entertainment. Fortunately, I got a firsthand look at what was about to happen, as Warner Amex became a client of Scali McCabe Sloves. At the time, the company was beginning to explore the concept of using cable TV for narrowcasting: Nickelodeon was aimed at children and The Movie Channel at adults. Both became clients. John Lack was executive vice president of marketing and programming. Lack, a 33-year-old former executive at CBS Radio, liked music. Nesmith approached him and pitched his idea for a music video show in the United States. It seemed like a natural fit. So Lack hired Nesmith to produce a 30-minute pilot for Nickelodeon called "Popclips." The program was so popular it inspired Lack to try to create a cable channel dedicated entirely to music videos.

IGNORE THE NAYSAYERS

John Lack's vision was wise from a commercial point of view. The record companies were experiencing an unprecedented industry recession; they needed a shot in the arm. And there were other industry trends that supported his vision. The majority of U.S. radio stations ignored the more controversial punk movement in Europe, along with its protégé, new wave. New music wasn't being heard much on the radio, so people weren't buying new albums. Lack was convinced that MTV could become a venue in which record companies could introduce new artists to consumers. With some difficulty, he convinced top-level executives at American Express and Warner of the value of their idea.

NONLINEAR THINKING . . . AND ANOTHER CREATIVE LEAP

When Bob Pittman was brought on to design the format for MTV, he envisioned a television station with no programs: no beginning, no middle, no end. Pittman, who in his early twenties had had a short but wildly successful career as a radio programmer, was responding to what he described as the nonlinear thinking of the next generation. This was a true creative leap. Dubbing his targeted audience "TV babies," Pittman designed the product for a generation that had grown up with the TV on. That audience sought heightened stimulation, had shorter attention spans, and would welcome a loose, amorphous format.

Pittman knew he had to promote the channel itself—not individual shows, as the networks did. So he and former on-air radio promoter Fred Seibert worked to design a logo that would express the spirit of rock music. When they arrived at the "M" as a brick with the spray-painted "TV," they had to fight for it over the loud protests of in-house sales and marketing people, as well as the advertising firm with which they worked. Everyone argued that it didn't conform to traditional standards for successful logos. Which was exactly their aim.

I Want My MTV: Making Consumers the Brand's Ambassadors

Perhaps the most powerful communications victory was the "I Want My MTV" campaign. One year after its 1981 launch, MTV was facing extinction. It was having a difficult time convincing local cable companies across the country to carry the network. Advertisers were growing more and more reluctant to support cable in general, and record labels were hedging over providing videos free of charge. But the founders knew the channel had a kind of grassroots power.

After the first few weeks of airing, Pittman sent scouts to conduct field studies of what would later be dubbed "the Tulsa virus." The intent was to find out whether MTV was having an effect on record sales in areas of the country where the channel was available. What they discovered in Tulsa and in other small cities such as Wichita, Des Moines, and Syracuse, was astonishing. Record stores were seeing dramatic increases in sales of albums whose artists could be seen on MTV. Local radio stations were inundated with requests for new music groups that had been featured on the network, including Squeeze, the Tubes, and Talking Heads. But even more interesting were stories the scouts heard about the change in behavior of young people. Kids without cable were traveling to visit friends who had cable, just to watch videos. They started changing the way they dressed. One barber in Wichita told MTV scouts that boys were coming in asking for "Rod Stewart haircuts." The irony was that MTV wasn't yet available in large, culturally sophisticated cities such as Los Angeles and New York. Progressive music, through the medium of MTV, was reaching young people living in quiet, conservative American towns, allowing them a kind of identification with a larger, more radical world.

The "I Want My MTV" slogan took on a life of its own. The campaign lit a fire of protest—an activity to which young people are intrinsically drawn—and cable companies across the country began receiving phone calls and letters from young would-be viewers. In

New York City, negotiations with the Manhattan Cable Company that had been dragging on for about a year were at last finalized, thanks to the extra nudge of incessant phone calls from young fans demanding their MTV. The arrival of MTV in Manhattan set off a national media buzz that legitimized and solidified the network's growing reputation as a cultural force.

PRODUCT OF THE YEAR

In 1981, *Fortune* magazine declared MTV one of the products of the year. In December of that year, the release of Michael Jackson's *Thriller* video spurred a *Time* magazine cover story that declared a revolution in music, describing "the great video blitzkrieg . . . that has shaken up Hollywood, salvaged the record business and set up a whole new way of responding to music."

MTV has transformed not only the record industry, but also television itself. It has changed the way music is marketed and experienced and has had a lasting impact on the style of cinematography. It has created a commercial avenue to a huge and previously untapped market and serves as a pulpit for the younger generation. In 1992, some credited MTV's "Rock the Vote" as a critical factor in Bill Clinton's winning the presidential election.

That's one powerful Creative Business Idea. And it was made possible by MTV's recognition of what business it is in. It's not in the television industry. It's not in the music industry. It's not even in the music-video industry. MTV is in the business of serving as a voice—and an outlet—for a generation of young people around the world.

> **BEFORE YOU LEAP:** In trying to apply creative thinking to business strategy, a myriad of lessons can be learned from MTV. Here are two:
> - A creative leap does not necessarily demand an idea that springs from pure innovation. It can come from looking at long-standing ideas with fresh eyes and discovering a radical new way of seeing something old.
> - When it comes to brand ambassadors, enthusiastic, unpaid customers are usually far more valuable than highly paid celebrity spokespeople. Don't ever forget how important they are.

HALLMARK FLOWERS: THE VERY BEST

The creation of Hallmark Flowers was one of the ideas that initially led me to further articulate and develop the concept of Creative Business Ideas within Euro RSCG. What was so inspiring was that the assignment to think creatively about the Hallmark business came from the client. It is incredibly exciting when a CEO turns to a group of really talented art directors, copywriters, production people, strategic planners, and interactive people and asks them to think about the business. It is even more exciting when that same person tells us, "Don't do any advertising." Those are real breakthroughs.

What emerged from those creative sessions enabled Hallmark to  enter an entirely new business, one that could become a valuable source of revenue. And I think it all started there, with opening the door to rethinking the business—and, while decoding the brand DNA, discovering what Hallmark really means to its customers.[9]

AN INDUSTRY LEADER

Hallmark Cards, Inc., a family owned, privately held company, was founded in 1910 by Joyce C. Hall. Working out of a rented room at the YMCA with a shoebox full of postcards, he created the greeting card industry. And for decades Hallmark was the industry's undisputed leader. But by the end of the 1990s, the company knew that it would need to identify and build new categories to experience its desired level of growth.

As early as 1917, when the company introduced decorated gift wrap, Hallmark had extended its greeting card business into other ventures—and had done so quite successfully. By the mid-1990s, President and CEO Irvine O. Hockaday Jr. saw that the Internet and the global business climate would make the marketplace in which Hallmark competes much more complicated and fragmented. He needed to take this very traditional company into the next century.

A NEW KIND OF CREATIVE BRIEF

To get there, Hockaday did something completely unconventional. He wrote a letter outlining his assessment of the Hallmark brand—what it was, what it stood for, his belief in what it could represent and how the brand could be extended in the future—and he sent the letter as a proposition to a number of advertising agencies. His conclusion was that even though the core business of greeting cards was flat and he didn't expect significant growth in the foreseeable future, the Hallmark brand retained a great deal of value in the minds and hearts of consumers. He believed that the brand had the consumer's permission to expand into other areas—he just wasn't sure what those areas should be. And that was his charge to the agencies: He wanted Creative Business Ideas.

Hockaday acknowledged in his letter that it might seem odd that he was reaching out to advertising agencies for services that consultants typically provide. However, he chose to engage advertising agencies because of his belief that they would have a better understanding of consumers and brands.

> HOCKADAY UNDERSTOOD ONE OF THE BASIC PRINCIPLES UNDERLYING THE CALL FOR CREATIVE BUSINESS IDEAS—THAT THE CREATIVE THINKERS CONCENTRATED IN THE ADVERTISING COMMUNITY SHOULD BE TAPPED AS A RESOURCE IN DEVELOPING TRULY INNOVATIVE BUSINESS STRATEGIES.

THE LEAP

In their bid for the job, Barry Vetere, managing partner of MVBMS/Euro RSCG, and his team took Hockaday's input and analysis, examined Hallmark's brand, and then took a long, hard look at what new product categories Hallmark could put its name on. They knew that the idea had to be founded on some intrinsic truth about the business itself—the starting point for all great CBIs.

> THE CREATIVE BUSINESS IDEA MUST BE ROOTED IN THE BRAND, GROW FROM IT, AND BE AN ORGANIC EXTENSION OF IT. IN SOME CASES, THE PRODUCT IS EVEN CREATED OR TRANSFORMED AS A RESULT OF THE CREATIVE IDEA.

Ultimately, the agency realized that Hallmark wasn't really in the business of greeting cards or gift wrap. Nor was it just in the business of giving people a very personal way of expressing themselves—after all, you buy Hallmark "When You Care Enough to Send the Very Best." The Hallmark brand was bigger, broader, deeper. Its true DNA had to do with traditional values, family, morality, decency.

What enabled the agency to make the leap, to go from A to B to M, was its in-depth understanding of the consumer . . . coupled with its depth of understanding of the client's business and the brand DNA. As I said,

CREATIVE BUSINESS IDEAS EXIST SOMEWHERE IN THE SYNAPSE BETWEEN UNDERSTANDING THE CONSUMER AND THE COMPANY. ONLY BY KNOWING THE POSSIBILITIES OF THE BUSINESS CAN WE MAKE THE LINK TO THE CONSUMER.

This is the space where Creative Business Ideas are born, and it's that space that the agency discovered.

For years, Hallmark had indulged in what is not an uncommon practice in corporate America: It kept marketing to its traditional customers—older women. But once the agency had uncovered the brand DNA, new worlds opened up. New markets, new targets. Traditional values? Why not target Gen Xers, the generation that, unlike the baby boomers, had exhibited a gargantuan move back to traditional values? Instead of just older moms, why not target the new moms, who just happened to share the same values for which Hallmark has always stood?

In the initial pitch, which lasted some five hours, the agency identified numerous areas into which it felt Hallmark had the consumer's permission to enter. The agency recommended creating a new category of cards, "story cards," greeting cards for children that were more like books. That would drive up the price of cards, because it would increase their perceived value—the customer would want to keep these cards.

The card idea dovetailed with another idea: to become a resource for parents, which included developing a reading program for parents and children and offering products and programs about parenting. The agency proposed a line of Hallmark books for kids and recommended expanding further into family-oriented entertainment and programming. It suggested that Hallmark start its own TV channel, and it also explored the idea of a kids' TV show, which I'll come back to in a later chapter.

Then there was the flower business. . . .

FROM GREETING CARDS TO FLOWERS

It's not that expanding into flowers was something that Hallmark hadn't explored before. But Barry Vetere made the distinction to the company between "selling flowers" and "being in the flower business." In the past, the company had ventured into arrangements with flower businesses by licensing its name. MVBMS argued that licensing agreements were dangerous, because the brand was too valuable and came with too many equities to risk damage by association with products that weren't up to the quality of Hallmark.

The sale of flowers in the United States is a $14 billion a year business. As large as it is, it has room to grow—the purchase of flowers is much lower in the U.S. than in Europe, for example, where people are likely to buy fresh flowers daily. But there is a downside to the flower business: the lack of freshness. Ironically, people often are disappointed with the flowers they receive.

The agency's studies showed that the most critical three or four days in the shelf life of a flower were being lost in transportation. What if you could eliminate those three or four days? Hallmark was intrigued. The flower idea was one that had the potential to achieve profitability in the short term—even though it would mean a significant up-front investment. So Hallmark asked the agency to research it further.

Among other things, the team looked at how FedEx was managing to deliver fresh products such as steaks and seafood. Based on that knowledge, MVBMS came up with a business model: Whether tulips from Holland or roses from South America, flowers would be

Unless you wipe the slate clean and do a proper audit of a brand's business, it's difficult to truly get at the critical issues, the key barriers to a brand's continued growth. All the sacred cows need to be slaughtered and the business needs to be viewed through an objective lens and dissected if you are to have any hope of uncovering new target-audience insights.
—Marty Susz, Euro RSCG MVBMS, New York

What is sacred to any company is the core brand idea. But understanding what that is, distilling that idea down to its essence in order to be able to reinvent ideas around it, is what CBIs are all about. It is very easy to get caught up in the idea of what you think your business is about. For instance, Hallmark is a greeting card company, right? In fact, greeting cards are not sacred and are not the essence of the brand. Instead it is the high-quality demonstration of caring and sharing that is sacred to the business idea called Hallmark. Only by understanding this are Creative Business Ideas, like Hallmark Flowers, made possible. No one who thinks they are in the greeting card business would ever create the kind of successful line extension that the flower business is for Hallmark.
—Beth Waxman, Euro RSCG MVBMS Partners, New York

shipped straight from the grower to a Hallmark facility in Memphis, where the bouquets would be created. They would then go out the next day via FedEx's Memphis hub. Hallmark could promise the freshest flowers, with just a single stop between the hands of the grower and the hands of the person receiving them. As a result, the quality of flowers would be drastically better than anything available. The business would be built online.

THE COURAGE TO CHANGE

For Hallmark, offering flowers meant entering an entirely new business. Because it's easy to ruin one's brand by creating overinflated expectations, Hallmark first decided to test-market the idea, to give the operational side of the project a chance to be understood and analyzed. Five markets around the country were selected for the testing phase. The team had six months to put the plan into action. Six months to, in essence, create a small business, virtually from scratch. The management team created to run the test was composed of both Hallmark and MVBMS people. As then senior account director Jim Huffstetler recalls, that was one of the most exciting parts of the project—it was a true collaboration. MVBMS creatives were very much involved in the design of the bouquets, participating in a three-day session with floral design experts. They also designed the original packaging for the flowers, with help from Hallmark and FedEx, so that it would be totally functional. Importantly, our agency was part of the executive committee, which was charged with all approvals.

To get the business off the ground in only six months, the management team had to work at lightning speed. Looking back, Huffstetler is convinced they succeeded in great part because the project was essentially autonomous—it was treated as a freestanding business. If the project had been caught up in the internal approval process at Hallmark, he doubts it ever would have happened as quickly as it did.

LIKE RATP'S "BRAND TEAM," THE PROJECT MANAGEMENT TEAM IS A POWERFUL DEMONSTRATION OF WHAT CAN HAPPEN WHEN AGENCY AND CLIENT WORK TOGETHER, AS PARTNERS, IN TRUE COLLABORATION.

The results of the five-city market tests in 2000 were remarkably positive—the Hallmark brand awareness surpassed that of the leading flowers-direct supplier, 1-800-Flowers. Even more impressive, more than 80 percent of consumers indicated brand satisfaction. As a result, Hallmark executives voted to launch the brand nationally, which required another major financial investment. The makeshift facility in Memphis was replaced with a permanent one, which opened in the fall of 2001. Hallmark Flowers is now a national venture.

Hallmark always had a good sense of what the brand means to consumers, but it was very much focused on the card industry, where ink meets paper. As Huffstetler puts it, "What we recognized at the time is that the company had a good sense of itself in terms of greeting cards. Yet the CEO had a strong notion that the brand could be a lot more, that it had great elasticity. We brought clear definition to [the CEO's] intuitive sense. We were able to energize them to understand what they could be. And that's what we heard back from them: We had helped them to see what their company could be."

Hallmark is a perfect example of how critical it is to understand what business you're really in. The agency never would have arrived at the Creative Business Idea of flowers without first understanding Hallmark's personal meaning to people.

THE AGENCY WAS ABLE TO PROVIDE HALLMARK WITH A BUSINESS SOLUTION THAT INFLUENCED THE NATURE OF THE COMPANY'S CORE BUSINESS, LED TO PROFITABLE INNOVATION, AND GAVE HALLMARK A POWERFUL NEW WAY TO MAXIMIZE THE RELATIONSHIP BETWEEN ITS CONSUMERS AND ITS BRAND.

Hallmark got to that space where Creative Business Ideas are born because it understood the possibilities of the business and made the link to the consumer.

One of the marks of a great CBI is its ability to refract the unerring soul of a brand in new ways and perspectives that enliven its current franchise and extend it to new franchises . . . much like the myriad ways in which one can view the refractions of the unerring light of the sun.
—Denis Glennon, Euro RSCG Tatham Partners, Chicago

Hallmark Flowers

Agencies have always strayed occasionally into applying their creative skills to business strategy. Although typically this was the exception rather than the rule. Many agencies have at different times grafted a strategic consultancy business onto their core offer, but almost invariably as an adjunct to the main agency and quite blatantly in pursuit of incremental revenue streams. These businesses operated as separate, autonomous entities—staffed from the world of business consultancies rather than with the creative talents of agencies. What is fundamentally different about a CBI culture is that it forces an environment in which business strategy and creativity coexist. It's the business equivalent of going coed—interesting things happen!
—Glen Flaherty, Euro RSCG
Wnek Gosper, London

BEFORE YOU LEAP:

- Know that behind every Creative Business Idea is a single-minded focus on brand essence. Waver from that focus and you dilute the value of the brand. Conversely, by not straying from your focus, you can profitably take your brand in new directions and into new product lines and categories.

- Set no limits for your brand. The quickest way to squelch creative thinking is to insist on talking only about the practical, the highly possible. Sometimes it's the "impossible" ideas that uncover a pathway to a better future.

CREATE A NEW CATEGORY: MCI

Understand the business you're in, and not only can you expand into other categories, you can create categories where none existed. MCI did that brilliantly, with a product that would transform the way we call collect: 1-800-COLLECT.

Back in 1993, when MCI and MVBMS introduced 1-800-COLLECT, there was no collect-calling category. You picked up the phone, dialed 0, reached an operator, and announced that you wanted to make a collect call. It was a $3 billion a year market, with AT&T sitting in the catbird seat.[10] MCI's innovation was that customers could call 1-800-COLLECT from any phone, anywhere, no matter who the long-distance carrier was. You didn't have to be an MCI customer to use the service and neither did the person you were calling. For the first time, consumers had a choice in making collect calls.

THE LEAP

The service was positioned as "America's least expensive way to call collect" and was advertised as offering savings of "up to 44 percent over AT&T." There's a psychological catch here: Collect callers have no real incentive to try to save money—they're not the ones paying for the call. So how do you motivate consumers to switch providers and call 1-800-COLLECT instead of dialing 0 and reaching AT&T?

Knowing that it's primarily young people and college students who call collect, MCI's president, Jerry Taylor, along with his marketing team and our agency made an important decision: MCI would position 1-800-COLLECT as the "cool" way to call. "We decided to create a brand that would be based on emotions," remembers John Donoghue, former senior vice president of consumer marketing. "The image is young, it's hip, it's a little bit edgy." Adds Timothy Price, former CEO of MCI, "It's an amazing thing: Taylor took a hundred-year-old product, collect calling, and, on the basis of personality, turned it into a huge business" (see Note 9).

MCI was famous for marketing its products through telemarketers and customer service reps. For this product, however, it would rely almost exclusively on advertising. Blimps took to the skies emblazoned with the 1-800-COLLECT logo. One of the most popular commercials was an ad featuring onetime David Letterman sidekick Larry "Bud" Melman dressed in a bumblebee outfit. The advertising was hip, young, slightly irreverent. And it was the sole marketing vehicle. If it weren't for the advertising, you never would have known that this product existed.

It took MCI only two and a half years to capture 30 percent of the $3 billion collect-calling market. And operating costs are minimal. Dialing 1-800-COLLECT simply gives you access to the MCI network. There are no salespeople. Three employees take care of the marketing effort.

THE POWER OF CREATIVE THINKING

When I look back over the past 30 years, it's clear that 1-800-COLLECT is the single biggest new business success I have ever witnessed. MCI created something where nothing existed and, in a very short time, captured a huge share of a market no one had identified. It did it with creative thinking.

IT TOOK CREATIVE THINKING TO DEVELOP THE IDEA FOR 1-800-COLLECT, CREATIVE THINKING TO EXECUTE THE IDEA FROM A SYSTEM STANDPOINT, AND THEN MORE CREATIVE THINKING TO DESIGN COMPELLING, FUN ADVERTISING FOR THE PRODUCT, WHICH GAVE IT A VIBRANT AND APPEALING PERSONALITY.

It was without a doubt a brilliant Creative Business Idea. And it could not have been accomplished had MCI failed to recognize the business it was in: MCI was never just in the business of providing long-distance phone services. It was in the business of providing a youthful, hip alternative in an industry just opened to competition. Its status as a young, brash contender colored its communications and helped to shape its strategic decisions.

ORANGE ONE

MCI created an entire category. Before 1-800-COLLECT, collect calling was a default position that led customers to AT&T. For one of our telecom clients on the other side of the world, in Australia, the challenge was the exact opposite. The category was saturated. And that inspired the company to create an entirely new one.

Hutchison Telecommunications (Australia) Limited wanted to build a wireless phone network in one of the country's most competitive service categories. There was only one problem: There were already four companies in that category—research showed that Australians were not looking for a new wireless brand.

Together with one of our agencies there, Euro RSCG Partnership in Sydney, Hutchison brainstormed strategies for introducing its new product, named Orange One, in this highly saturated market.

THE LEAP CAME WHEN COMPANY EXECUTIVES REALIZED THAT THEIR ONLY HOPE WAS TO LOOK AT MOBILE IN A COMPLETELY DIFFERENT WAY.

The germ of the idea began when they looked closer at the technology that was unique to the Orange One network; it had the slight difference of a triangular configuration of base stations. This meant that Hutchison's technology allowed it to offer different charging structures, depending on where the call was made. The phone would pick up where the user was at the time of the call, allowing Hutchison to charge a low flat rate when a call was made from home and competitive mobile rates away from home.

If Hutchison could exploit that technological point of difference—and communicate it in a meaningful way to consumers—it would have a compelling message: Orange One would be the one and only phone that customers would need. Matt Cumming, executive creative director who worked on the account, describes the thinking behind it: "The idea was to not call it a mobile phone, but to call it a home phone that charges you home phone rates. It would be your landline, but you could take it out with you when you go out. Changing the paradigm."

This was an idea with particular appeal to Australians. As research showed, Aussies thought it was strange and overly complicated to have two phones; Orange One would give them the freedom to take their home phone with them anywhere they went. And who doesn't like ease of use without the complications of technology?

COMMUNICATION BEYOND TRADITIONAL MEDIA

Instead of using conventional imagery associated with telecoms—people out and about, talking on their mobile phones—the agency pushed the concept of freedom one step further. It invented an icon: an orange hot air balloon that symbolized the lack of restrictions. When the balloon is tethered, it represents calls from home; when it's flying, it symbolizes mobility.

The hot air balloon drove home the message: No strings attached. The future's bright. Simple? Very. Easily understood? Extremely. Effective? Totally—the balloon iconography became a recognized symbol in Sydney and Melbourne, and brand awareness quickly reached 82 percent.

A NEW WAY OF SELLING

The sales strategy took some unusual approaches. Orange One chose door-to-door selling rather than retail stores as its primary sales channel, something unheard of in Australia's mobile phone business. This emphasized the home-phone aspect of the product and reinforced the theme of simplification. Customers could also buy Orange One over the Internet or by phone.

Second, Orange One targeted the market of Internet users with a simple, appealing product benefit: You can be on the phone while your kids are surfing the Internet. Direct mail and e-blasts went to decision makers in Internet homes—which constituted one-third of Australian households. After four months of operation, Orange One had 76,500 customers.

Orange One was an idea that came out of strategy development, not simply proprietary technology.

It arose from and influenced business strategy, not just communications strategy. It combined creativity and strategy in new ways, which resulted in breakthrough solutions and industry firsts. It led to innovative execution across traditional and new media, and to brilliant execution beyond traditional and new media.

Research had shown that Hutchison was going to have a very hard time launching a new mobile phone in that market; in essence, it was a market in which it couldn't compete. The technology allowed the company to make a paradigm shift—and it made Orange One a brilliantly successful Creative Business Idea. Indeed, it would become the first-place winner in our very first Creative Business Idea Awards.

But technology is not the only reason for Orange One's rapid growth. The company understood the business it's in. Not technology. Not telecommunications. Not mobile telephony. *Freedom and mobility.* Making your life easier with one phone.

Orange One TVC

BEFORE YOU LEAP: Cut loose any and all ropes that are tethering you to convention, to notions about "that's the way things always have been done." Orange One succeeded because it didn't take on the market giants in their own game. It made a new game for which it set all the rules.

GUINNESS: WITNESS

Imagine you're a brand director or an advertising director of a major company. As long as you're imagining, why not make yourself chief marketing officer or CEO? You have a brand that is essentially an institution—it has been around since your grandmother was in bobby socks. But that institutional status is now hurting you. Your brand holds little appeal for the younger generation. Worse, this generation actively rejects it, as it rejects everything that is associated with the older generation.

I could be talking about Oldsmobile. I could be talking about Volvo, at least where it was 10 years ago. But the brand I'm referring to is Guinness beer. Now, consider two problems:

1. You're trying to rejuvenate an age-old brand like Guinness.
2. Your advertising agency recommends that you launch a new product specifically targeted to the younger generation— but hide the fact that it is a Guinness brand.

What do you do?

THE CHALLENGE

KLP Euro RSCG looked at two contradictory facts. One, Guinness had the biggest single market share of any beer in Ireland—the brand is so entrenched you can hardly drive a block in an Irish city without seeing some mention of Guinness beer. Two, Guinness had been showing a gradual decline in patronage over the past 20 years among 18- to 24-year-olds. Why is that such a big deal? Because Ireland has the youngest population in Europe. Seventy percent of the Irish are under 40 years of age; half the population is under 25. And

60 percent of Guinness's targeted audience—the young—rejected the brand flat out.[11]

Here was Guinness, a powerful global brand, facing potential failure at home.

A Widening Generation Gap

It is also true that the generation gap in Ireland today is no ordinary generation gap. It has widened to unprecedented proportions by the major social changes and dramatic new economic growth taking place in the country. Known as the "Celtic Tiger," the Irish economy has grown at an average rate of 8 percent since the mid-1990s. Agriculture, once the most important economic sector, has taken a backseat to foreign investment.

One of the most dramatic factors in the changing economy is the explosion of high-tech and Internet-related business, especially in Dublin. Government-sponsored tax incentives and a young, English-speaking, and highly educated workforce have attracted large multinational computer companies. As a result, Ireland has become the world's biggest software exporter.

What the agency quickly realized is that young people living in Ireland today are living in a very different Ireland than the one in which their parents grew up. As Frank McCourt, author of *Angela's Ashes,* puts it, "Ireland is a booming economy now. It has drugs and fornication and divorce—it has everything. And U2 and Van Morrison and Sinead. And traffic jams."[12] So the young, ambitious men and women who used to leave Ireland to find work are staying—and Ireland is seeing an influx of workers of many nationalities. Moreover, Irish women are increasingly entering the workforce. All this leads to a richly varied youth culture that—in Dublin, in particular—emphasizes the ever-widening generation gap.

The Leap

As it set out to tackle the client's problem, the Euro RSCG team quickly recognized that anything with the Guinness name would be rejected by this new generation. So the team began to work closely with Diageo, Guinness's parent company, to get to the root of the brand DNA. In this case, the company's strength—a brand whose affinity with Irish culture had made it a global institution—was becoming its weakness. So the goal was to reconnect Guinness to young people in Ireland and to the rapidly changing ways in which they live their lives.

Ultimately, the agency realized, Guinness needed to create a new face for the beer, one that would reinforce the brand and ensure its future. The goal: to get young rejecters of the brand to say, "I never thought of Guinness in that way before."

THE AGENCY TEAM'S RECOMMENDATION WAS TWOFOLD—AND RADICAL: FIRST, INTRODUCE A NEW ENTITY, WITNESS, AND *NOT* IDENTIFY IT CLEARLY AS A GUINNESS BRAND. SECOND, PROMOTE IT THROUGH A SERIES OF ROCK MUSIC FESTIVALS. WITNESS WOULD BE THE REBELLIOUS SON TO THE FATHER GUINNESS.

BE BRAVE

Phil Bourne, CEO of KLP Euro RSCG, stresses that agreeing to launch a new entity and forgo the use of such a powerful and valuable brand name was a brave decision on the part of the parent company. The agency seemingly was asking the company to abandon both its brand heritage and its tried-and-true methods of marketing. The campaign strategy required the client to spend marketing money in ways very different from what it was used to. For Euro RSCG did not simply want to advertise this new brand—it wanted the target audience to experience and identify with Witness. If Witness was launched correctly, it would represent the new, young, rebellious, and outward-looking Ireland.

In meetings with the most senior-level Guinness management, the agency convinced the client that Guinness wasn't abandoning its brand heritage. A critical step—and one that could not have been accomplished had senior management not been open to creative thinking.

Beyond Traditional and New Media

The creative concepts for the Witnness campaign came about through a collective process at the agency, a series of brainstorming sessions that included Euro RSCG people in the entertainment division, experienced pioneers in branding through festivals, the agency's promotional team, experts in the drink market, and strategic planners. Another newsflash here:

The best creative thinking comes through collaboration.

The centerpiece of the campaign was the Witnness weekend rock festival.

Promotion was interactive in all respects. Guerrilla marketing techniques created a mystique around Witnness and encouraged active discovery; authenticity was built through word-of-mouth and underground, noncorporate modes. The agency created real-life irreverent stunts—from graffiti art to police-style incident boards placed at roadsides with cryptic references to Witnness.com. At the time, in-bar drink promotions that typically employed young models were quite popular. Witnness spoofed those with what it called "grannies visits"—women over the age of 65 made visits to Dublin's hippest bars to distribute the Witnness URL. In addition, set lists for the upcoming concerts were "accidentally" left behind in bars. Clues were also placed in unexpected places and ways, such as dropping little plastic strips that read "www.witnness.com" in the pockets of clothing items sold at trendy stores.

To reach this well-educated and Web-savvy population, the agency team used the Internet as the primary communication vehicle for the brand. With its fully interactive media launch and extensive online coverage of the festival, Witnness was the first branded music program to fully exploit the digital potential of the Internet. TV ads were used but they were unconventional, 10-second bursts meant to cause a stir.

THE WITNESS ROCK FESTIVAL

The Witness concerts proved to be a success that surpassed simple event sponsorship. The two-day-long outdoor festival featured five theme stages and a one-night party at Dublin's Ambassador concert hall. A report published on the Witness site describes the Ambassador event, held in July 2001:

> For weeks Dublin has been abuzz with rumors about this gig. From sniffy "more-indie-than-thou" types on various online chat lists who had already worked out the guest headline band to excited enthusiasts with just an inkling of what was going to go down, there was no doubt that this was the hottest ticket in town for a long time. By 7:30 P.M. an hour before doors opened, the queues were five deep and stretched from the Ambassador down the street and past the Rotunda. It was clear from the outset that tonight was in a different class.[13]

There was an overriding sense among young people that the concerts and the upsurge of activity surrounding them were long overdue. BBC1 radio followed the performances closely: "Wilt front man Cormac told Radio 1 it was about time Ireland got its own big music event and as a Paddy, he's especially pleased it's sponsored by Guinness. 'It should be good. I'm hoping the backstage area will be a Guinness free for all! That's important!' "[14] Witness had successfully fused the traditions of the old Ireland with the new Ireland.

Witness rock festival

The goal, long term, was that a newfound affection for Witnness would translate into improved image for the Guinness brand, coming full circle. It has worked. In the first year of the initiative, decline in market share was halted for the first time in 20 years. Talk about a transformed marketspace . . .

The makers of Guinness were smart enough to understand that beer is only one part of their business. Guinness is also a face of Ireland, a brand intrinsically connected to that nation's history and people and folklore. And, as the face of Ireland, the brand must evolve and grow as its national base evolves and grows. Witnness allowed the company to fulfill that brand promise for a new generation.

> **BEFORE YOU LEAP:** Figure out which aspects of the brand DNA communicate with each audience. As long as you remain true to the brand's fundamental essence, you can successfully extend a brand into new directions—and a new era.

SELECT COMFORT: MAKING A MATTRESS MOD

Just as Witnness breathed new life into an aging brand, this CBI breathed new life into a tired category—and that's what made it so compelling.

The category was the sleep industry. The product was a bed. The client of Euro RSCG MVBMS was Select Comfort. Up until the Creative Business Idea that would transform its business, Select Comfort had positioned itself as "The Air Bed Company." Its beds contain a patented, digital, remote control that adjusts the firmness of the mattress to a specific numerical setting, from 0 to 100—the more air, the firmer the mattress.

THE CHALLENGE

The mattress business is not exactly booming. In any given year, only 8 percent of the population shops for a mattress, and the average life span of a mattress is 10 years. Select Comfort had seen declining sales for the past two years, not only because of those realities, but because its niche market—older, back-pain sufferers—was saturated.

The company also suffered from both low brand awareness and image problems—historically, brands like "The Air Bed Company" are promoted almost exclusively via late-night, direct-response TV. Not exactly an approach that confers a sense of status.

Another obstacle: Unlike mattress manufacturers that offer competitive pricing and make their products available via mass-market distribution channels, Select Comfort are premium-priced beds, in the $1,000+ range, and are sold only through two channels: factory direct or via retail stores located in major malls.

WHAT DREW EVERYONE TO THIS CREATIVE BUSINESS IDEA, I THINK, WAS THAT THIS NEW IDEA FOR AN OLD CATEGORY WAS BORN OF THE PRODUCT ITSELF.

The agency decided to turn the bed's key product feature—a level of firmness from 0 to 100—into a unique, ownable point of difference called the Sleep Number®. The idea was that, whether you knew it or not, you have an individual Sleep Number, and once you discover your number, you'll have the key to a perfect night's sleep.

But a Sleep Number was not just the firmness feature of the bed. It was a language and measure that had never before existed—a new way for consumers to measure their personal comfort.

Do You Know What Your Sleep Number Is?

Do you know what your Sleep Number is? Consumers were invited to find out by visiting their local Select Comfort stores—which were renamed and rebranded as "Sleep Number Stores." The Sleep Number now permeates every facet of the company, including the brand name, the brand image, the logo, the sales process, and the product itself. The idea transformed the business—it directly impacted not

Sleep Number store

just communications strategy, but business strategy. Even more, it introduced a powerful selling idea to a business that is not idea-driven.

Select Comfort is not in the business of selling mattresses. It's in the business of selling a perfect night's sleep. Once the company understood that, everything else fell into place.

> **BEFORE YOU LEAP:** Find the unique creative proposition that will speak to a coveted audience. And make sure that the UCP is communicated through everything the company does.

DEAN'S® MILK CHUG®

One of the Creative Business Ideas from our first awards program also brought new thinking to an old category, a category that, at least in the United States, has been promoted so heavily in the last few years that you'd think it would have already been rejuvenated. The category is milk.

A DECLINING MARKET

Milk has been suffering a steady 20-year downturn, despite years of a highly visible creative campaign and countless celebrity endorsements. Our Chicago client Dean Foods®, one of the largest regional dairies in the United States, wanted to drive distribution into nontraditional outlets and create a stronger brand presence in the dairy case. The goal was not to convince non-milk drinkers to start drinking milk, it was to better reach people who do like milk, to differentiate Dean's from other brands, and to increase consumption. Our agency—Euro RSCG Tatham Partners—wanted to create a milk brand that could compete with all the other choices in the beverage case.

THE LEAP

In order to do that, we had to revolutionize the milk category.

WE HAD TO CHANGE THE WAY PEOPLE THINK ABOUT AND DRINK MILK.

Target consumers included young men who already drink a lot of milk and mothers who thought their active children weren't drinking enough. The solution was to repackage milk in light plastic containers, styled after old-fashioned bottles—in 8-, 16-, and 32-ounce sizes—with resealable lids, in a variety of flavors. It would be called Dean's® Milk Chug®.

As with Witnness, the Dean's Milk Chug campaign aimed to turn something tired into something cool. Highly visible TV spots aimed at children and young teens featured the Milk Chug animated character, Chazz. An interactive website, hosted by Chazz, has a soccer theme and includes online chats with soccer stars Carlos Valderrama and Shannon MacMillan.

PROFITABLE INNOVATION IN ALL ITS GLORY.

The results of the campaign surpassed expectations. Dean's Milk Chug was the first milk product in recent history to increase sales. And the rise was dramatic—Dean's Milk Chug led to a 200 percent sales increase, with profitable chocolate milk sales increasing 347 percent. It also returned true brand value to the company. The visibility effort of the campaign helped boost Dean Foods Company stock price more than 30 points in one year.

A SHIFT IN BUSINESS STRATEGY

The success of Milk Chug allowed Dean's to pursue an aggressive shift in business strategy, moving its focus from local dairy acquisitions to creating innovative single-serve products. The success of the brand differentiation has opened up new channels of distribution and has also led the company to continue to pursue the launching of new products.

What business is Dean's in? With Dean's Milk Chug, it went from being in the dairy business to being a provider of fuel and nutrition for consumers on the go.

Dean's Milk Chug ad

BEFORE YOU LEAP: Take a close look at consumer trends that could potentially impact your category. At Euro RSCG, we continually drive trendsightings throughout the agency via our STAR (strategic trendspotting and research) team. The Dean's Milk Chug campaign benefited from an understanding of the new demand for portable, ultraconvenient food and beverage products. In a world changing as rapidly as ours, it is essential to focus on what is real today and what will be real tomorrow, rather than accept that what worked yesterday is still the best approach.

GREEN GIANT® CANNED CORN

Dean's Milk Chug went beyond just innovative new packaging. The idea changed the distribution channel for Dean's milk. It changed the way people think about milk and when they drink it. It ultimately had a direct and significant impact on the company's business strategy. The same was true for a Creative Business Idea that focused on what at first seems the most unlikely of products: Green Giant® canned corn, sold in France.

WHERE'S THE DIFFERENCE?

General Mills Niblets variety canned corn, marketed for decades under the powerful Green Giant® brand name, is seen as the highest-quality product in the category. Green Giant has tried to improve market share through intensive promotion programs, but refuses to use price cutting or product giveaways, and thus needed new and

Green Giant® La Maïssette

qualitative ways to offer value to consumers. General Mills has searched for marketing campaigns that both reinforce the brand's image of quality and increase sales during the summer season, as the French eat corn mainly cold in summer salads.

THE LEAP

Our agency, Euro RSCG Manille, focused its attention on two target audiences. The primary target was mothers and the secondary target was distributors. Green Giant® bans price promotions as part of its marketing policy, so Euro RSCG Manille had to come up with a way to grab attention for the brand without reducing the price or significantly increasing the cost of the corn. The campaign had to be strong enough to make the distributors buy Green Giant® and display it in a prominent location. To do that,

THE AGENCY MOVED BEYOND MARKETING AND INTO BUSINESS STRATEGY. IT REVITALIZED THE PRODUCT'S FUNCTIONALITY WITH A SIMPLE, YET TRANSFORMATIVE IDEA.

Euro RSCG Manille created a plastic cap that went over the outer metal top of Green Giant® Niblets. The plastic was perforated so it functioned as a strainer. The strainer proved to be very convenient, enabling consumers to easily separate the corn from the water. The agency named the cap "La Maïssette" (from the French word for corn, *maïs*). The plastic cap was included with every three-can package of Green Giant® Niblets. It was inexpensive enough to produce that the company was able to include it in Green Giant® products for a one-month period, resulting in a million and a half La Maïssettes being used by consumers throughout France. The business objectives were met, and Green Giant® sold every can of corn packaged with La Maïssette. The idea set a new standard in the French market and is being explored by Green Giant®'s other markets. In addition, Green Giant® has already produced a smaller size of La Maïssette.

Green Giant® understood an essential truth about its business: It isn't just in the business of selling canned vegetables and other food products. It's in the business of meeting families' everyday needs through products that combine wholesome nutrition, convenience, and ease.

> **BEFORE YOU LEAP:** It is important to recognize that CBIs don't always have to be expansive, far-reaching propositions such as those developed for RATP or Hallmark. It is not necessary to transform an entire industry or create a new business in order to be a powerful CBI. Even a smaller-scale CBI can create a high impact . . . as long as it adds value to the company, to the brand, and to the consumer.

CREATIVE BUSINESS IDEA . . . OR "GOLDEN TICKETS"?

Do you remember the "Golden Ticket" in *Willy Wonka and the Chocolate Factory?* It's the ultimate "collect $200 and go to the head of the class" prize. So is a Creative Business Idea—but not forever.

Consider MTV. The strength of the original idea was an endless loop of videos, with no delineated programs. That worked for a long time. But, as with all products directed at the young, it became old. MTV faltered. The mechanism of its recent recovery? An unlikely at-home series with Ozzy Osbourne and his family. Osbourne himself is not an obvious draw; his music career is, for the most part, behind him. But his family is so eccentric that *The Osbournes* drew a larger audience than many shows on the major networks. It is MTV's most popular show ever. Proof of the Osbournes' importance? When it came time to renew the show for a second year, MTV had to pay the family an undisclosed sum that has been estimated as high as $20 million.[15]

Consider Virgin. For a decade, slapping the Virgin name on any product category conferred immense cachet. But the numbers don't lie. Recent figures show that Virgin Cola never really damaged sales of bigger brands. And in other launches, the numbers are equally underwhelming.[16] Has Richard Branson gone to the well too often? Can you be in your mid-50s and still market yourself as a rebel? Can you be on the cutting edge with a muted Internet presence? These are some of the questions Virgin faces today. I wouldn't count Branson out, though; if anyone is capable of generating a successful Creative Business Idea, he is.

We'll end on a happier note: If you have ever been to Vienna, you know it's famed for its coffeehouses. There is one for every 530 people. And Austrians drink about 1,000 cups of coffee outside their homes and offices each year. Recently, Starbucks decided to invade Vienna—with four Starbucks cafés. Even more shocking, it would maintain the American no-smoking standard there—even though approximately 40 percent of European adults smoke. How did these cafés do? Well enough to delight the Viennese and win Starbucks millions of dollars in free publicity in a front-page story in the *New York Times*.[17] Howard Schultz's original idea was to bring European culture to America; now he's bringing Europe back to Europe. Clearly, he has added something to make his import such a viable export—a Creative Business Idea.

Chapter 7 – The End of Advertising . . . the Beginning of Something New

And we wonder . . .

WHY ARE WE NOT IN THE THROES OF A NEW CREATIVE REVOLUTION, A NEW DEFINITION OF CREATIVITY?

Why is there no new twenty-first century bonanza for advertising?

A generation ago, television created a new structure for advertising and for advertising agencies. It also created great opportunity. An advertising agency could make its creative reputation on one brilliant commercial, become a great agency with two, and become immortal with three. And those of us who were part of that time often miss its clarity and simplicity of purpose. Perhaps that is why—despite the rise of interactivity and media convergence—we still mostly award, and reward, creativity only as it is seen on television.

The irony is that we all know that network TV is a medium in decline. We read daily about the rise of cable, the fragmenting of the network audience, the changing economics, the aging demographic. Our clients watch the slow demise of mass commercial television with enormous fear in their hearts. Because that's how mass brands were created. That was the formula for success. But it's over. Yet here we are, still obsessed with creating commercials for television, even as the latest generation of smart TVs with digital recorders (e.g., TiVo and ReplayTV) gives consumers the ability to bypass all advertising with the press of a button.

There are those who hope it all goes away. In my view, the revolution must begin with those of us who realize that the old advertising model is obsolete, that the old platforms no longer apply, that we have to break the rules and create new rules.

What does this revolution in advertising look like to me?

For starters, it looks like awarding and valuing creativity not based on reels of work, but on the brilliance of Creative Business Ideas—ideas that transcend advertising and lead to brilliant execution across the business itself.

It looks like, in short, the twenty-first century version of a reel.

We all need to adopt a different attitude to the way we have historically viewed ourselves and our jobs. The industry has pigeonholed us into thinking of ourselves as account handlers or creative people who make TV spots or print ads, or direct marketers or sales promotion people, or PR people, or interactive people. We need to stop thinking of ourselves in that narrow light . . . and begin to think of ourselves more as general marketing practitioners whose job it is to develop the most powerful creative idea to move a client's business forward regardless of the medium. From a developmental concept, it's an exciting and empowering way to redefine our jobs.

—Marty Susz, Euro RSCG MVBMS, New York

I've had the opportunity to speak at the International Advertising Festival at Cannes on a few occasions. I've used this platform to talk to the world's creative community about the changes, realities, and great new opportunities of creativity—and the need to stop rewarding creativity based on reels. It was difficult to know how my message would be received. Here I was, at an event that rewards television creativity, in a room filled with people hoping to be honored with a prestigious award for television advertising. Was this the right forum in which to make this argument? In fact, my message was well received—which helped to confirm for me that my ideas were on target.

It was at Cannes that I met Romain Hatchuel, who was head of the festival at the time and who later served as a juror for our first Creative Business Ideas awards. When Romain first took over the Cannes Awards in 1997, they were generally given for excellence in television or print. But Romain recognized that the rest of the world was radically changing while the advertising industry seemed to be standing still—and he set out to change the awards. Just a year later, he added a category for interactive advertising. The following year, he added media planning, an area that had tremendous opportunity for creativity, especially in Europe, which has seen a proliferation of magazines, newspapers, cable, and other communication channels in the past decade. The year after that came awards for creativity in marketing services, such as promotion, and direct mail. And just before he left the position nearly five years later, Romain began talking about another new awards category: one that would recognize integrated advertising and solutions that actually influence a client's business strategy.

Rewarding creative business ideas . . . perhaps there are more lessons to be learned from the Europeans.

BEYOND MASS MEDIA

In 1997, an article in the *Harvard Business Review* on brand management reinforced my sense that Europe was ahead of America in this area. In "Building Brands Without Mass Media," Erich Joachimsthaler and David A. Aaker argued that "U.S.-based companies would do well to study their counterparts in Europe. Because they were forced to, companies in Europe have long operated in a context that seems to mirror some of the harsher realities of the post-mass-media era." In Europe, consumers see fewer commercials. Media outlets typically stop at every border. And the costs of mass-media advertising have been disproportionately high.[1]

Which leads us to an old and universal truth: When you have limited resources or face seemingly overwhelming obstacles, your brains and imagination—in short, your creativity—become your greatest asset. Samuel Beckett was once asked why so many of the greatest writers in the English language were Irish. His response: "When you are in the last ditch, all you can do is sing."[2]

Joachimsthaler and Aaker discuss several European companies that have come up with wonderfully innovative and creative ways to build brands without mass media.

- One classic example is The Body Shop, which Anita Roddick built into a global brand—without advertising. Her business strategy was centered on activism. The Body Shop received widespread exposure and support for its work for social and environmental causes. Her message was powerful and consistent. Her consumers felt directly involved with the brand. Her success was theirs.

- The brand-building efforts behind Swatch not only created a powerful identity, but also redefined a product category and reinvigorated the entire Swiss watch industry. The strategy was simple: Imbue watches with personality; turn watches into fashion. So the Swatch marketers hung replicas of 500-foot Swatch watches from city skyscrapers. They found sponsorships that made them a part of global pop culture. Their media became the message. By 1992, Joachimsthaler and Aaker report, Swatch was the best-selling watch in history.

- Cadbury invested nearly £6 million in a theme park—Cadbury World—that takes visitors on a journey through the history of chocolate and the history of Cadbury. The park drew nearly half a million visitors a year between 1993 and 1996. Six years after its opening, Cadbury was named the most admired company in the United Kingdom.

What all these brands share is great creative thinking that led to innovative execution beyond traditional and new media—and way beyond mass media. In this case, the lesson lies not in the end point but in the starting point. None of these companies started with the proposition, "Hey, we could use mass media if we wanted, we've got the resources, but let's get creative and see if we can come up with something else." They brought creative thinking to their businesses because they had no other option: They *had* to get creative. As an exercise, maybe we should impose those same shackles on ourselves.

BEFORE YOU LEAP: Ask yourself: If I were forbidden from using the power of mass media, what would I do to build my brand?

A MUSEUM AS A BRAND?

Your company is well known. But times have changed. Now you're flailing. You need fresh energy—and new consumers.

Thomas Krens faced just that challenge in the late 1980s. As director of the Guggenheim Museum in New York City, he needed to revitalize the once-hip institution to reflect the changed times. But how? Krens made a radical decision: He would look at his "product" as a brand.

The Guggenheim was a fantastically interesting case of an institution that, because of economic and competitive changes, needed to be rethought from a creative standpoint. But what really interested me was that Krens's solution lay in thinking about the museum as a global brand rather than as an eighteenth-century institution.

THE LEAP . . .

When Krens took over the helm of the Guggenheim Museum in 1988, he saw two challenges facing the museum industry. First, the huge growth rate among cultural institutions had slowed dramatically. The long-term revenue growth curve was flattening. Expenses were on the rise due in part to competitive pressure among museums to win audience. At some point, expenses were destined to overtake income.[3]

The second challenge was more philosophical. As Krens was fond of saying, "The art museum is an eighteenth-century idea—the idea of an encyclopedia, offering one of everything—in a nine-teenth-century box, which is an extended palace or series of rooms . . . that more or less fulfilled its structural destiny sometime in the middle of the twentieth century." And that is now, I might add, competing with twenty-first-century entertainment.

Krens's creative leap was to challenge every assumption under which the museum world operated and ask *why*. Why does the art museum have to remain an eighteenth-century idea, with an ency-clopedic offering? Why does it have to be housed in a nineteenth-century box, with rooms that go on ad infinitum? Why can't the museum be redefined for the twenty-first century?

AS IS THE STARTING POINT WITH ALL GREAT CREATIVE BUSINESS IDEAS, EVERY ASSUMPTION WAS QUESTIONED—AND, IN THIS CASE, EVENTU-ALLY OVERTURNED.

Krens had a clear objective: to develop a vision for the institution for the twenty-first century. But first he had to achieve a near-term

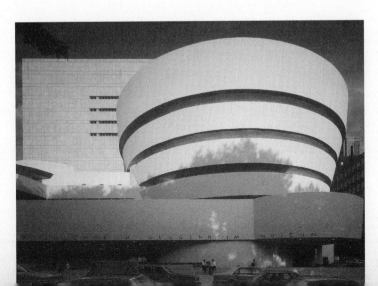

Solomon R. Guggenheim Museum, New York

objective: to make sure the Guggenheim made it to the twenty-first century in the first place.

CHALLENGING TIMES

At the time Krens took over, the Guggenheim ranked fourth among the museums in New York, behind the Metropolitan Museum of Art, the Museum of Modern Art (MoMA), and the Whitney Museum of American Art. It had acquired art way beyond its ability to show it—98 percent of its collection was in storage. And of that, the postwar collection was not strong. Worse, the Guggenheim was operating at a loss. At $24 million, the museum's endowment was considered modest, at best.[4] The size of the Met's endowment was the equivalent of 11 years of operating expenses; the Guggenheim's, in contrast, would fund it for just two years. And while the Met received 25 percent of its funding from New York City, the Guggenheim received very little civic or government money.

In essence, the Guggenheim was well known, but not particularly successful.

Krens believed the situation called for "a reexamination of the basic function of the museum." Soon after his appointment, he went to the board and explained that the international strength and reputation of the Guggenheim as an institution was a function of six things: its collection, its physical plant, its endowment, its operations, its program, and its staff. And that "if the institution were going to strive for a certain kind of excellence, i.e., to be one of the best in the world at what it does . . . it was going to have to improve itself in each of those areas simultaneously." He set out to ensure the survival of the Guggenheim Museum. In the process, he would transform the Guggenheim . . . into a global brand.

THE PHYSICAL PLANT

The now famous Frank Lloyd Wright masterpiece that is the Guggenheim Museum was designed in the 1940s for a completely different concept. In 1983, former director Thomas Messer had set in motion plans for an expansion and renovation, but these were now long overdue. The projected budget: $55 million. But where would the money come from?

Krens became creative. New York State had a piece of legislation that allowed cultural institutions to issue bonds for construction purposes only. The bonds were triple tax exempt—which meant very low interest rates. The state granted the bond issue to one institution each year.

Krens decided to leverage the reputation and collection of the museum to take advantage of the legislation. He hired a leading architectural firm, Gwathmey Siegel & Associates Architects, to design a 10-story adjoining tower. His lobbying efforts were successful. The bond issue raised some $56 million, enabling him to restore the famous spiral building and extend its exhibition space by 60 percent.

That's creative thinking applied to the most unlikely of business fundamentals: financing.

BEFORE YOU LEAP: When bringing creative thinking to your business, start by challenging every assumption. Continue by looking for every opportunity to apply creativity to business strategy, across the spectrum, even in the most unlikely of places. Leave no doors unopened.

As his next step, Krens turned his sights across the Atlantic, to the Peggy Guggenheim Museum in Venice. When the museum acquired Ms. Guggenheim's collection and palazzo in the 1970s, it intended to bring the works of art to the Guggenheim in New York. It didn't work out that way. The Italian government declared the palazzo and its contents a national treasure—the art wasn't going anywhere.

Krens believed the city of Venice to be an ideal location—and one worthy of investment. With 12 million visitors a year, as he puts it, "it in effect exists for cultural tourism." So he focused resources to the Peggy Guggenheim collection there in order to turn it into a first-rate cultural facility. His second move was on a grander scale. Krens's thinking was that, if you had a museum in Venice and one in New York that were of similar size, you could achieve the economies

of scale for which he'd been looking. Mount an exhibit in one location. Restage the exhibit at a second location for a fraction of the
cost. Unfortunately, the palazzo in which the Peggy Guggenheim
collection was housed was much too small. So he set his sights on
another location, this one just across the canal—the Punta della
Dogana, a late-seventeenth-century classical pavilion at the very end
of the Grand Canal opposite St. Mark's. It took more than a decade
to reach an agreement with the Comune of Venice, and negotiations
are still under way.

Again, great creative thinking applied to yet another fundamental of the museum business—and a sacred one at that: location.

With the bid for that seventeenth-century pavilion, Krens put
into motion the concept that would eventually redefine the idea of
art museums in the twenty-first century: the concept of a Guggenheim constellation. The way Krens saw it, the Guggenheim would be
one museum that happens to have discontiguous gallery space, placed
all around the world, but with one collection, one programming
concept, and one coordinated approach to understanding and presenting culture. All of the museums would be called Guggenheim.

In 1992, the Soho Guggenheim opened in New York's trendi-
est neighborhood. The brand was on the move.

ZERO FOR SIX

In addition to a master's degree in art, Krens also holds a master's
in public and private management from the Yale School of Management. Perhaps that accounts for his businesslike mentality. As he says,
"You have to see yourself as an investment banker. You develop 10
projects. You expect that your success ratio is one in five."

Krens had no problem developing multiple projects simultaneously. It's just that, in the early 1990s, none of them were coming
to fruition. A deal to open a museum in Salzburg, Austria had stalled,
as had deals for four projects in Japan and one in Massachusetts. Little did Krens know that his next stop would be an industrial port city
on the Northern coast of Spain. . . .

Bilbao

Bilbao is home to some 1 million Basque—nearly half the inhabitants of the surrounding Basque country. It was once thriving, but by 1989 it was in a state of deterioration. That year, the Basques hatched an ambitious urban-renewal program to transform the city into a modern-day commercial, cultural, and recreational center that would attract businesses and tourists from around the world.

Part of this plan was to create a museum of contemporary art, designed by one of the world's great architects. Who did the leaders of Bilbao want to run the museum? Thomas Krens.

When the invitation came, Krens had been looking at locations for a satellite museum in Spain. But Bilbao wasn't one of them. He wasn't interested. Still, he met with the president of the Basque country—and gave him a list of conditions he never thought would be accepted. For openers, the president would have to agree in advance to build the greatest building of the twentieth century—and not only would the Guggenheim get to pick the site, Krens would submit the names of three architects from among which the president could choose. In addition, the Basques would have to subsidize the cost. The Guggenheim would loan part of the collection, but Krens would need a multi-million-dollar acquisition fund to buy new works of art. And he'd need $20 million just to go forward, nonrefundable. When Krens was finished, he got up to leave. Suddenly, the president reached across the table and said, "You've got a deal." It happened just like that.

Guggenheim Museum, Bilbao

At the initial meeting, Krens had told the Basque president to "think big." The Guggenheim Bilbao, designed by Frank Gehry, is nearly double the height and length of the Centre Georges Pompidou. A single gallery is large enough to hold two 747s.

Krens always believed that if the museum were interesting enough, people would go to it—wherever it was. The Guggenheim Bilbao proved that theory. The Guggenheim had projected 485,000 visitors in the first year—it lured in 1.5 million. In one stroke, it changed the fortunes of the Basque country. In the first year alone, the museum brought in $250 million in increased tourist spending and $45 million in new tax revenues. The second year the numbers were even better. As of the end of the year 2000, the Guggenheim was receiving almost 4,000 visitors a day. The only museum in Spain that gets better attendance is the Prado.

McGuggenheim

"Krens-bashers had a field day. They accused him of being a wheeler-dealer, of franchising art, of creating 'McGuggenheim.' They hated the fact that he talked like an entrepreneur."[5]

Krens was unfazed. Now that his expansion plans were well under way, he could turn his attention to programming.

Krens had always questioned why *art* had to be defined as either painting or sculpture. He was also acutely aware that, to draw more people into his museums, he needed to make art more accessible to today's consumers—and to make the experience entertaining. As Krens put it, "The audiences for art museums have become more sophisticated, more specialized in some ways, and art museums have a certain amount to do with that—it's a leisure time activity, so we're really a part of a larger entertainment business."[6]

But when Krens turned to motorcycles and fashion, the inevitable question arose: Was this really art?

Art or not, the controversial *The Art of the Motorcycle* exhibit opened in New York in 1998 and drew the highest daily attendance of any show in the museum's history.

Frank Gehry's monument to the city and people of Bilbao, Spain, is a brilliant example of doing something differently, with unquestionable authenticity and uniqueness. The city of Bilbao could have very easily hired another architect to do the job Gehry did, but they didn't because they had a vision for what they wanted their city to be, to look like, and to be perceived as by the tourist industry. We need to have that same passion for difference, for superiority, for uniqueness and authenticity in all areas of our marketing communications. What a pity it would be if we, as a company, were ever accused of doing our jobs without such a passion. . . .
—Daniel McLoughlin, Euro RSCG MVBMS Partners, New York

What Krens had done was to apply creative thinking to the most sacrosanct area of them all: to the museum world's very reason for being, art itself. The result? He drew people to the Guggenheim who had never entered a museum in their lives. With one exhibit, he made relevant again the art museum—an institution that he believed had fulfilled its destiny in the twentieth century.

KRENS TRANSFORMED ART INTO TWENTY-FIRST-CENTURY ENTERTAINMENT.

Two years later, Krens once again incurred the wrath of critics, this time with an exhibition devoted to Italian fashion designer Giorgio Armani. The show was sponsored by AOL Time Warner's fashion magazine, *InStyle,* and also was reportedly accompanied by a multi-million-dollar gift to the museum from the Italian designer.

Art? Vulgar showmanship? Either way, Krens had successfully achieved something to which none of his contemporaries had even aspired—he had essentially redesigned the concept of museums for the twenty-first century. And because Krens was able to make that creative leap, he was able to triple the museum's attendance between 1989 and 2000.

Krens questioned the status quo. He was open to new ideas and new ways of thinking and new ways of doing business. He asked not just *why* . . . but *why not.*

In the process, he also employed a principle that is at the core of every great Creative Business Idea: He remained fiercely loyal to the brand history, the brand integrity, the brand essence. The Guggenheim's mission statement, created in 1937, was "to engage people in art for the larger social good." And with every move Krens made, he never strayed from that.

The Art of the Motorcycle
installation view, 1998.
Solomon R. Guggenheim
Museum, New York

As of this writing, there are two Guggenheim museums in Las Vegas. In the meantime, the Soho Guggenheim has closed, and, following September 11, plans for a new Guggenheim near Wall Street are on hold. Will Krens have more successes? I expect so. More failures? Without doubt. Mistakes and failures mean that Krens is still engaging in great creative thinking.

> **BEFORE YOU LEAP:** There is one final lesson to be learned from Thomas Krens: Don't give up. When Krens was being denounced by others in his industry and accused of turning the Guggenheim into "the Nike or Gap of the art world,"[7] he never wavered in his vision and his conviction. He exhibited the level of strong leadership that is integral to all Creative Business Ideas. You have to be bold. You have to take risks. It takes courage.

YOU NEVER KNOW WHO'S WATCHING . . .

Thomas Krens's expansion plans were being covered extensively by the press the world over. Little did he know that they were also being followed closely by an advertising executive in the city of Buenos Aires, Argentina.

When Jorge Heymann opened his own advertising agency in January 1999, he was a seasoned veteran of the business. But running his own agency gave him the chance to do something of which he had always dreamed: to create not just advertising, but communications.[8]

About 10 years ago, one of the things that I began to notice when I went to Cannes—where you have the opportunity to see ads from all over the world—was the exceptional creative work coming out of Latin and South America, Brazil in particular. When I became CEO of Euro RSCG and started traveling more, I became aware of Argentina's work as well.

The Latin countries, I saw, represented a very interesting marketplace. A lot of creative thinkers are there. In part, it must be because many of them were trained in U.S. advertising; they studied all that great advertising from the 1960s and 1970s. But the innate creativity of Latin cultures also plays a role—there's a great emphasis on and appreciation for thinking that is both left brain and right brain. The end of the twentieth century also saw lots of deregulation and explosive media growth in the region, which meant more advertising, more creative thinking. And as opposed to being U.S.-centric, they had the advantage of European influence. I think they were able to take all of that in, absorb it, and then develop their own creative approach.

Eduardo Plana, our CEO for Latin America, introduced me to some agencies he thought we might want to acquire. And he told me that if I wanted to see firsthand the latest creative thinking that was going on there, I should meet Jorge Heymann. As it happened, we met in my New York office.

WHEN I SHARED WITH HIM MY THOUGHTS THAT CREATIVITY WAS GOING WAY BEYOND ADVERTISING, HIS EYES LIT UP. HE SAID, "LET ME TELL YOU A STORY."

THE INSPIRATION

Heymann had been inspired, some 15 years earlier, by the work of design firm Pentagram. Intrigued by that firm's creative approach to communications, he went to visit its creative team in London. "There were five partners: three graphic designers, one industrial designer, and one architect," Heymann recalls. What he admired was the team's total approach to the design process: "For instance, for the Reuters headquarters in London, they had designed everything: from the building to the logo to the look of the lobby, right down to the ashtrays."

His second source of inspiration was Bilbao. He was fascinated by what the Basque authorities in Bilbao had done: the way they had attracted people to the city not through mass media, a huge promotional campaign, or traditional forms of communication and advertising, but through the use of architecture.

BUILD ME AN AD CAMPAIGN

Jorge Heymann was determined to do the same for his clients: to create communications that went far beyond advertising. In the late

1990s, he got his chance. It all started with a seemingly straightforward request from a former client, who needed an ad campaign to promote a new riverfront real estate development in Buenos Aires. Covering a seven-block area, the complex included a Hilton hotel—the first in Argentina after years of failed attempts—a convention center, an apartment building, three office buildings, a mall with an 18-theater Cineplex, the first IMAX cinema in Argentina, a sea museum, recreational areas, and a 700-meter-long pedestrian street for outdoor events. It would be more than a new neighborhood. It would be a city within a city.

The development was located in the Buenos Aires' equivalent of London's South Bank, a historic area of the city known as Puerto Madero. It even resembled the old wharves on the Thames; the bricks had been brought over from London. But although Puerto Madero was one of the hot, up-and-coming areas of Buenos Aires, it had one big drawback—it was off the beaten path. The complex was by no means in a high-traffic area.

The ad campaign had clear-cut objectives: to generate awareness and drive visitors to the complex. The budget: $4 million.

GET IN ON THE GROUND FLOOR

Heymann and his team were fortunate enough to get in on the ground floor—even before the complex had a name: "We had the opportunity to work with the client on brand definition and on creating the brand image and a brand identity. And, eventually, on how to communicate its existence." The brand name would become Madero Este. But even as the brand identity took shape, the question of how to build awareness kept nagging at him.

The typical recommendation—and the one that the client was expecting—would have been a comprehensive ad campaign, one that used print, television, radio, and other forms of mass media to say "Come to Madero Este" and tout the advantages of having everything in one place. But Heymann couldn't help thinking that spending $4 million on an ad campaign would be a mistake. "If you have to reach 10,000 or 20,000 people, why should you have to produce a commercial or a print ad?" he says. Given its location, he was convinced that no campaign would drive the level of traffic to the complex that was needed. There was too much competition from other malls. He decided that to promote the complex using mass communication would be a bad idea.

He began to explore other ways to communicate the existence of Madero Este. As he puts it, "I wanted to devote the resources we had to create something, to add something to the product which came from the product itself." Heymann wasn't out to create a CBI. Yet instinctively he understood the importance of the product component: The idea has to be rooted organically in the product itself.

THE LEAP

Heymann and his agency team began conducting research. Where would the traffic come from? What would be the most compelling reasons to go there? And how would people get to this out-of-the-way location? It was while pondering this last question that Heymann made the leap: Instead of building an ad campaign, why not build something that would literally and physically bring people to the complex? Why not build a bridge? A pedestrian bridge across the river would provide easy access, it would generate traffic, it was just what the development needed.

And then he and his creative team pushed the idea a step further. They recognized that, unlike in many of the world's major capitals, city landmarks were scarce in Buenos Aires. "In Sydney, you have the

Puerto Madero footbridge,
Buenos Aires

Opera House. In Paris, the Eiffel Tower, the Arc de Triomphe," Heymann notes. "Here, we have only an obelisk, just like dozens of other cities have. That's it. And not a very impressive obelisk at that. It's shorter than the obelisk in Washington, D.C."

What if, instead of building simply a utilitarian bridge that would get people from one side of the river to the other, the bridge itself were to be an attraction? An impressive architectural structure that would draw people to the riverfront and the new complex? A world-class structure designed by a world-renowned architect?

And a great Creative Business Idea was born.

BANNED FROM THE BOARDROOM?

If you were a CEO who had requested a new advertising campaign from your agency, and the agency came back to you with a recommendation to build a bridge . . . what would you do? I have known quite a few CEOs, and I know that most of them would like to think they would have embraced the idea. They're open to great creative ideas, naturally. Who isn't? But, most of them, in the end, would probably have passed on the plan. By the time the board members had dissected the idea, my bet is that very few CEOs would have been willing or able to sustain that kind of battle—and win.

Fortunately, Heymann and his agency team didn't have to worry about a board. There was none. The complex was owned and developed by a family-run company composed of the 70-year-old CEO, who was Heymann's client, and his two sisters. He was the key decision maker. The sisters typically supported his judgments.

PRESENTATION MATTERS

When it came time to make the agency's presentation, Heymann knew he had to make the idea as easy as possible to understand. So he kicked off the meeting with the story of Bilbao. He told of how a dying city had been brought back to life, transformed from an industrial wasteland into a thriving tourist destination. He talked about how great architecture had been used to attract people. He talked about the results, how millions of visitors now flock to Bilbao every year.

And then he gave his recommendation: Build a bridge at Puerto Madero.

Fortunately for Heymann, his client was a man of vision. He understood the idea, he had the ability to imagine what it would be like, and he had the foresight to see that it was a brilliant move. Heymann and his team had encouraged the CEO to let them help him make his product—his brand—more attractive and more successful. He agreed.

And the fact that the cost of the bridge would be 50 percent higher than the original advertising budget? The CEO not only had vision, he also had the ability to put things into perspective. Compared with the $180 million cost of the complex, a $6 million bridge was relatively insignificant.

The project was a go.

BE CRAZY

So far, so good on the bridge plan. But it's never quite that simple. In the case of Madero Este, while both agency and client understood the power of the CBI, others were not so sure. In the early stages, Heymann says, the press dismissed the idea, and many in the advertising industry thought it was a waste of time and resources. Besides, how is an agency compensated for helping to build a bridge? There were even those who thought the CEO was crazy, which earned him the nickname "El Loco."

Puerto Madero, Buenos Aires

The local architectural firm that had been contracted to build the entire complex drew the initial designs for the bridge. But there was a problem. As Heymann puts it, the designs were "pretty common. It was a commodity bridge." His new objective was to cancel the contract with the local firm and call for an international competition of well-known architects.

But this was not Bilbao. It was Buenos Aires. And that's not the way things were done in Argentina. It was uncommon to go outside the country for creative talent—what would be the need? But Heymann stood his ground, and eventually he was able to secure one of the most important architects in the world today, Santiago Calatrava—the same architect who had designed the spectacular footbridge in Bilbao. It would be the first Calatrava structure in all of South America.

As Heymann explains it, "What we proposed to Calatrava was how we would build a new landmark to symbolize the new Buenos Aires. An icon which would become a symbol of the rebirth of Buenos Aires, a symbol of the city's potential for the future." Heymann and his team played an active role throughout the design process. "We acted as the intermediary between the client and the architect, on the client's behalf. Partially because we didn't want to scare them with the lack of processes in our country!" The team even carried the client's business card with their names on it. "For all practical purposes, we were acting as the client," says Heymann.

That's true partnership. Based on an enormous level of trust and respect.

BE INSPIRED

The outcome? A stunning work of architecture. "Hilton is very excited about the idea of having a major city landmark so close to the hotel," says Heymann. "The different presidents of the country have all been tremendously excited about the idea. And the press coverage has been unprecedented. We could never buy that kind of publicity."

In some ways, Heymann was lucky. His client welcomed creativity. The client also had the vision to realize that spending $6 million on a stunning bridge as opposed to $4 million on an ad campaign was no contest. But Heymann's idea was also brilliant. And modest. "It's an inspiring case, though not the first. The work of Pentagram inspired me 15 years ago, then the work being done in Bilbao. We are all human beings, inspired by the experiences of our fellow humans."

In any business, that's a good thing.

HERO PUCH POWER XL

When was the last time you were on a moped? If you live in the United States, chances are you have never even grazed the seat of one of these zippy two-wheelers. Despite the fact that Harley-Davidson was making mopeds in this country nearly 100 years ago, the moped fad of the 1980s quickly ran out of gas.[9]

But if you've spent much time in any of India's major cities, the evidence is everywhere: Mopeds are big business.

Mopeds in India have traditionally been used as personal transport vehicles. They've been popular with women, because they're light and easy to handle. They've also been popular among those men who couldn't afford the more expensive motorcycles. The selling proposition? For not too much money, you get your own set of wheels. Mopeds are inexpensive to own, inexpensive to maintain.

Then along came another zippy little two-wheeler that threatened to undermine the selling proposition of the moped . . . the scooter.

At first, the higher cost of scooters kept them a safe distance away.

Desirable to the traditional moped owner? Yes. Affordable? No. But as prices gradually came down to the level of mopeds, those traditional moped owners began migrating to the newer, sleeker scooters and scooterettes. And the moped market started to sputter.

Such was the situation when moped manufacturer Hero Puch approached Euro RSCG India with the question: How do we revive the category?

The agency knew that any great Creative Business Idea starts with the pursuit of knowledge. To revive the category, the agency would first have to know the category—inside and out. And so the creative team took to the streets. But not just the city streets. The agency also studied suburban and rural markets, where small traders and vendors used mopeds. These Indians couldn't afford motorcycles or scooters to cart their goods—let alone a truck. So they used their mopeds. Vendors would carry goods to a larger city to sell there, or they would carry goods from a larger city to sell in the village.

And out of that knowledge . . . eureka!

THE LEAP

The agency realized that not all moped uses are equal. One group used it for personal transport, as a way to get around. The other was using it for an entirely different reason. Not to transport themselves, but to transport their goods and wares. And therein lies the leap: Why not revive the category . . . by creating an entirely new market? Why not shift the category from mopeds as personal transport vehicles to mopeds as business utility vehicles (BUVs)?

A cosmic leap, you might say, but repositioning alone—is that truly a Creative Business Idea? In and of itself, no. But this one not only influenced communications strategy, it influenced business strategy—and the manufacturing process.

THE AGENCY TEAM DIDN'T RECOMMEND JUST REPOSITIONING THE MOPED—THEY RECOMMENDED REDESIGNING IT.

Hero Puch Power XL

In pursuit of the perfect design, the team once again took to the streets and made visits to small towns. They spent hours hanging out where vast numbers of moped drivers congregate—in parking lots—and they talked to customers about what they needed and wanted from a business vehicle. They also targeted industries that use mopeds to make day-to-day deliveries, such as newspaper vendors, pizza parlors, milk deliverers, and so on.

THE BUV

The redesigned moped was named the Power XL and included a special plank in front, a removable pillion seat (for accommodating extra loads), and adjustable shock absorbers to withstand the heavier loads. Later design modifications were made specifically for those in the delivery industry, including extra sections such as compartments for milk containers and a space for courier packets.

Why invest in four wheels when you can get everything you need in two? The new moped was positioned as "the truck on two wheels." The promotional message reinforced that the Power XL can carry loads that would be torture for a normal two-wheeler. It makes more commercial sense than a bicycle or scooter—and more economic sense than a truck. It's the ideal business utility vehicle.

In five months, sales of the Power XL went from 0 to 3,000, with no cannibalization of Hero Puch's existing line. Not a bad acceleration rate for a brand-new category.

What the agency brought to Hero Puch's business was great creative thinking: creative thinking that resulted in carving out an entirely new market . . . and started to define a new category. That's the kind of creative thinking that every agency should be bringing to their clients' businesses.

Yes, it's the end of advertising. But it's the beginning of something new and something far more exciting and rewarding. It's the beginning of the opportunity to think creatively across larger and larger business issues—and to redefine businesses in the process. What would *you* rather do?

Chapter 8
The Entertainment Factor

For the first half of the twentieth century, entertainment wasn't at the center of life; it was on the sidelines. It was what you did on Saturday night—a movie, a dance, a concert. Later, with television, entertainment got bigger. You no longer had to go out to be entertained.

In the twenty-first century, entertainment is America's national pastime. Beyond the outrageous amounts of entertainment-driven media we consume each day, the entertainment experience has pervaded even the most mundane activities of our daily lives. Supermarkets, retail stores, airlines, banks, restaurants, hotels . . . more and more, entertainment is the deciding factor in where we shop and what we consume. We don't simply run errands anymore, we consume experiences. The bigger, the better.

Adding to the pressure on retailers and service providers is the fact that we're becoming more and more choosy. Not just any form of entertainment will do. And what we clamor for one month may well be passé the next. In the post–September 11 America, the most highly prized entertainment is the most escapist. In the realm of films, we're flocking to action-packed movies that have only the most modest connection to our daily existence. For those films, it's bonanza time: Box-office revenues for the first five and a half months of 2002 are up at least 20 percent over that period in 2001, which was already a record year. And this cannot be attributed simply to slightly higher ticket prices: The number of people going to movies is up around 16 percent from 2001.[1]

The blockbuster box office receipts of recent years confirms Michael J. Wolf's contention in *The Entertainment Economy: How Mega-Media Forces Are Transforming Our Lives*: Every business must now have some entertainment element if it intends to survive in today's and tomorrow's marketplace.

Selling widgets on a website? You're not exempt from the need to captivate before you get the chance to take an order. Want more business for your bank? If you're Citibank, you don't stop at using an Elton John song in your commercials. You get into the entertainment

Your starting point is people. . . . You explore their lives, their problems, and the brand will find its place, its role. The starting point is not the brand. You have to start by speaking about people's passions.
—Mercedes Erra, BETC Euro RSCG, Paris

business by creating an exciting, content-rich online service that both engages and entertains your customers. You don't just tell them that banking can be fun. You make them feel it.[2]

THINK BIG . . . REALLY, REALLY BIG

With the demise of advertising as we know it, our revolution—our future—must be connected with that kind of thinking. Entertainment is the Esperanto of our age, a universal language that draws people in almost hypnotically, a powerful magnetic force that, in many cases, serves as a bigger draw than the products themselves. This is going to have a huge impact on advertising and marketing in general. It will influence how we meld wisdom and wonder and magic; how we create and craft the brand experience. In the future, I can't imagine that any creative idea will be executed until the entertainment value has been explored—and embedded into the brand experience. We are now in the entertainment business. Full tilt. And our imperative is to connect entertainment with ideas.

THE LION KING

For the past few years, I've been using a wonderful example of what I mean by "brand experience" and how vital entertainment is to that experience and to the future of brands and creative business ideas. That example is *The Lion King*.

Let me show you why. . . .

ONE-UP YOURSELF

Disney didn't break the rules of branding when it created *The Lion King;* instead, it pushed them to their very limits. At every step in the brand-development process, the company pushed a little—or a lot—further than it had for any other product. Remember how it started: Disney released an animated film that became one of the 10 highest-grossing films of all time. Bravo! But it didn't end there. . . . That film then became the best-selling video of all time. Also fabulous, but not wholly unexpected in the film-to-video era. But the company kept pushing. The soundtrack, written in part by none other than pop icon Elton John, won a Grammy Award. Then came the Broadway musical. You know . . . the one that dominated the theater world and picked up all those Tony Awards. Not a bad run for a kids' cartoon.[3]

The Lion King's unprecedented success stems directly from the fact that Disney was savvy enough to start its mega-merchandising from the start. Released as part of the Disney Classic Series, *The Lion King* was named the number one best-selling children's book of 1994 by *USA Today* and was a contender on the *Publishers Weekly* and *New York Times* best-seller lists. Before the release of the film, product tie-ins with such brands as Burger King, Eastman Kodak, General Mills, Nestlé, Mattel, and Payless ShoeSource amounted to a marketing blitz of $100 million. It was the largest set of promotional tie-ins in Disney's history. And that's saying something!

Then Disney launched the Broadway musical, not as an opportunistic add-on, but as a full-scale, box-office-stomping event. It won six Tony Awards, a Grammy for "best musical show album," and accolades from the New York Drama Critics' Circle, among numerous others. When the show roared into London, it enjoyed a similar success, cementing its power as a truly global brand.

UNIVERSAL APPEAL

When I saw the show in London, there were just as many adults in the audience as there were young children. Very few shows have that kind of broad, ageless appeal—you have to suspect

Lion King *marquee*

that *The Lion King* was designed to be translated into multiple languages for a global audience right from the start.

What Disney did here was to elevate its brand, in the process appealing to those who felt themselves too sophisticated for anything "Disney." As Disney CEO Michael Eisner said, "*The Lion King* . . . enhanced our brand. We've been O.K. around the world, but the intellectual community in New York, we surprised them with *Lion King*."[4]

PROFITABLE INNOVATION

If you add up all of the products, many of which have income streams that will continue for years to come, what's the lifetime value of *The Lion King?* As a business idea, it has to be in the billions. It's a great example of an enormously powerful Creative Business Idea that transcended industries and mediums. And it continues into markets around the world, from film to CDs to cereal boxes to Broadway to backpacks and, naturally, to theme parks. At Disney's Animal Kingdom in the Walt Disney World Resort, the Circle of Life has given way to the Tree of Life—and the Festival of the Lion King stage show.

THE CREATIVE LEAP

THE BRILLIANCE OF *THE LION KING* IS THAT DISNEY FOUND AN IDEA WITH UNIVERSAL APPEAL AND STRATEGICALLY IMPLEMENTED THAT IDEA ACROSS MULTIPLE MEDIUMS, AND WITH THAT SINGLE IDEA, GAVE CONSUMERS A PLETHORA OF CHANNELS THROUGH WHICH TO EXPERIENCE THE DISNEY BRAND.

What, exactly, does *The Lion King* have to do with creative companies? It's an example of taking a company's brand essence and creating a multilevel experience that reaches into the lives of a far broader audience in a much deeper way. *The Lion King* isn't simply a movie. Nor is it just a book or play. It's a brand experience. And one that offers numerous lessons to all companies looking to connect their brands to consumers.

BEFORE YOU LEAP: Clearly define the brand experience. What is the entertainment factor? What are you delivering to your audience? How are you capturing them in ways they have not experienced before?

DRAW OUTSIDE THE LINES: CRAYOLA CRAYONS

I'll bet you didn't know that, if you're the average American, you used up 730 crayons by age 10. Or that Hallmark owns Binney & Smith, the company that owns Crayola. Or that when Hallmark first opened its doors, nearly a century ago, there were eight colors in a crayon box—black, brown, blue, red, violet, orange, yellow, and green (what, no Burnt Sienna and Raw Umber?)—and they cost a nickel. Today, Crayola crayons come in 120 colors. And these crayons are as popular as ever; in 1998, Crayola ranked as the number two top-selling "toy," second only to Mattel's Hot Wheels.[5]

I don't know exactly what Crayola's market share is, and I'm sure there must be other people who make crayons, but can you name another brand? Ninety-three years after their introduction, Crayola's 100-*billionth* crayon rolled off the production line. And visualize this: Binney & Smith produces nearly 3 billion crayons a year, which if placed end to end would circle the earth more than six times. The Crayola brand name is recognized by 99 out of every 100 American consumers. (What I can't figure out is who that hundredth person is.) And it's a global brand: Crayola crayon boxes are printed in 12 languages.

The success of the Crayola brand owes much to its strong and consistent brand image: Crayola has always stood for color, fun, quality, creative development. Go to the Crayola website and you'll discover a

CBIs have no set boundaries, no predetermined definition, no single source. Every element of the marketing mix—strategy, media (both new and traditional), geographies, copy lengths, products, packaging, distribution channels, local events—can be the catalyst for a new CBI. From a broader perspective, consumer and industry trends, the media, movies, books, even personal experience can be the basis for a new CBI. Ultimately, all CBIs come from synchronic thinking, the ability to see multiple connections on multiple levels where none were seen before.
—Cynthia Kenety, Euro RSCG MVBMS, New York

Crayola crayons

creativity center for kids and special areas for parents and educators that spread the message about the importance of art for children and the power of creativity. In 1993, when Crayola added new colors, consumers named all 16 of them. Burnt Sienna, meet Macaroni and Cheese, Purple Mountain's Majesty, and Tickle Me Pink.

THE LEAP

What would you do if presented with a brief from the CEO of Hallmark that asked you to think about how to expand the business, but not to do any advertising? Part of Euro RSCG MVBMS's recommendation was to expand the Hallmark brand into new markets by targeting a younger generation of consumers, Gen Xers, and to do that by building on the family values of the Hallmark brand and the tremendous equity Hallmark has in family entertainment.

The agency made the leap not just from A to B to C, but from A to B to M. Why not create a TV show for the kids of those target Gen Xers—starring Crayola crayons?

The agency came up with the idea of creating an animated children's show with crayons as the characters. (Imagine what you could do with a bunch of characters named Mauvelous and Cerulean and Atomic Tangerine and Jungle Green and Wild Watermelon.) The agency even created an animated character named Red the Fireman that morphs into a red-hot chili pepper and a friendly red-hot devil—among other things—and then back again. When you're a crayon, he explains to his young viewers, you can be anything you want to be.

> **IT WAS A CBI THAT WAS BRILLIANTLY ROOTED IN THE ESSENCE OF THE CRAYOLA BRAND: ENCOURAGING KIDS TO EXPLORE THE POWER—AND THE SHEER JOY—OF CREATIVITY.**

THE BIGGER IDEA

Here was an entertainment vehicle that Hallmark could use to create a really fun brand experience around Crayola crayons (and other Binney & Smith brands like Silly Putty). But it could also create a much bigger brand experience around the core values of the Hall-mark brand—family, morality, and the return to traditional values. I thought it was a brilliant way to appeal to a much broader target base, to appeal to the moms of today just as the Hallmark brand appealed to the moms of the 1950s and 1960s. Above all, it was a great way to cre-ate an entertainment experience for the brand.

Innovative? Yes. Profitable innovation? Perhaps eventually. Unfortunately, at the time, this idea didn't generate quite enough interest between Binney & Smith and Hallmark Entertainment to move it to its next phase. I still wonder, though, what it would have been like to follow the escapades of Red the Fireman. . . .

> **BEFORE YOU LEAP:** Know that, while passion and pushing may not always be enough to get a particular CBI off the ground for a partic-ular client, the effort that goes into developing that CBI will be rewarded. It will inform the agency's work on behalf of that very same client—the better you know the client, the more you can do for them—and it will further reward you by clicking the "on" switch to an idea that may be translatable at a later date or in another industry.

BILLIKEN: LIKE TAKING CANDY IDEAS FROM BABIES

One of our agencies in Latin America faced a similar challenge, with a brand that is also primarily targeted toward children. In this case, it was an old brand, with an old-fashioned image, one that des-perately needed to be rejuvenated. The agency's solution is a great example of what can happen when we make consumers fully vested participants in the brand itself.

In fact, this effort not only boosted sales, it won first place in our 2001 Creative Business Idea Awards.

YOUR DADDY'S CANDY

Billiken is a very well known candy brand in Argentina—the company makes soft and hard candy, fruit jellies, and mints. It has a long history and is known as a high-quality brand. But the brand was in trouble.

The candy market is an interesting one—what the agency team in

CBIs need not be only sexy and hip. Nor should it be the exclusive terrain played out by the new media and technologically savvy. Really, the more focused and simple it is, the better. The net result is a solution to make one's experience better.
—Eugene Seow, Euro RSCG Partnership Asia Pacific, Singapore

Argentina calls "hyperactive." Because the primary consumers in that market are children, kids dictate a lot of the market dynamics. Here is what we know about kids: They have short attention spans. They get bored easily. They crave what's new. As a result, the product life cycle of candy is typically short; kids flock en masse to the next new product. For the candy companies, that means a company's growth is heavily dependent on the ability to continually launch innovative new products.

When the client approached our agency, CraveroLanis Euro RSCG, the Billiken brand was a very weak competitor in this hyperactive market. There was nothing wrong with the quality of the product or with its brand awareness. It's just that the brand wasn't attractive to consumers—Billiken was the candy that Mommy and Daddy ate when they were kids.

THE LEAP

The agency was quick to recognize that Billiken needed more than an ad campaign or a makeover—the brand needed to be relaunched. Nothing less would make the brand appeal to children, revitalize the brand's image, and differentiate Billiken from its competitors.

How do you come up with ideas that will appeal to 6- to 12-year-olds? How do you take a tired old brand and make it attractive to them?

What's so exciting about this story is that the agency turned to a partner that seems like such a natural. But no other candy company in Argentina and maybe anywhere else, to my knowledge, had ever done anything like this: The company made its consumers its partners.

Brand image is often only the reflection of what the brand has steadily told consumers year after year. We push our clients to temporarily forget their brand identities and focus on consumers' aspirations, and further imagine ways for their products or category to meet these aspirations. Only when this is clear can we come back to the brand heritage and leverage it to meet consumers' evolving needs.

—Marianne Hurstel, BETC Euro RSCG, Paris

Billiken website

It makes perfect sense: Who better to create candy that children will like than the children themselves? Include them in the candy-making process, invite them to literally help design the candy, and kids would be getting exactly what they want. It would be *their* candy, but you would be making it for them. What a great way to differentiate one's brand from the competition.

This approach could make the brand the most widely recognized in Argentina, but it had the potential to do something far greater: to create brand loyalty among these easily bored consumers by, in essence, making Billiken *their* company, their brand partners.

So Billiken invited children to actively participate in the creation of the company's candy, in its design, and even in evaluating the candy once it had been produced. Billiken sounded the call to children everywhere in Argentina:

> *Be part of the dream. You create the candy . . .*
> *Billiken makes it for you.*

The implications of such a major shift in strategy for such a traditional company are staggering. Product development, manufacturing processes, packaging, marketing, logistics, distribution—most of it would have to change in one way or another. Fortunately, there were leaders at Billiken who welcomed creative thinking.

INVITING KIDS INTO THE BOARDROOM

Imagine walking into a conference room for a big meeting and discovering a group of kids sitting around the table—talking about your products, your brand image, and what they like and don't like. Sort of like Tom Hanks in the movie *Big,* only here everyone is Tom. Well, that's what happened on a regular basis at Billiken. Four panels of kids—"candyologists"—met every month for a full year.

But these candyologists in the boardroom represented just a small fraction of the children who got involved with the brand and provided their input and advice. To launch the concept of candy "for kids, by kids," the agency turned first to mass media. A series of TV spots introduced children to the concept, encouraging them to "become a part of the dream" and create their own candy, then vote for their favorite idea. Kids had the option of sending in their ideas through traditional mail. But the tool that was most essential to developing the project? The Internet.

BEYOND TRADITIONAL MEDIA

Think Santa's workshop. Now imagine a candy workshop where the workers are—no, not elves—kids. Next, take it a step further and make the leap to the first-ever online candy workshop. Now, you're there—at the Billiken Club website, where the dream of every kid comes true. Kids get to draw their candy ideas online. Plus, they get to become a member of a very exclusive club—just for kids!—complete with their very own membership card and very own member number.

The ideas the kids submitted were screened by a committee for technical feasibility. Those that passed the test were then posted on the website, where kids could vote for their favorites. The winning ideas showed up at the candy counter.

Is this the place where dreams come true or what?

FORGE ALLIANCES

Concurrent with the launch of the Billiken Club website, the agency undertook a massive promotional campaign: posters, fliers, inserts in newspapers and magazines, direct-mail samples. It even redesigned the workers' uniforms. Beyond that, what most struck me was that the company forged alliances with schools, not just to distribute samples and information pertaining to the contest, but also to offer activities that would stimulate group creativity.

BILLIKEN WASN'T JUST PROMOTING ITS PRODUCTS. IT WAS PROMOTING CREATIVE THINKING—AT AN EARLY AGE.

And *creative* is certainly a good descriptor for what came out of the children's imaginations: A chocolate spoon that dissolved in milk.

A bubble gum–flavored cookie. It's like peanut butter and jelly. These were definitely kids' ideas.

The Consumer as Partner

Billiken was hoping that 40,000 children would visit the website by the sixth month. It drew twice that number. Billiken was hoping for 2,500 proposals for new types of candy. It received 11,000. Within two months, more than 12,000 children had registered for the club. Billiken contacted them directly every week—giving the company a valuable database and a direct line into the mind-sets of its customers.

But I don't think the real story here is in the numbers. It's in connecting the idea, the brand, with consumers in a way no one had ever done before, developing not just a great interactive brand experience, and an entertaining one, but making the consumers fully vested participants in the brand itself. And it all started with the premise: candy created by and for children.

> **Before You Leap:** Imagine all the ways you can compel your target audience to act on the brand's behalf. People want to be involved with brands. They want to be the first among their peers to be in the know. They want the special sense of connection and ownership that comes from a personal relationship with a brand. What are you waiting for? *Give it to them.*

Nokia's Game

How do you use the power of entertainment to connect consumers to your brand? Before you leap, get to know Nokia. . . .

A hundred and fifty years ago, Nokia was in the business of selling paper. Once it got into the business of making mobile phones, it took the company only 11 years to become a market leader worldwide. All fine and well, but then the trick becomes how to stay on top. To remain the dominant brand in a rapidly growing market of evolving technology, Nokia needed to get creative in an increasingly saturated and confusing marketplace.[6]

WHAT'S YOUR FUTURE?

The year was 1999. Nokia had seen its future, and it clearly wasn't limited to handsets. Industry watchers had come to realize that consumers would eventually be using their phones to listen to streaming music, watch a movie preview, or check stock quotes—because the next generation of phones would be a lot less like the traditional telephone and a whole lot more like a computer terminal. Nokia was smart enough to realize that it wasn't just in the business of making mobile phones; it was in the business of connecting people through mobile services. And to do that well, it needed to connect mobile consumers to the Nokia brand. For that, it turned to its PR agency and interactive agency in Rotterdam, Bikker Euro RSCG and Human-i Euro RSCG.

THE LEAP

At the time, Nokia's advertising tag line was "Connecting People." The agency team began to think of ways to make Nokia's tag line come to life. The team ultimately settled on the idea of connecting with consumers by, essentially, drawing them into a really good story. "We wanted to show Nokia that there was another way of connecting people, not just by product but by communication of the Nokia brand itself," says Marco Boender, chief operating officer of Human-i Euro RSCG. "That's where the creative leap began. We thought, what would be a better way to connect people? What do people talk about? People talk about good stories, about good challenges." What the agency team had discovered was the essence of the consumer DNA. They had tapped into what the consumer wanted to experience. Now they just had to connect the consumer to the brand.

Eventually the team came up with a James Bond–like adventure story that would be called "Nokia Game." Created by Sicco Beerda and Joost van Liemt, at the time creative directors at Bikker Euro RSCG, Nokia Game was designed as an interactive adventure that would fully engage consumers in the brand experience.

THINK BEYOND YOUR CUSTOMER BASE

The plan was to offer Nokia Game to all mobile phone users—not just Nokia users—with a primary target of Europeans ages 15 to 35 who had Internet access. This would allow the company to connect with consumers beyond its core customers.

Though it's primarily an online adventure game, Nokia Game uses all kinds of media: TV spots, short message text on a player's cell phone, mysterious phone calls, and hidden messages in newspaper, and magazine ads, in addition to the Internet. All of these elements work together to tell the story. Players have to interpret the game clues they are provided as though they are the main character in the story.

LET THE GAMES BEGIN

Following a pilot project in 1999 in the Netherlands, the game kicked off in 18 countries in November 2000. By way of introduction, consumers across Europe were told only that "Nokia Game is coming—be ready—subscribe on the Internet." Their attention piqued, nearly half a million people registered for the game, not knowing exactly what it was they were registering for. They knew it would last three weeks. And they knew it would be an all-media adventure. That was it. On the day prior to the official start date, registered players received a cryptic mobile phone message from a woman who would become one of the main characters in the adventure. She told them, "I need your help in the coming weeks to safeguard the future of mobile gaming."

The game was afoot!

The next day players received an e-mail message directing them to tune into a TV spot, which in turn directed them to a Web address and then to a newspaper. Thus began a series of messages, found in newspapers, heard on the radio or Internet, left on mobile phones. . . . The evolving story line also included communication between players, who essentially "lived the adventure" for three weeks, day and night. All 500,000 players started the game at the same time and lived the same

> *Breaking the shackles of traditional campaigns is absolute in the CBI strategy. You must become an "extreme thinker." Look for extreme business solutions. Think of yourself as an explorer in a new territory pushing to extreme regions to discover new lands to settle.*
> —John Dahlin, Euro RSCG Tatham Partners, Salt Lake City

story in their own languages. The buzz generated around the brand even led to the creation of some 30 "shadow sites"—Internet sites that players created on their own to discuss conspiracy theories and share information.

With Nokia Game, client and agency succeeded in their mission to connect mobile consumers to the Nokia brand, not just as a company that manufactures handsets but as a provider of meaningful and entertaining mobile services. They wanted to change the way consumers think of Nokia by delivering on a brand promise that said this product helps you shape your life and connects you to others and to the world around you. The game did just that. And for good measure, the integrated multimedia campaign picked up a Gold Lion Direct award at the 2002 International Advertising Festival in Cannes.

> **BEFORE YOU LEAP:** Consumers are bombarded with thousands of messages every day. Why not shape that chaos into something entertaining? Provide fresh and satisfying experiences on an ongoing basis, and you will soon have a loyal customer base. But a word of caution: Entertain, don't bombard.

A SHIFT IN MIND-SET

I was drawn to Nokia as an example of a CBI by one factor that will be increasingly important in the years to come: its global nature. Nokia set out to create a community, much as Guinness set out to build a community of young people around Witnness rock festivals. Both brands used entertainment to connect consumers to their brands. Both brilliantly understood the community-building potential of the Internet. But what's intriguing about Nokia is that it was able to do it simultaneously across 18 countries. People from different time zones and in different countries were comparing notes and sharing clues and even getting together in cafés and bars, all the while playing exactly the same game at exactly the same time. Nokia Game achieved the kind of cross-border brand awareness that is invaluable, and it did it through a truly interactive form of entertainment.

ROOM SERVICE®

Hallmark wasn't ready to embrace the idea of a children's television show based on Crayola crayons. It may have been the right idea—but it definitely wasn't the right time. One of our agencies in Sweden, on the other hand, created a TV show that was rated number two on its channel in the first year.

LOOK FOR WHAT'S EXCITING IN THE UNEXCITING

It all started in what seems the most unlikely of places: Sweden's paint industry. (It just screams "prime-time TV," doesn't it?) Ten years ago, Malaremastarna (the Swedish Association of Painting Contractors) created an association for the paint and painters industry in Sweden called Färgdepartementet—which roughly translates as "Institute for Color." The association is a consortium of 15 companies, seven of them direct competitors. Other members include all of the paint producers in the Nordic countries, plus the trade union and the painters' association in Sweden. The corporate members contribute the funds. The role of Euro RSCG Söderberg Arbman is to recommend the best way to use those funds to promote the paint industry.

Since the organization's inception, the goals had remained consistent: Defend the market of paint and paint services against other markets; expand the market; and, ultimately, place painting high on the priority list in consumers' minds. To accomplish those goals, the agency had relied primarily on traditional media, including one commercial that featured some of Sweden's top politicians.

Then the home decorating trend hit. Suddenly, decorating became fashionable, trendy, a cool thing on which to spend time— and money. The paint association wanted to be part of it. But in order to capitalize on the trend, the association decided it first needed to overhaul its image. Painters had been perceived as not-so-bright, not-so-creative guys who paint only in white. The industry wanted to make painting and painters more fashionable, more artistic.

Technology and new media, or traditional media, will be accelerators only when they connect with the true essence of the CBI. Today's prosumers are savvy, more sensitive than ever to hype they see as superficial and irrelevant.
—José Luis Betancourt, Betancourt Beker Euro RSCG, Mexico City

THE LEAP

The ad campaigns created by the agency up to this point had been reasonably effective. They had shown audiences the importance of having nice surroundings at home and in the office—even in public facilities. But now it was time to break new ground. The agency knew what it needed to do: bring fun and fashion into painting and show viewers the simple, even inexpensive things one could do to improve one's decor with paint.

The agency thought it had come up with an idea that perfectly met every objective. It would showcase fresh new decorating ideas that were extremely affordable. It would demonstrate that painters can be creative types who can work wonders in one's home. It would help to give consumers a new attitude toward the painter's trade. And, ultimately, it would get more people to hire professional painters in addition to selling more paint. It might even get people interested in becoming professional painters.

Boldly, the agency presented the idea. The response reminded me of the time early in my career when the head of British Motor Company responded to a great idea I had with the less-than-supportive "Just remember, I warned you." This time was worse. The idea actually drew laughter. "If you can do that," the members of the Färgdepartementet said, "we will certainly go along. Good luck, and report back to us."

PAINTING IN PRIME TIME

What the agency had proposed was a television series, to be aired on national TV in Sweden. The series of 10 half-hour shows would introduce viewers to fashion trends in home decorating, feature young, artistic painters, and include new ideas for decorating with paint—and lots of rock 'n' roll. A young, fun, hip TV show with a rock feel seemed like the ideal vehicle with which to reach the primary target: young people (ages 25 to 35) living in small apartments with equally small budgets, people who care about their living space but have no idea how to redecorate.

Promoted as "a new way to look at decorating," each show in the *Room Service*® series featured a different decorating makeover, carried out by a team of young people consisting of a decorator, a painter, and a carpenter. This was real reality TV. These were real people in real spaces.

To recruit people for the show—both those who wanted to have their spaces redecorated and those who would make up the *Room Service* decorating teams—the agency distributed leaflets in coffee shops, game centers, and other places where young people hang out. The show was promoted in all paint stores in Sweden. A *Room Service* website was launched. Ads ran in print and on television. The TV channel also provided the agency with a lot of airtime prior to the show—the agency cut together trailers, which teased upcoming episodes.

PURE ENTERTAINMENT

Everyone agrees: *Room Service* is highly entertaining. You watch these young people go about designing and then redecorating what-ever space they're working on. You see the before and after and get to watch the owner's reaction. They take their jobs seriously, but obviously they're also having a good time. Also, there's no how-to in the show. It's pure entertainment. For the how-to part, viewers can go to the website, where they can also enter competitions and play games.

Room Service ad

The ratings for *Room Service* exceeded estimates by 100 percent. In fact, it was

The real value of these great brand ideas is that they're inherently flexible. They have a clear center of gravity but, around that, their shape is constantly changing. . . . The incredible value of great CBIs is that they're powerful enough to influence, and more important direct, the way our customers reinterpret what our brand means to them.
—Glen Flaherty, Euro RSCG Wnek Gosper, London

the second-highest-rated program on the channel. The show was so successful that Channel 5 has signed up for another season and the paint association has agreed to fund it. *Room Service* has even spawned a new logotype called "Johnnie Starpainter" (Johnnie is the name of the painter in the TV show), which is being used in a recruitment campaign to attract young people, both men and women, to the painting trade.

MAXIMIZING THE BRAND EXPERIENCE

Room Service is a great Creative Business Idea. As an example of a new way to maximize relationships between consumers and brands, I don't think you can get much better.

It's also a wonderful example of using entertainment to connect the consumer to one's brand, of using entertainment to create a powerful new kind of brand experience.

HOW MANY PEOPLE WOULD HAVE THOUGHT OF PROMOTING SOMETHING LIKE THE PAINT INDUSTRY WITH A YOUTH-ORIENTED HOME DECORATING TELEVISION SHOW?

That was brilliant creative thinking. It was a great creative leap.

EXPAND YOUR HORIZONS

And there's another lesson I think we can learn from *Room Service,* one that is vitally important to our future. In order to make *Room Service* a reality, the agency had to get into an entirely new business, one it knew absolutely nothing about: television production. The agency conceived and created the show. It had complete control over every creative and production element. Bottom line, the agency realized it wasn't just in the advertising business anymore.

BEFORE YOU LEAP: It doesn't matter whether you're a corporation or whether you're a creative company delivering services. We all have to ask ourselves, "What business am I really in?" (For those in my industry, it's no longer just straight advertising, that's for certain.) We then need to ask, "Am I willing to radically alter my business—or even get into an entirely new one?" Euro RSCG Söderberg Arbman was when it got into TV production. Billiken was when it revamped its manufacturing process. Hallmark was when it got into the flower business.

Finally, do a self-check on your excitement level. This is the end of advertising and the beginning of something new. To me, it is so exciting, so stimulating from both a left- and a right-brain point of view, and also potentially so much more rewarding in every way than the "old" advertising business. I believe it's absolutely the most exciting time to be working in this industry . . . as long as we constantly remind ourselves of what business we're really in.

PROJECT GREENLIGHT

Even the entertainment industry is beginning to see the importance of adding entertainment to the brand experience. Film marketing, for example, is finally being reinvented beyond the traditional blitz of TV advertising and fast-food tie-ins. One of the most brilliant examples, I think, is the partnership among Miramax Films, HBO, and actors Matt Damon and Ben Affleck, along with producer Chris Moore. Called Project Greenlight, it is revolutionizing not just the way films are marketed . . . but the way they are made.[7]

THE LEAP

The genesis of the idea came from Damon and Affleck, who wanted to offer aspiring screenwriters the chance for a career break like the one they received with the script for *Good Will Hunting*—a break that catapulted them from unknowns to Hollywood superstars virtually overnight. Once again, the idea was strongly rooted in the product, in this case, a great script that otherwise never would have seen the light of day. The two actors invited would-be writer-directors from all over the world to submit their screenplays, with the winning entry to be made into a feature-length film by Miramax. The budget for the film was promised to be at least $1 million; the winner would also direct the film.

The way the contest played out online is a great example of how the Internet can create global communities. Writers reviewed each other's submissions to help narrow down the finalists. Chat rooms stayed active long after the competition was over. With more than

7,000 submissions, this was the largest active screenwriting community in the world.

A BIG IDEA GETS BIGGER

HBO produced a 12-part documentary series on the making of the movie, which was broadcast in the winter of 2002, prior to the film's theatrical release. From a business standpoint, the financial risk was negligible. A documentary shot on videotape with ready-made material that had been used for a low-budget HBO series. And it turned out to be very compelling television. Viewers experienced what it was like for a complete novice—the winner's only film experience had been a couple of stints as a production assistant—to direct a film. Actors came on board for far less than their standard wages, and the company was able to procure the workforce for below-standard union pay scales.

Though critics had mixed reviews of the final movie, *Stolen Summer,* the HBO Project Greenlight series was a critical and popular  success. The *Los Angeles Times* called the series "a compulsively watchable word-of-mouth hit."[8] Viewers witnessed every mistake, argument, and crisis. Real-life Hollywood characters lived up to, and beyond, our stereotyped expectations of outrageous behavior. Some cynical critics even suggested that the director had been chosen precisely for his inexperience and naïveté, to create drama between him and the personalities of the film business. Whether by carefully laid plans or just plain luck, the people behind Project Greenlight had managed to create a compelling and highly entertaining brand experience.

Add up the elements: The Project Greenlight team created a global screenwriting community, then allowed this community to select the contest winner; they produced the film, and then leveraged it with a hit HBO TV series. That's a big Creative Business Idea. And it led to another breakthrough business idea. Damon and Affleck are now cofounders of a venture called LivePlanet, which was formed with the specific intent of creating integrated media entertainment experiences. Their plan is to use traditional media, new media, and the physical world to provide a new kind of entertainment. "Live-Planet is taking things that people already know and do," says Live-Planet CEO Chris Moore, "like watching television, using the Web and wireless devices and going to events—and making them better, more complete and more accessible. We think that means that people will have more fun."[9]

BEFORE YOU LEAP:
- Know the consumer DNA as well as you know the brand DNA—the space in between is where CBIs happen.
- Make the brand experience fun, make it entertaining. In the future, the entertainment factor associated with your brand may be as much of a draw as the product itself.
- As the world turns, the consumer changes. Keep redefining the consumer relationship and the brand experience. People's passions change.

ED SCHLOSSBERG AND ESI

In the future, we will be turning more and more to nontraditional partners, those outside the traditional business universe we used to be in. This is particularly true as we begin to transform all brand experiences into entertainment experiences and as it becomes imperative to connect consumers to our brands and our ideas in new ways.

IT'S ALL IN THE GAME

I regularly meet with people outside of our industry, and one person I have gotten to know is Edwin Schlossberg. Schlossberg has a doctorate degree in Science and Literature from Columbia University. He is the author of a number of books, including a collection of poetry, and has coauthored several game books. One of them, *The Pocket Calculator Game Book,* came out in the early days of electronics, and it was a kind of "101 games you can play with your calculator." They were literally games you played with just the calculator—and as twentieth century as it now sounds, it was a very original concept, and the book sold a great number of copies in several languages.[10]

In 1977, Schlossberg founded Edwin Schlossberg Incorporated (ESI), a multidisciplinary firm that specializes in interactive design for public places. His company has done work for museums, zoos, parks, cable channels, and utility companies. He designed the lobby in the AOL Time Warner building and programmed 1,000 square feet of signage space to display an ever-changing video presentation of animated logos, movies, television, and live broadcasts. The way it's designed, no two visitors will ever see the same presentation.

He also created the science and technology museum at Sony Plaza, Sony Wonder Technology Lab, where children learn about technology as they play with it. It's a free public space where the visitor is at the center of the experience and invited to become a "media trainee." As you go through your "training," you see and hear great moments in the history of communication technology and participate in a high-definition-television training experience. Then you can use your new skills in activities that simulate a variety of media professions, such as robotics engineer, camera operator, and video game designer.

What Schlossberg has gravitated to more than anything else is the possibility of interactive experiences, not with advertising or with brands necessarily, but creating experiences to enable people to know something better by experiencing it. He describes traditional exhibits, such as what's typically seen in museums, as being set up like puzzles, based on ideas that are understood, and it's the audience's job to find its way. He describes interactive exhibits, on the other hand, as being like games. And what do games provide? Entertainment.

THINK LIKE AN ANIMAL

Back in 1981, Schlossberg did a project for the Massachusetts Society for the Prevention of Cruelty to Animals, a working farm that is designed to provide visitors with a compassionate look inside the world of animals. The exhibit encouraged visitors to understand an animal's needs and behavior by actually experiencing what it's like to perceive the world the way a particular animal does.

There were more than 60 different interactive activities with which visitors could experience what the world looks like to a goat, for example, or how it feels to work like a horse. Schlossberg accomplished the visual effects through fiber-optic Sight Masks. In the Stride Game, for instance, you could match an animal's gait and get a sense of its size and movements. There was even a Scent Maze, where visitors sniffed their way from one point to another just the way a pig does by following a maze of scented poles. What a great, interesting idea.

GET ENGAGED

Ed Schlossberg also designed the Ellis Island website and museum exhibit, which, as anyone who has been there will attest, is incredibly compelling. If you know that your family emigrated to the United States during the great surge from 1892 to 1924, you can search a database containing 22 million passenger records of those who passed through Ellis Island at that time. At the museum, visitors use computer stations to search, view, and print out digital records of ships' manifests containing passenger records and pictures of the ships themselves. You can also add to the permanent record of Ellis Island by adding relics of your own family's history, such as photographs and official documents, and create a virtual scrapbook.

BEFORE YOU LEAP: Take the time to look beyond the realm of advertising—or even commerce—to understand the full impact and power

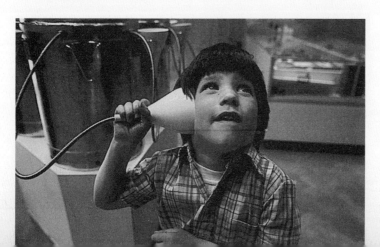

ESI: Macomber Farm

of truly creative ideas. Talking about his larger goals, Schlossberg says, "My concerns are social in the sense that I can't imagine our culture taking all the steps it needs to take unless we're all actively engaged in the creative process—as opposed to simply traveling along with the most sophisticated inventors or artists."

The things Ed Schlossberg has done may seem to have nothing to do with creative thinking in the business world. But I think they have everything to do with it. His projects are all about connecting people to Creative Business Ideas and creating new kinds of entertainment experiences. They are all about powerful creative ideas.

Chapter 9
A Structure for Creative Thinking

Breakthrough creative thinking is not simply a matter of having a spark of inspiration that miraculously works its way into a business plan. It requires teamwork and a process—and a total commitment to seeing great ideas come to fruition. And that's not something that the average company can achieve on its own.

MEMO TO CORPORATE AMERICA: THE CASE FOR COLLABORATION

Not every company has a Richard Branson or a Thomas Krens or an Akio Morita or a Frank Perdue. For those that don't, it shouldn't be too much of a stretch to realize that your best bet is creative collaboration. By that, I don't mean a committee of the usual suspects—the in-house "creative" people you call upon when you're facing a challenge that requires communications cleverness. Those folks can solve many problems. But it's very unlikely they will give you the breakthroughs that lead to Creative Business Ideas.

To wind up with breakthrough CBIs, your best bet is to take on a strategic *creative* partner that can bring creative thinking to your business—that can help you make the leap. And from where I sit, your best bet is to partner with an agency. Why? It's simple: No other industry is so densely populated with creative people. Hell, half of them are paid just for coming up with creative ideas.

Those of you who work for management consulting firms—or hire them—might take umbrage at what you see as my oversight. But if you are looking to consulting firms for truly creative thinking, you're looking in the wrong place. Their specialty isn't creativity, it's analysis. And even though analytical people can amass data, study markets, track consumer trends, and come out with some intriguing conclusions, they're not likely to present you with the kind of breakthrough thinking I'm talking about. Could they have transformed the Paris Metro? Made the Swedish paint industry suddenly fashionable? Recommended building a bridge in Buenos Aires? Invented MTV or Yahoo! or a brand of chicken? I think not.

In the business environment in which we exist, strategic thinking—no matter how brilliant and on target—is not enough. It won't accomplish what more and more clients are asking their partners to do: reinvigorate brand strategies that have gone flat, help them take advantage of all media, be expert in how to build their brands and their businesses, and help them revolutionize their own industries.

Hallmark's Irv Hockaday knew that. That's why, after rounding up the usual suspects yielded no great ideas, he turned away from management consulting firms and turned instead to advertising agencies. He understood that what he needed was people who could bring creative thinking to his business. It's when right brain meets left brain, when creative thinking is applied to business strategy, that one arrives at ideas with the ability to be transformational—and we in the agency business can do this without having to transform ourselves into consulting firms.

How can you structure your own company so that Creative Business Ideas can flourish? And how can agencies and clients structure the relationships between them to maximize the level of creative thinking that takes place? Read on.

HOW TO STRUCTURE YOUR COMPANY FOR CREATIVE THINKING

Just how does one structure a company to elicit the highest levels of creative thinking? At our agency, we believe that great creative thinking starts not with individuals, but with teams—teams made of people who bring different perspectives.

In Chapter 4, I discussed the views of *Fast Company* founder Bill Taylor on corporate innovation. He contends that one reason companies fail to innovate successfully is that they've got the same old kinds of people, using the same old kinds of tools, asking the same old kinds of questions. It's an imperative that you can either heed or deny, but I think we have to find ways to introduce into our organizations what Taylor calls "weird new strands of DNA" and weird new points of view about the future.[1]

I don't think that imperative has always existed, at least not for those of us in the marketing communications business. In the days when our work was being judged by reels and books, having an organization made up of the hottest talent in the industry was a coup. If you could attract and retain the best in the business, why look anywhere else?

Welcome to the new world.

Today, putting together the right group of talent isn't just about finding the smartest or most creative people. It's about striking the right balance among thinking styles, personalities, and skill sets. We are constantly working to integrate "weird new strands of DNA" into our network. Some of our people grew up in advertising; this is where they've built their careers and spent much of their lives. Others know very little about advertising in the traditional sense, but are savvy and seasoned veterans at exploring ideas outside of traditional campaigns—and they thrive on it.

But just because you've assembled the right team of people doesn't mean you can then sit back and wait for the creative juices to start flowing, hoping that eventually the proverbial sparks will start to fly. You can't put a group of highly creative, highly enthusiastic people in a room and simply wait for creative ideas to emerge, any more than you can put together a group of skilled football players and expect them to hand you the Super Bowl. You need a game plan. A system. A strategy. A process—even if that process relies less on regimentation and more on feeling and flow.

CREATIVITY IS NOT A LICENSE TO "PLAY"

Albert Einstein's creative method was to outlast a gray, dull day and hope for late-afternoon inspiration. For Isaac Newton, the way was to think without limits—to go beyond the apple falling from the tree to wonder whether the force of gravity also applied to the moon.

Creativity is liberating. But that is the result of creativity—not the process. Disappointing, I know. How much more fun life would be if it were as simple as Zorba the Greek proclaiming, "Take off your belt—and live!"

"Two heads are better than one" drove creative teams of the twentieth century. The twenty-first century team looks more like a football team. Managers of agencies need to become more like managers of top sporting teams. They have to assemble the best playing roster of stars with complementary skills.
—Matt Donovan, Euro RSCG Partnership, Sydney

Getting the right balance of human talent is the essence of creating powerful winning strategies in a true CBI environment— throw that talent together without a moment's thought and your chances of success are already diminished. So why trust it to luck? Understand the talent around you, what motivates them, inspires them, challenges them, and use that knowledge to build a collective set of skills with the power to turn talent into genius. In the CBI world, and like any team sports, there is an energy and power in the fusion of different skills that you can see come to life—and that is when you can create ideas which truly change the shape of accepted thinking.
—Fergus McCallum, KLP Euro RSCG, London

In fact, creativity is a hothouse flower, if you will forgive the metaphor. You have to plan far ahead to create the conditions that will induce it to appear. And then, once it sprouts, you have to nurture it. You have to channel the creative energy that feeds it. You have to focus it. And you can't do all of that without a methodology.

BUILD A PROCESS

So where do you begin? How do you bring methodology to the madness and magic of creative thinking? Before you leap, get to know an organization that has done it brilliantly. One great example: IDEO.

At one of our 100-Day Meetings at IMD in Lausanne, Switzerland, we studied a business case of a very creative product design company named IDEO, one of the most innovative design and development firms in the world and a great example of brilliant creative thinking applied to product design. It has worked on the design (or redesign) of literally thousands of products, from toothbrushes to shopping carts, remote controls to high-speed trains. Among other things, IDEO brought the world the Palm V, the Apple mouse, and the Polaroid i-Zone camera. General manager Tom Kelley and his colleagues believe that the goal of any company should be to tap into and encourage creativity, and that you can build a routine and process that allows you to come up with great ideas time and time again. He has a unique understanding of the way creativity can shape business, because creativity *is* his only business.

IDEO has devised a well-developed, continuously refined— and deceptively simple—methodology for innovation, which Kelley discusses in his fascinating book, *The Art of Innovation*. At the heart of the IDEO method, as at our network, are teams. As Kelley puts it, "Quite simply, great projects are achieved by great teams."[2] But not just any old team. An IDEO team is a carefully constructed group of individuals from diverse backgrounds. The team engages in a very distinct process, which involves analysis and understanding, observation, a highly structured brainstorming process, which Tom calls "visualization," extensive prototyping, evaluation and refinement, and, finally, implementation.[3] Let me give you an example from the book.

THE SHOPPING CART

Back in the late 1990s, ABC approached IDEO with an intriguing proposition. If IDEO would demonstrate innovation in action—by reinventing a product category—ABC would showcase that process on *Nightline*. There were two catches: The network got to pick the category, and the firm would have only five days to complete the project.

What ABC picked was the toughest challenge it could think of, an old product in an unexciting category: the shopping cart. Think about it. When's the last time anyone redesigned the shopping cart? Has it *ever* been redesigned?

The first thing IDEO did was put together a diverse team. There was the usual smattering of engineers and industrial designers. But there were also people with backgrounds in biology, architecture, linguistics, business administration, and psychology—people who don't look at the world from an engineering or design standpoint. A deliberate combination of left brain, right brain.

With the team assembled, they hit the streets—and the stores. As Kelley puts it, the goal was ". . . to immerse ourselves in the state of grocery shopping, shopping carts, and any and all possibly relevant technologies. Blending our 'understand' and 'observe' phases into a single day's work, we were practicing a form of instant anthropology. We were getting out of the office, cornering the experts, and observing the natives in their habitat."[4]

Some team members flocked to grocery stores. Others paid a visit to a bike store to catch up on the latest materials and designs being used in the cycling world. One group focused on the child-seat component of shopping carts and decided to check out car seats and strollers. Another interviewed a shopping-cart repairman. Kelley chose to interview a professional shopping-cart buyer who worked for one of the big chains.

By the end of the day, as Kelley recalls, "Three goals had emerged: Make the cart more child-friendly, figure out a more efficient shopping system, and increase safety."

The Idea Engine of IDEO's Culture

The second morning was devoted to brainstorming, what Kelley calls ". . . the idea engine of IDEO's culture."[5] The walls were quickly covered by hundreds of sketches and ideas. Then team members voted for their favorites. After lunch, the team leaders, who had reviewed the votes, decided where to focus prototyping—based on the technical feasibility given the time frame—and divided the team into four groups, each assigned to build a mock-up focused on a different concern.

The speed with which the teams worked was absolutely amazing: Within three hours, the mock-ups were ready. The design team then convened in the company's shop, along with the model makers and machinists, and picked the best feature of each prototype. For the next two days, the design and shop teams worked hand in hand, practically around the clock, to finish the new cart by the Friday deadline. When the finished cart was finally revealed, to a television audience of nearly 10 million viewers, it bore little resemblance to the cart that has been around since time immemorial. Sleek, curved lines, a system of nesting handbaskets so you could go down an aisle with just a basket instead of the whole cart, two cupholders, a price scanner, wheels that locked, and a safety bar and play surface for the child's seat. True to IDEO's ideology, it hadn't just redesigned the shopping cart, it had redesigned the shopping experience.

The phones started ringing early the next morning—largely from corporate executives. "Most of them didn't give a damn about shopping carts," says Kelley. "They wanted to know more about the process we used to bring the cart into being. One CEO told me that he understood, for the first time, what creativity really meant and how it could be managed in a business environment."

THE IDEA ENGINE OF OUR CULTURE: WAR ROOMS

Bringing weird new strands of DNA and weird new points of view about the future into the organization is something that Tom Kelley and the IDEO organization have done exceedingly well. They have also brilliantly managed to channel the creative energy generated by all that weird DNA.

The last thing the business community needs is yet another analysis of what went wrong with the dot-com phenomenon. So I'll spare you. Except for this: I don't know if I had ever before seen such a massive explosion of creative thinking in such a concentrated period of time. So many great creative ideas emerged out of that era. But so much of that energy was unchanneled and random. If the marriage of business strategy and creativity is to be a marriage of equals, the concept of discipline had better be invited to sit side by side with creative thinking. That's what our war rooms are all about—discipline.

SHARE THE KNOWLEDGE!

The idea of creating war rooms actually stemmed from an observation that I made early on in my career—account people were constantly hiding facts from creative people. They were almost obsessive about owning knowledge and keeping it away from anyone else; it was theirs and theirs alone. At first, I couldn't figure it out. What was with these people who were so possessive with these facts?

Then it dawned on me. Over my 30 years in advertising, it was the account people who clung desperately to information because information was how their worth was measured by the agency—in the same way that creatives are measured by their book, portfolio, and reel. And that's why they didn't want to share the information. How could they have any measurable worth if they shared ownership of the facts?

But breakthroughs in creative thinking come only with shared information—not with fiefdoms focused on protecting their turf. It was during my years at MVBMS that I came up with the idea of war rooms as the way to change this and more. And since we were already a decentralized, democratized, totally flat organization, we didn't have to tear down any walls to do it.

What is a *war room*? It's a physical place where pertinent information is housed and made accessible to all. Just as important, it's a team learning and idea-building process that takes place in a common, dedicated central location. In short, it's a place where random creative thinking is transformed into the only kind of creative thinking that is valuable to any of us: targeted creative thinking.

Every organization needs the ability to channel creative energy. War rooms are part of a process that we've put in place to force people to be disciplined in their creative thinking. Today, war rooms are totally integrated into the way we do business; they're the idea engines of our culture.

RANDOM ACCESS, TARGETED THINKING

Walk into a war room at any one of our agencies and you'll find the walls covered with information—what we call "windows of knowledge." What's there are insights about the client's business, organized to include consumer perceptions, polling data, competitive analysis, market trends, industry dynamics, tracking studies, and any other kind of research we've undertaken. This information enables us to be totally objective about our client's business. The "windows" concept came from the computer culture fostered by Microsoft, which gave users the ability to have multiple sources of information open at the same time. The premise is that if you look at different windows of information simultaneously, as opposed to having to view pieces of information one at a time, you see things differently. It's the difference between taking a photograph with a telephoto lens or a wide-angle lens.

In our war rooms, the windows of knowledge serve as the backdrop, the constantly changing, interactive wallpaper. By bringing every discipline together in one physical space—by exposing everyone to the same information, at the same time, in the same place—we generate better thinking. Also important, the war room is a way of engaging a group in a nonhierarchical way, with everyone at a similar level of knowledge; it's a stake in the heart of the old-school hierarchical method that saw each discipline briefed, individually, by the account executive. We cut across those barriers, share the same information with everyone, and then turn that information into useful insights that, we hope, will in turn generate big ideas. The media people know the same thing as do the planners as do the creatives as does the client.

Yes, the client. Those days when the account executive was the client's greatest protector? They're over. In our methodology, the client no longer briefs the account executive. The client briefs the team, in the war room. And the team is organized around the client. Ideally, the client participates from day one. War rooms are holistic. And because the client is an integral member of the team, the door is open for a creative leap to take place at the very beginning of the process—where it can help to define the primary business idea and can be used to invent and reinvigorate both brands and businesses.

BEFORE YOU LEAP:
- Be ready to take a totally objective—and painstakingly thorough—look at the client's business.
- Have a process in place that enables you to share information in a nonhierarchical way.
- Make the client an integral member of the team.

FROM INFORMATION TO INSIGHTS

What kinds of insights can emerge out of all these windows of information? Allow me to return to the company where I first discovered the joy of applying left-brain/right-brain thinking to business . . . yes, Volvo.

Being totally objective about Volvo's business—the facts, please, just the facts—is what led us ultimately to recommend that Volvo Cars not only could reclaim the safety positioning, but absolutely had to. It also led us to the realization that, because every other car company

When you start with the goal of thinking about Creative Business Ideas, what happens is extraordinary. Creative people are delivering strategy. Account people are being creative. Strategists demonstrate their business acumen. And, even more so, when you operate this way across marketing communication disciplines, direct marketing people, interactive specialists, public relations professionals, everyone, forgets about the application of their individual discipline for a moment in time. But they still bring to the team effort their unique points of view that have been developed through their practice. Big Creative Business Ideas quite reliably create passion and energy and excitement—which is exactly what every business needs.
—Beth Waxman, Euro RSCG MVBMS Partners, New York

was claiming safety based on hardware, Volvo had to shift the conversation away from hardware to one that focused on the benefits of all that hardware: saving lives.

The insights garnered in the war room also led us to an important piece of creative work: the original Survivors campaign. During a session in the war room, we discovered that Volvo had a network of owners who passionately believed that their Volvos had saved their lives. They sent in shots of their crumpled cars, together with pictures of themselves and their families. As you can imagine, it was a poignant experience to discover the impact our client company had had on all these lives. The lengthy, heartfelt letters usually cited the professional opinions of safety experts and mechanics who had told them they probably would not be alive if they hadn't been driving a Volvo. Volvo had always known those letters existed, but had seen them as pieces of information. It wasn't until that information was shared that it was transformed from a file folder filled with letters—information—into useful insights that, eventually, would help us to generate big ideas.

In fact, insights from the war room eventually led us to change Volvo's entire positioning. Through the war room, we learned that, across the board, the primary purchasers of Volvos were men. Technically, the men were the consumers. But while men were buying the cars, it was the women who were driving them. So, in essence, women were driving the sales of this brand. As a result, Volvo shifted its targeting from the male purchaser to the female driver. A major shift. A mini-revolution.

BEFORE YOU LEAP: It's important to understand that the springboard for making a creative leap is facts and data, not fiction. The best creative thinking comes out of discipline, not unbridled brainstorming. And when gathering information, fight the urge to censor it. What one person sees as unimportant may lead another to a revolutionary idea.

BE SPECIFIC, BUILD ON THE KNOWLEDGE

"How to achieve world peace" would not be a good war room topic. It's too general, too broad. War room topics need to be very specific, like, "How do we launch this product?" or, "How do we gain market share?"

War rooms are also not immersion tanks. You can't just bring everyone together in a room, expose them to all this information, decide what you've learned . . . and wait for the ideas to percolate and rise to the surface. You have to build on the knowledge you have acquired. And it has to be an ongoing process. The windows of knowledge and the learning that come out of our first war room session allow us to find out what we know and what we don't know. What we don't know, we go out and investigate. Then we return with the new information and reevaluate and build on what we've learned. Inevitably, after the reevaluation, something new emerges that we realize we don't know. And off we go again.

This process of building our knowledge from the ground up is extremely valuable as a tool for new business. And when new people join the team, they can be led through the thinking in an hour—no big learning curve here. That allows them, from the beginning, to start their thinking from a place much further along than they would otherwise have.

It's an Ongoing War

War rooms have become a metaphor for the Euro RSCG culture. At one point, at MVBMS, there were 10 war rooms going on at once, some of them fully dedicated. Instead of holding meetings in their offices or in conference rooms, people began to congregate there. This is, I think, fuel for the idea that people might be more productive working in less square footage, as opposed to big open spaces—as long as it's the right square footage.

War rooms go on as long as they need to, sometimes for the life of the project. The Volvo war room's been up and running for 11 years now. And war rooms aren't limited to our own real estate. Knowing how vital the war room is, we eventually took to developing acetates of all the windows of knowledge, so we could take the "room" with us and work in it wherever we happened to be. At

We can't live and breathe CBIs unless we have a culture of dialogue that spans every discipline. We can have all the greatest data in the world, but generating a CBI is not about the data. It's about the interpretation that stems from the dialogue about the data.
—Sander Flaum, Robert A. Becker Euro RSCG, New York

times, we re-create the war room in clients' offices, so that the knowledge can be shared there, ensuring that they are involved every step of the way. Certainly a big advantage when we need them to sign off on something.

DON'T DO IT!

Sometimes the insights gained in war rooms can take you to a place you never ever intended to go. Case in point: Regina, one of my first clients when I joined what was then Messner Vetere Berger Carey, was primarily known for its vacuum cleaners, though it also manufactured steamers and tried to use its vacuum/steamer technology to get into the home spa market with a gadget that turned a bathtub into a whirlpool.

When Regina came to us, its executives were thinking of expanding into the water purification business. They were eager to create an over-the-counter device, the kind that attaches to a faucet. What did they want from us? To tell them how many speeds it should have.

To find the answer, we had to learn everything there is to know about the water business. Our initial thinking was that it was a simple proposition—how complex could the water purification market be? We could not have been more wrong. The complexity of the issue was mind-boggling. We ended up learning more than any of us ever thought we'd know—and certainly a whole lot more than we ever wanted to know.

We never got to the part where we determined how many speeds Regina's water purification device should have—we didn't have to. Because once we had collected all the information and started to build on these windows of knowledge, we ended up at a totally different place. We never intended to go there; it's simply where our investigation took us.

I'll never forget the meeting when we presented our findings to the client. We were in the war room, surrounded by all of these windows of knowledge, and we started at the beginning and began to walk the Regina executives through what we had learned. We started

Combining disciplines under one roof (or, more important, one leadership) is a prerequisite of stimulating the move toward uninhibited thinking. Being stuck within the confines of your own discipline is the death of what I understand to be true creativity, and indeed the death of CBIs.
—Mark Wnek, Euro RSCG Wnek Gosper, London

with our initial findings, then explained how those prompted us to look at something else, and once we knew that, the next logical thing to look at was this, and from that we learned something else, and so on. At the end, I announced that we had come to a conclusion, and it was unanimous: There was no opportunity for an over-the-counter purification device. It was not a business Regina should get into.

The company had previously done a lot of this research, but they didn't know how to look at it or how to build on the knowledge. We had done the heavy lifting. At the end, they thanked us profusely.

We had basically just talked ourselves out of a job. But it was the right thing to do.

THE STRATEGIC TOOLBOX

War rooms force our people to be ruthless in their creative thinking. It starts with thinking objectively about our client's business. But just doing that gets people out of their comfort zone; soon they're thinking way beyond the traditional promotional mind-set. Bottom line: War rooms enable us to channel all of that random creative energy and turn it into targeted creative thinking.

Euro RSCG Worldwide is made up of 233 offices located in 75 countries. In order to drive CBI thinking into every outpost, we needed to provide a clear and easily understood system. One that would serve as a universal tool but be easily adapted to diverse local environments. With the Euro RSCG Five Points™ process we have done just that. Across the agency, it serves as a framework for the creation of Creative Business Ideas.

Why is such a system necessary? Because we believe that, just as you can't paint without learning perspective or getting your hands dirty, and you can't write a symphony without knowing chord structure, you can't consistently come up with breakthrough Creative Business Ideas without discipline and process. The process isn't my dictate, and it doesn't come from headquarters; it reflects the ongoing efforts and input of top planners around the world and across disciplines.

Planners use the process in conjunction with the account and client teams, but it's not some rigid set of rules we've laid down with the mandate that they be followed. Nor are the actual five steps in the process rocket science—you'll see that they are sequential and logical. They provide guidelines for channeling creative energy. They keep people focused. Essentially, they're a way of bringing discipline to the process of creative thinking . . . which gives us the right to demand that creativity and business be a marriage of equals. It's our entrée into the boardroom.

Point 1: Get smart about the brand, the prosumer, and all known touch points. (We define *prosumer* as today's more proactive, and empowered, consumer—those people who are marketing-savvy and more demanding in their relationships with companies, retailers, and service providers.) Decode category targets and conventions.

Point 2: Determine where the brand currently lives within the mind-set of prosumers and influentials.

Point 3: Determine what objectives, marketplace variables, and realities must factor into the creation of a CBI.

Point 4: Bring everyone and every tool together to generate the CBI. It doesn't matter what briefing format you use—just use one.

Point 5: Finally, evaluate the success of the program. But don't stop there. Use that information to refine and reinvigorate the strategy. And never stop asking the question: Does the idea lead to profitable innovation?

Then start the process all over again . . .

I have impressed on all of our offices the value that the agency and our clients derive from this systematic approach to the creation of CBIs. We have also found that learning by doing is the very best way to master this new thinking style aimed at producing profitable innovation. We have teams that we send out to train planners and others in the Five Points process and to let them experience firsthand the energy that comes from focusing all of one's efforts on this single-minded goal. The training takes CBIs out of the realm of the theoretical . . . and makes them tangible. As our chief strategy officer, Marian Salzman, describes it, "Over the course of the three-day training course, we immerse our people in the world of Creative Business Ideas and teach them how to use our proprietary Five Points process to create a CBI of their own. We call it a 'Playshop' rather than a workshop because once you start flying toward such creative solutions, it's downright fun! We use case studies to inform the leaps, the transformations, the germ of genius that can be blown up and out to become an action plan. The energy that results is mind-blowing!"

In this way we have been able to start imbuing our unique thinking style throughout the agency, one office at a time—one team member at a time.

> **BEFORE YOU LEAP:** Recognize that generating CBIs isn't intuitive. It requires discipline and practice. Our Five Points process is not complicated; your process doesn't have to be, either. What's important is to have one. When you get to the end, go back to the beginning. After you've implemented the CBI, revisit the strategy and start over again.

PLAN ON IT

If branding is no longer simply about communications strategy but about business strategy, it doesn't take much of a leap to realize that the role of strategic planning had better be elevated from that of a bit player to a leading role. How can you expect client companies to actively involve you in their strategic planning processes if planning doesn't hold an exalted position within your own agency? It's not enough to talk about it. You actually have to do it.

What's our take on the role of strategic planning?

At the annual Account Planning Group (APG) meetings some time ago, account planning legend Jane Newman flattered me by introducing me as having been the first "legitimate planner" in the United States. Coming from the person typically credited with

CBIs are about "transforming the business itself," providing "profitable innovation." Following that line of logic, it seems to me the only metric that matters is the bottom line: profit, share price. I think if we stray too much from those criteria, we muddy the meaning. Increased brand recognition is just not enough in this brave, exciting new world.
—Ira Matathia, Euro RSCG MVBMS Partners, New York

bringing account planning from the United Kingdom to the United States, that meant a great deal to me. Although I'm quite certain I have never had that exact title on my business card, I can tell you that since my early days at British Motors I have been absorbed in continually attempting to understand the connections between the brand and business needs and between the brand and the consumer. It all comes down to psychology. And asking the right questions is only half the strategic process. Planning must force original perspectives, challenge conventions, and create stimulating disruption. Great planners don't respect the status quo. They provoke and defy.

In the years I've worked in marketing communications, this is what I have come to know about planning—when it's done correctly:

> Planning is storytelling. The planner's challenge is to find patterns and coherence in the chaos of information and opinion and then to craft a simple, compelling narrative.
>
> Planning is also futuristic. While research is about monitoring the now, or analyzing events through the rearview mirror, planning lives is in the future tense. It's not just thinking about what *is,* but thinking about what's possible, about anticipating and even initiating change.
>
> Planning is a defender. Planning plays a vital role in nurturing and protecting infant work and sustaining and developing existing work. As Charles Brower said, "A new idea is delicate. It can be killed by a sneer or a yawn; it can be stabbed to death by a quip and worried to death by a frown on the right man's brow."[6] Planning is motherhood and fatherhood. It's parenthood.
>
> And one more thing: Planning is not only visionary, it requires being a good translator. Planning transports the brilliance and insight of the vision to a place where team members can see it, smell it, and taste it.

Where does planning best occur? In a place where thought runs wild, information is freely shared, all contribute to the unfettered flow of ideas, and there's a discipline in place to channel that great unleashing of creative energy.

For us, it's our war room. What's your war room?

MAKE MISTAKES

BEFORE YOU LEAP: Understand that you can't create a structure giving people permission to unleash great creative thinking and then sit back and expect that only great creative thinking and innovation will come out of it. If you're not ready for mistakes and failure, too . . . don't even go there.

Whenever things were going really well, when the business was running so smoothly it was hard to imagine how things could get any better, I remember that Jerry Taylor used to tell his people at MCI, "You're just not making enough mistakes." Meaning that if nothing's failing, you're not taking enough risks, which means you must be missing some big opportunities. By definition, if you have a flat organization—if democratization is your organizational mantra—and if the imperative of coming up with breakthrough creative thinking is embedded in your corporate culture, people should be taking risks, and they should be making mistakes. And everyone should be totally okay with that. Not sent to the guillotine because of it.

I've always said, "I'd rather be wrong on Monday than right on Friday." Why? Because if you've waited till Friday, chances are, the ideas you're presenting are probably your safest ideas, but not necessarily your best ideas. It's the notion of having the courage to act before you're 100 percent sure. So what if it's wrong? At least you took the risk. If it's wrong on Monday, you have from Tuesday to Thursday to fix it and still be ahead of your competition.

When Franklin Roosevelt boldly claimed that "The only thing we have to fear is fear itself," he could easily have been addressing everyone in our industry, especially the way fear seems to permeate the souls of our organizations in times of recession or when there's even the remotest hint of an economic downturn. Fear is our worst enemy. Because when people are afraid, especially the creative people that make up the vast majority of our organizations, they have a tendency to do things that they would otherwise never dream of doing—and the things they do are usually not very smart. The greatest danger, especially in tough times when people are afraid of losing their jobs, is not that great creative thinking will come to a roaring halt. It's that brilliant creative thinking will continue to go on, but no one will present their ideas because they are afraid. Afraid of being rejected. Afraid of being fired. Afraid of losing the account.

I'm asked all the time, "What should I do, Bob?" And I always say, "Do the right thing. Do the right thing for the client and the right thing for the business." Because if you do what you truly believe is the right thing, you can't go wrong. We might lose the account, but you won't be wrong.

THE FEAR FACTOR

Bill Taylor makes an interesting connection between fear and creativity. As he puts it, "Any company that is serious about creativity and radical innovation has to figure out what it thinks about fear . . . and about fear as a motivator. Because it's a powerful motivator and oftentimes a very good motivator."

Taylor makes a distinction between who should be fearful and who should not, and points to Intel as a company that gets it. "Fear is a very good thing for a company to have," says Taylor. "It's a very bad thing for an individual to have. The challenge is, how do you have a paranoid company without paranoid people? Intel has figured out how to do that. When Andy Grove talks about how 'only the paranoid survive,' he's talking about the company. The trouble with most companies, though, is that the organization is not willing to confront its own demise, but everyone within the organization is— that's all they think about, all the time. So you have a blindly confident company, and utterly fearful people, as opposed to Intel, which has figured out how to be a relatively paranoid company, without too many paranoid people."

Taylor also relates a wonderful story about Marc Andreesen, cofounder of Netscape. Andreesen keeps a list—and updates it every month—of the top 10 reasons his enterprise is going out of business. As Taylor explains, "He doesn't use it to scare people, he does it to constantly shake the organization out of complacency. Kind of a neat little gimmick."

THE PHYSICAL STRUCTURE

Let's say you've created a corporate culture where ideas are free-flowing. You've structured your company for creative thinking. You have a discipline and process in place, whether it's 5 points or 8 points or 20 points. In your view, you've created a decentralized, democratized, totally flat organization. Are you done? Maybe, maybe not. Depends on what your office looks like.

Pick up any business publication today, and chances are good you'll find lots of corporatespeak on the need to create nonhierarchical organizations and delegate the decision-making process. If you do that, these articles claim, you'll soon see a transformed organization and empowered employees.

I think it's great for companies to aim to tear down metaphorical walls and create flat organizations. I've been working in one since the late 1980s—that's what MVBMS was founded on. And I've seen the benefits. That flat culture was the engine that powered the creation of war rooms—without it, the concept would have remained trapped in the limbo of business school theory.

What surprises me, though, is that so much of this conversation about "corporate culture" is psychological and theoretical. In my view, we could benefit from some focus on the other critical ingredient in creating the right culture—the physical space. It's not an afterthought. It's not a footnote to the adjustments you might make to the corporate culture. The physical space may actually be the most critical component of corporate culture—it's its manifestation. I have seen, time and again, how one can change behaviors and mind-sets just by changing the physical environment.

THE IDEO OFFICE

Tom Kelley is a great believer in the importance of the physical space. As he puts it, "Space is the final frontier. . . . You can shape the activities of your organization if you change the physical environment of where you work."[7]

Kelley's belief is that, just as innovation comes from teams, teams need places to thrive and grow. That's what the workplace is—a greenhouse in which innovation can flourish. And every company should consider that space one of its biggest assets.[8]

IDEO's offices follow what Kelley calls a "neighborhood" concept. It has open workspaces that function like "parks" for the team members. It also has "translucent Lexan barn doors [that can be] closed if [team members] need to buckle down and work privately on something."[9] Everyone is encouraged to put a personal stamp on his or her space in the neighborhood; prototypes from projects on which IDEO has worked make for workspaces that are both colorful and cre-

IDEO, Palo Alto

ative. Simple foam cubes, dotted around the offices, can easily become temporary partitions. All office furniture, even partitions, are transportable, so that team members can easily move from one project to another. Nearly everyone has a vote in solving any space problems that crop up throughout the company. It goes back to the belief that the group brain rules over the individual brain, and that truly innovative solutions to problems come not from lone individuals working solo in silos, but from teams of people who bring different points of view to the challenge.

As IDEO has grown, the offices have expanded, but not under the same roof. Instead of putting everyone in a single building, the 160 or so workers are spread over seven buildings in close proximity, simulating what Kelley calls "a microcosm of a college campus. Each building's character and personality reflect its workers and their particular blend of projects."[10] The spaces and places between the buildings become impromptu meeting spaces where ideas and information are shared.

What IDEO has done that so many companies have failed to do is make the connection between the workspace and creative thinking. As Kelley points out, even after Amazon.com went public, Jeff Bezos remained in a cramped office that was no bigger than his assistant's; that was an expression of Amazon's corporate culture. Ditto for Andy Grove, who worked in a cubicle that was the same size as everyone else's. And he may well have been right to do that—what your workplace looks like sends a critical message to everyone inside your company and to the outside world about who you are. But as Tom Kelley puts it, "You've got to create a culture where space matters."[11]

FUEL NORTH AMERICA

Our war rooms are a part of our physical structure. They represent a process, but they are also a physical space. What transpires in that space—engaging a group of people in a nonhierarchical way and

Fuel North America, Euro RSCG MVBMS Partners, New York

having everyone come to a similar level of knowledge—is the embodiment of our corporate culture: flat, decentralized, democratized. But war rooms aren't some rare specimen that we showcase like a special exhibit. You don't walk out of the war room and into sectioned-off offices, separated by walls both metaphorical and literal. You walk into an environment that embodies what our war rooms and our culture are all about.

For instance, walk into the New York offices of Fuel North America, a unit of Euro RSCG MVBMS Partners, and you'll find yourself inside what looks like a Soho loft the size of two football fields. Surround yourself with windows, then add a river view plus 160 strategists, creatives, producers, and planners. Take away the secretaries and the barriers. Not just the psychological barriers, but the walls, literally. What you're left with is a space that promotes the free expression of ideas, a space that by its very structure encourages the marriage of business and creativity.

The company was designed just as the space was—to meet the marketing demands of the digital age. Fuel North America is an agency that was created for one reason only: to deliver better, more targeted business solutions to a single client, Volvo. It all started when, in an attempt to develop consistent advertising at the local level, Volvo decided to implement an internal tactical advertising program that would fund the local market media activities necessary to support local sales. To do that, the company put together 20 local retailer groups—who in essence became our clients. But there was a big question: How do you coordinate advertising at the national level with 20 local market retailer groups spread out all over the country and do it in a way that will deliver the timely responsiveness that local markets demand?

Instead of restructuring our existing agency, we created a totally new agency: Fuel. It is a separate, tactical agency—fast, responsive, and structured exclusively to deal with the local account directors while simultaneously interfacing with the main agency in order to maintain strategic and creative continuity. It's what we always talk about when we stress the importance of "glocal" branding: To be successful, global brands must work to marry a single global brand essence with the local nuances of particular markets. It is the only way to fully speak to the wants and needs of one's customer base.

At Fuel, information travels fast, whether through conversation, telephone, or e-mail. Multimedia cables crisscross exposed stainless-steel air ducts. Rows of cubicles are topped with frosted glass panels that serve as projection screens for graphics and TV spots. The furniture is sleek, modern, and functional. Meetings are as often impromptu as they are scheduled. There are no physical departments to separate disciplines. No hierarchy. Not one window office. No executive lavatories. Everyone is out in the open, partners included. It is integrated to the nth degree. The space doesn't just define the culture; it is the culture. And it's been hugely successful.

BETC Euro RSCG Paris

If you've spent any time in the tenth arrondissement of Paris in the last few years, the last thing you'd expect to find is a thriving agency—which is one of the reasons BETC Euro RSCG was deeply drawn to this working-class, multiethnic neighborhood.

When BETC set out to decide what its new home would look like, the creative team envisioned a workplace that would be close in structure and feel to the comfort and freedom we find at home. Why put people to work in a constrained, formal, anonymous, rigid office environment when the thinking you want them to do is anything but that? The executives envisioned

BETC Euro RSCG, Paris

more big, wide-open spaces, more light, and more fluidity—a space that would reflect their own seamless flow of ideas and information from one discipline to the next. They envisioned lots of common areas in which to share ideas and relax, as well as smaller spaces and cubicles for those necessary moments of isolation. They firmly believed that the physical workplace itself has a huge and direct influence on how we work. But they also recognized that a sense of place extends beyond the four walls of a building. It is of equal importance where the building is located.

Their search for the ideal location took three years—it's not easy to find space in a homey neighborhood anchored in the heart of city life. The answer was a large, old, five-story department store that had been closed in the 1960s. It had been converted into a furniture store at one point, then abandoned, and for the past 15 years had been used as a parking garage. But many of the original features were still intact: soaring atriums, sweeping archways, massive windows, vast open areas, and great light.

If you walk into this building today, it does feel more like a home than an office. Salons on every floor almost beckon you

BETC Euro RSCG, Paris

to gather with colleagues there. The entire fifth floor, with sweeping views of Paris, has been transformed into a café, complete with chaise longues for those needed moments of relaxation. (There are no executive suites with penthouse views in this organization—here the proletariat rules.) Vast open areas give way to small rooms and cubicles located around the perimeter of the building.

The fluidity of the space mirrors the fluidity of the organization. There's also an undeniable sense of playfulness: The small conference rooms on each floor are in bold primary colors and are identified not by sterile numbers but by name. Instead of meeting in conference room 2206-3W, you gather in *box rouge, box blanc, box bleu,* or *box vert.*

CraveroLanis Euro RSCG

The agency world in Buenos Aires is a lot like Manhattan, at least when it comes to location. Just try to find an ad agency on Madison Avenue—most of them have migrated south. When CraveroLanis Euro RSCG decided it was time to find new quarters, it also decided to look beyond city center, eventually selecting a former shipping warehouse at Puerto Madero.

As is the case for many agencies, the move to a new location was dictated by the need for more space and plans for future expansion. But square footage was far from the only consideration. CraveroLanis took the opportunity of its move to create an entirely new kind of space.

The office's open spaces follow a geometric diagram, which evokes transparency and simplicity. The agency doesn't have private places, except for the client meeting rooms. It has a bar in the middle—complete with pool table—and a beautiful view of the river and docks. The grounds are covered with expansive gardens, filled with flowers and trees. There's even a punching bag that management encourages employees to use whenever they need to work off a little steam. And a British-style phone booth outside the entrance for a bit of privacy while making one's cell-phone calls.

When I take my clients on a tour of the agency, and I show them the planning and research department, everybody is very surprised. For the first time, they see all the investment that goes into the idea. What I like about CBIs is that we are at the crossroads of two things: looking for the business idea and communicating this idea to consumers. So there are two parts: the strategic creativity and the executional creativity. Until now, most people have only thought about the executional creativity.
—Mercedes Erra, BETC Euro RSCG, Paris

CraveroLanis Euro RSCG, Buenos Aires

The intent of the agency's design is to invoke creative thinking, eliminate hierarchies, and diminish bureaucracy. You can see everyone, find everyone, have access to everyone—they're all right there.

Is it coincidence that CraveroLanis was the place that gave birth to Billiken, recognized as the number one Creative Business Idea within our network in 2001? Or that it was cited by *Ad Age Global* as the most creative agency of the year in Latin America? Or that the *Gunn Report* named CraveroLanis the sixth most creative agency in the world in 2001? No other Latin American agency has ever been ranked so high.

I do not believe it's a coincidence, any more than I believe it's a coincidence that BETC and Fuel North America were both top-three winners in our CBI Awards—for RATP and Revolvolution, respectively. This is no coincidence; it is solid evidence. Evidence that flat, nonhierarchical structures foster great creative thinking and that physical space matters.

STRUCTURING RELATIONSHIPS BETWEEN CLIENTS AND AGENCIES

Are we there yet? Let's say you've structured your company for creative thinking. You've got a flat organization in which all contribute to the free flow of ideas. You've unleashed creative thinking, albeit in a disciplined way. And your physical structure is a manifestation of your corporate culture. Are you ready to make the leap? Almost.

> **BEFORE YOU LEAP:** Here's another reality check. If you're really serious about delivering Creative Business Ideas to your clients, be prepared to do whatever it takes. Including restructuring the way you do business—on behalf of your clients.

That's what we did with Fuel North America. There is no way we could have coordinated advertising at the national level with 20 local market retailer groups all over the country and delivered the timely responsiveness that local markets demand . . . without creating a separate agency totally dedicated to doing just that. So that's what we did.

We have our people working full time in their offices. And by doing that, we've been able to deliver more than just great advertising—we've been able to deliver totally integrated communication solutions . . . and great Creative Business Ideas.

THE POWER OF ONE

Within our network, we had already seen how flat, nonhierarchical structures lead to innovative solutions for our clients. The question that we posed was, "Could we go beyond a nonhierarchical structure for people . . . to a nonhierarchical structure for companies?" We'd already seen how breaking down barriers, both physically and mentally, can foster creative thinking—we'd seen what can happen when you go beyond the titles of creative director and copywriter and media planner and account executive and instead become nonhierarchical and integrated to the nth degree and—very important—media neutral, where all media are created equal. What if you took that concept to the next step? What if you ramped neutrality to a new place and applied it to the corporate level? What if advertising, direct marketing, interactive, sales promotion, PR, and consulting services—instead of being individual fiefdoms fighting to get the biggest share of the client's budget—were also all created equal? And what if they were working together toward a common overarching goal: delivering great Creative Business Ideas regardless of discipline?

The result was the consolidation of 11 of our U.S. agencies into two new agencies that bring together all of the disciplines into one organization. Under the new business model, each agency works under a single profit and loss center, with a single CEO and a single management team. All of the traditional barriers to true integration have been eliminated—financial, structural, and physical. There's no incentive for an individual discipline to focus on its own bottom line.

The New York headquarters of one of the new agencies houses a representative of every discipline, along with the management team. Everyone sits on stools, at high desks. Open areas abound, with sofas and intimate seating areas where colleagues can discuss and chat.

Every generation or so an idea comes along and blows away all that came before it. Left brain uniting with the right brain to generate Creative Business Ideas truly is a new day in agency thinking. It will bring all disciplines into play at a far higher level of challenge, working toward far greater goals. Freeing the minds of media, planning, research, creatives, and account people to cross-pollinate sans territorial boundaries and restrictive thinking brings a whole new creative force into play.
—Jim Durfee, Euro RSCG MVBMS, New York

Two assistants—once again, there are no secretaries—sit in the middle. The physical space embodies the new business model—one focused exclusively on delivering totally integrated communication solutions . . . and great Creative Business Ideas.

While many of our competitors are busy trying to fix their outdated twentieth-century agency structures, we believe we have created the agency model for the twenty-first century. Think about it, and ask yourself: Are you trying to compete in the brave new world of the twenty-first century with an agency structure that fulfilled its destiny sometime back in the twentieth century? The rules have changed. Our clients' businesses have changed, and in revolutionary ways. Don't you need to change in revolutionary ways, too?

DEMAND A CREATIVE RELATIONSHIP

So you're there. You're ready to make the leap. You've got an agency that's been structured for applying creative thinking to your client's business strategy. You're willing to restructure your own agency to meet the needs of your client, if need be. No problem.

Now let's get to the other partner in this relationship: the client. Do you need to restructure the relationship between client and agency? You do if you're truly going to work together as partners, if you're going to create an environment in which the creative leap takes place at the very beginning of the process, when it can help to define the primary business idea and be used to invent and define both brands and businesses.

Every company, no matter what the industry, has a right to demand a creative business relationship from its agency. It's not just a right; I'd call it an imperative. And that creative business relationship needs to include the top management of both the company and the agency—we all need to recognize that those lessons of creativity begin at the top. It also cuts both ways: Every creative company has a right to demand a creative relationship from its client.

And don't fool yourself: Those reciprocal demands are going to change the nature of the relationship.

DON'T BE SO PROTECTIVE

Our old world was so comfortable, wasn't it? It was if you were a client, anyway. We put together a creative brief with your unique selling proposition: Your product is cleaner, it's brighter, it's stronger. Your account executive took that information and briefed the creative people, and the media people, and anyone else who needed to be privy to the information. All requests within the agency had to be funneled through the account exec. That was your primary contact. The more protective they were of you, the better they were doing their job.

Not that we didn't practice our own form of protectionism. In the old world, we religiously shielded people from certain levels of information. The theory: Give people only the information they need to know. If you're a creative person, in the process of creating a 30-second commercial, how much do you really need to know? You need to know the unique selling proposition, that it's cleaner, brighter, stronger. That should cover it. . . . Creative people rarely left their own floor; instead they holed up in their space and we left them to do what they do best. It was the Albert Einstein approach to creative thinking. Best not to interfere with the creative process, we said.

In the old world, the creative company was the supplier; the client was the purchaser. The creative company did the creating; the client did the judging. Under the old business model, that was fine. It worked. We created some great advertising together. Even won a lot of awards.

But advertising is no longer just about USPs. It's not just about marketing communications. It's about creative companies and clients becoming partners in solving strategic business problems. Which demands that all of us get out of our comfort zones.

I now arrive back at where we started. Namely, that Creative Business Ideas do not come from isolation. They come from teams of people who share the same broad base of knowledge. They arise when the understanding of the brand and the company DNA is just as deep as the understanding of the consumer. And getting to that place demands that everyone contribute information and ideas and knowledge, from the very beginning of the process, including the client. So, if you're a client, say good-bye to the days when your account executive was your greatest protector.

I guarantee, you won't miss those days. Because the process in which you'll be involved will be far more rewarding than deciding what your next 30-second spot will look like. I've seen it happen within our network, as people from all disciplines are given the chance to contribute beyond the 30-second commercial. And I've seen it happen with our clients, who truly enjoy the openness that redefined our environment. The spirit is contagious.

ARE AGENCIES UP TO THE TASK?

I posed the question to Bill Taylor, "Are corporations ready for their creative companies and agencies to help shape business strategy? Are they ready for a marriage of equals?"

Taylor's thinking is that good companies understand that traditional boundaries, at every level, are evaporating, evolving, and morphing. Just because you've been doing things a certain way for the past 30 years doesn't mean you should continue doing business the same way for the next 30 years. On the other hand, as he puts it, "It may be that agencies aspire to do things they're not really capable of doing, too. Lord knows, there's a difference between having ambitions to offer a wider variety of thinking and services and actually being able to deliver it."

Ultimately, Taylor points out, companies are now comfortable cooperating with the same companies with which they compete— and are engaging in modes of behavior that would have been unthinkable 20 years ago. "And so if you can be in business with your archcompetitors," he says, "presumably corporations can have the bandwidth to think that their agencies might be prepared to do more for them strategically and play a larger role in their business."

And once you have the bandwidth, you're missing only one element. A little thing called *trust*.

TRUST

MCI, Intel, Volvo, RATP, Room Service, Billiken. Every Creative Business Idea that I have ever witnessed would *never* have seen the light of day, let alone been executed, without a deep and enduring sense of trust. Trust enabled the people of RATP and our agencies in Paris to work together for the past seven and a half years in transforming the Paris underground. Trust enabled MCI to turn long-distance calling from a commodity into a brand. Trust enabled a Calatrava bridge to be built in Buenos Aires. It was because of a 10-year relationship based on a deep sense of trust that Volvo and MVBMS were able to create customized solutions.

Trust is fundamental to everything that we do. How fundamental? When I surveyed some of my colleagues regarding the elements necessary to create an environment capable of fostering CBIs, the word *trust* came up again and again in their responses. And I was intrigued to see that so many of them focused on very different aspects of trust. Taken together, they contained the following lessons:

- *Trust is about commitment—and about being comfortable that everyone else on the team is as committed to the idea as you are.* And that applies to both the client and one's own team members. Daniel Pankraz, at Euro RSCG Partnership in Sydney, told me that "when cracking a CBI, the trust between employees and agency/client is more about people's commitment to the cause." It's essential, he says, that "everyone be driven by the same unbridled passion to change clients' businesses in a positive way and not just be production houses for ads!" That makes sense. We all know how difficult it is to maintain a steady focus when you suspect that all your hard work might go for naught because of a lack of commitment on the part of others involved in the process.

- *Trust is based in a clear understanding of a common set of goals.* "The longer I am in business," says Tom Moult, of the Moult Agency, Sydney, "the more that I realize trust is the most important ingredient in any business relationship. Building that trust is the very first job in any new relationship. To do this, it's absolutely critical that everyone on both (or all) teams understand the overriding goals that are to be achieved. That sounds straightforward enough, but in practice, it requires strong, vigilant, and open management to keep everyone on the same page."

- *Trust requires openness and sharing.* "Only through complete collaboration of information, ideas, and intent can the optimum solutions be realized," writes Phil Bourne, of our KLP Euro RSCG office in London.

- *Trust is forged one relationship at a time.* There is no such thing as trust between a company and an agency. Trust is developed among people, and it ebbs and flows on an individual level. "In fact," says Aron Katz, of Euro RSCG Partnership in Sydney, "The trust between agency and client at a person-to-person level is the cornerstone of much of our current agency work!" I couldn't agree more.

- *There can be no trust in the absence of respect.* I might like someone at a client company an awful lot, and this person might like me, but if we don't respect each other's talents and experience and wisdom, we have nothing on which to build a working partnership. "Without an environment of trust, CBIs cannot work," says Euro RSCG Tatham Partners' John Dahlin. "The client must trust the agency team and their abilities before they will open the coffers to their real problems and opportunities in the marketplace." This cuts to one of the core truths about CBIs: If you cannot gain unrestricted access to a company—to its information, its ideas, its past failures, its leaders' vision—there is little point in investing the time and effort required to create a CBI. For a Creative Business Idea to be wholly effective, there can be no secrets. Glen Flaherty, of Euro RSCG Wnek Gosper, put it thus: "Without trust, any CBI an agency stumbles across is essentially going to be a random fluke. For a CBI culture to flourish there has to be genuine partnership. We have to get intimate. We have to get close to your business and you have to get close to ours. We need to trust each other enough to share our dreams, to bare our souls."

Importantly, trust grows stronger with mutual success—and that is one of the happy side effects of CBIs. "Over the course of a business relationship it generally follows that the larger the mission and the greater the success, the higher the mutual trust and respect," says Euro RSCG MVBMS's Jim Durfee. "In that sense, the CBI opens the way for a strong client/agency relationship to develop on a level quite above the narrow confines of traditional advertising."

A CREATIVE BRIEF FOR THE TWENTY-FIRST CENTURY

I sometimes wonder what the Hallmark business would look like today if not for the vision of Irv Hockaday. I try to imagine how different things would have been if Hockaday had gone to the agencies with a traditional creative brief and said, "Hey, business is flat. I need an ad campaign. Give me some spots." Instead, he told them that he knew the brand had lots of value in the minds of consumers. He knew the brand had the consumer's permission to expand into other areas. What he didn't know was what those areas should be. And that was his challenge to the agencies.

If you send out a narrowly defined creative brief to your agency or creative company and expect them to come back four weeks later, having had no contact with them in between, you're obliterating your chances of ever coming face-to-face with a CBI. Unless, of course, your agency has the courage and conviction to come back to you and defy your request.

But imagine the possibilities if we were to completely change the way we think about marketing communications. Imagine the possibilities if we were to abandon our twentieth-century thinking and start to do what we should be doing: creating a new kind of creative brief for the twenty-first century, for the times we live in now.

"At the edge of history, the wind is blowing in our faces," writes futurologist William Irwin Thompson.[12] Sounds exciting. Why not go there—and, together, invent the future?

Chapter 10
Make the Leap

All of this is not for the faint of heart.

Creative Business Ideas, on every level, take courage. It takes courage to develop them, courage to propose them, courage to fight for them, and courage to see them through.

It even takes courage to embrace the very concept of Creative Business Ideas. It means being open to creative thinking and being willing to apply it to business strategy. It means having the courage to make the creative leap and to transform your business in ways you never imagined. You need the courage to invite creativity into the boardroom.

Yet the irony is that, even as the need to bring creative thinking to business has never been greater, the act of being courageous has never been more difficult.

We are living in incredibly challenging times. Changes have occurred that are far beyond anything we could have imagined just a few years ago. These are changes that have made today's world a far more uncertain place in many ways. These changes have affected the advertising world, the business world—and the world of every one of you who is reading this book. Uncertainty has changed consumers' lives, agency economics, and our clients' businesses. It is changing the very nature of *all* our businesses—which is understandable, and concerning.

It's concerning because our work of building brands and building businesses is hugely important. In the face of adversity, the demand for creative ideas and leadership and brilliant branding is enormous. And given today's economic and social realities, capitalizing on creative thinking is crucial. Creative thinking, in some regards, represents the intellectual capital of our industry and, quite possibly, business in general. It's at the heart of the free economies that shape our way of life.

Yet uncertainty and fear are the enemies of the creative spirit. When people are afraid of taking risks or making mistakes, they are afraid of making the leap. And you can be sure that the best ideas will never be presented. Now more than ever, the success of all of us—

client *or* agency—depends on the courage and leadership that we represent together.

What we do isn't just about advertising, or marketing, or communications. It's about creativity. It's about creative insight, creative leadership, and creative ideas that foster new opportunities to build businesses. But how effectively we do that—especially during times of uncertainty and fear—is through courage. And not just the courage to be good, but the courage to be great.

"No fear" is the mantra within our network. We hope to fearlessly make leaps on a daily basis—or at least fearlessly attempt them—and we are fearless in our pursuit of great Creative Business Ideas. As you prepare to make the leap within your own organization, here are 10 key places to look before you leap:

1. *Say good-bye to advertising.* Bid a fond adieu, say your farewells, and then move on. This is the end of advertising, and it is the beginning of something new, something far more exciting and rewarding. Apply creative thinking to business strategy. Make regular nonlinear leaps, from A to B . . . to M or maybe even to Q. Ask not, "What is the creative advertising idea?" but, "What is the Creative Business Idea?"

2. *Reduce the casualty rate.* Take off the "Do Not Disturb" sign and invite creativity into the boardroom. In fact, demand that it be there—as a lifetime board member. And if you have no leaders at the top who embrace creative thinking? Hire some that do—and help reduce the number of CBI casualties. The one common thread in every Creative Business Idea I have ever encountered is a high level of acceptance of creative thinking at the highest levels of the organization. If the creative idea doesn't start there, it'll eventually get stopped there. And don't forget the future leaders. Nurture the up-and-coming leaders of tomorrow, and spawn a new generation of leaders and CEOs who embrace creative thinking.

3. *Choose a left-brain/right-brain partner.* For those CEOs who are uniquely capable of making leaps by themselves, may you soar higher

and higher. For those who need others to help bring creative thinking to your business, be selective and choose the right partner. Namely, the right creative agency. Because what you need is not simply a strategic partner, but a strategic *creative* partner, and half of the people in our industry are paid just for coming up with creative ideas. Agencies are best equipped to generate the right-brain-meets-left-brain thinking that has the ability to transform businesses. It's not my bias, it's a fact.

4. *Don't give the consumer your undivided attention.* The old business model of building meaningful brands was rooted in understanding the consumer. Change it. Deeply explore and become intimate with the DNA of the brand and the business just as well as you do the DNA of the consumer. The space between the two is where Creative Business Ideas are born. Ask about and come to know, in depth, what business you're really in (or what business your client is in) and where the consumer resides.

5. *Let the singers sing and the dancers dance.* Whether you're an agency or a client, create environments where singers and dancers can flourish. Start with the idea of a decentralized, flat, nonhierarchical structure. Then have a process in place that allows you to channel all of that creative energy into targeted strategic creative thinking. Allow yourselves to share information, make mistakes, and (yes) accept failure. Also remember, the physical space isn't an afterthought—it's the embodiment of your corporate culture. So go ahead, tear down the walls and get rid of the corner offices.

6. *Eliminate the fiefdoms.* Media-neutral is the mandate here, both in your corporate structure and creative thinking. Eliminate the warring fiefdoms and declare all communications disciplines created equal. And if you're really feeling fearless? Give them a common set of goals and a common P&L and let them soar. Instead of trying to fix your broken-down twentieth-century company structure, create a new business model for the times we live in.

7. *Be entertaining.* We are all in the entertainment business. With every Creative Business Idea, provide not just a strong product

component and a strong communication component, but a powerful, tangible, and highly entertaining brand experience. As we enter the age of the multimedia, multicultural, multinational brand experience, entertainment will soon be a bigger draw than even our products themselves. Entertainment value needs to be embedded into the total brand experience, right from its inception. With the new use of entertainment, we can regain the old mass-media power.

8. *This isn't dating, it's marriage.* Looking for a casual relationship? The occasional date now and then, but nothing too serious? Then don't make the leap at all. Creative Business Ideas are the result of a rigorous blend of solid teamwork and scrupulous discipline. And when it's over? It's not. Creative Business Ideas are not a one-time-only event. It's not one date and you're done. CBIs are a way of doing business.

9. *Bare your soul.* Open the closet door. Any proverbial skeletons hidden there? Then be prepared to drag them out. Creative Business Ideas are about companies and clients becoming partners in solving strategic business problems. And in a genuine partnership, we can't have secrets or hidden agendas. CBIs require complete collaboration and unrestricted access. You must share the same goals and dreams, with absolute trust at every level.

10. *Create a brief for the twenty-first century.* We all know that advertising is no longer just about USPs. It's not even just about marketing communications. The old creative brief is obsolete. Now it's in our hands to create a new creative brief—a new creativity—for the twenty-first century. If you're a client, demand a creative relationship from your agency. If you're an agency, demand one from your client. Go beyond asking for ad campaigns. Beyond asking for advertising. Instead, ask for creative thinking about your business. And when you get it? Reward it.

Courage is fear's enemy. What can make us courageous, especially in these fearful, uncertain times? Before you leap, there is one final place you should look: *inside*. And I'm not suggesting any deep, esoteric soul-searching.

I'm talking about enthusiasm.

Long ago, I pleaded guilty to being in the business of enthusiasm. Can the same be said of our global agency? What I can say is that I think our enthusiasm enables us to be fearless. We get passionately excited about the opportunity to ignite a new revolution in creative thinking, to create the twenty-first-century version of "the book and the reel," and to redefine the agency/client relationship for the times in which we live.

The sparks start to fly when we connect the creative and business worlds. And amazing things happen when we truly collaborate with our client partners and instill the magic of creativity into the very fabric and nature of business itself. I've seen it. We've done it. It's a big "Wow." And I think that's where the unbridled enthusiasm comes from.

All of this is, undoubtedly, a new way of doing business. Yet it is helping to create a future that holds unrestrained promise and potential. I think you will agree that it's so much more rewarding—for all of us—than the old world of advertising and business we left behind.

If you share our enthusiasm, be our guest. Try it out. You'll probably discover something else that we have. Whether you're a baby boomer, Gen Xer, or newly minted graduate, you'll find yourself doing important and satisfying work. And you'll be having fun doing it.

Go ahead. Make the leap.

ACKNOWLEDGMENTS

In Chapter 9, I made the case for creative collaboration. This book is the perfect example of just that: a collaborative creative effort. As with all great collaborations, there are many people I need to thank for their contributions.

First and foremost, thanks to Rebecca Leatherman, with whom I have had the pleasure of working for more than 10 years, and Lisa Fabiano, with whom I've had the pleasure of working for more than 15 years. Without them, this book would not have been possible.

Thanks to Jesse Kornbluth and Ann O'Reilly, whose contributions were invaluable.

Thanks to a core group of people whose collaborative teamwork made it all happen: Lillian Alzheimer, Johanna Berke, Roger Haskins, Sebastian Kaupert, Michael Lee, Carin Moonin, Peggy Nahmany, Sandra Riley, Marian Salzman, Amy Woessner, Nancy Wynne.

Thanks to all of the Euro RSCG people around the world who provided their thinking on Creative Business Ideas:

Thomas Bassett, Black Rocket Euro RSCG, San Francisco
Ron Berger, Euro RSCG MVBMS Partners, New York
José Luis Betancourt, Betancourt Becker Euro RSCG, Mexico City
Leendert Bikker, Euro RSCG, Northern Europe
Frank Bodin, Euro RSCG Switzerland, Geneva
Marco Boender, Human-I Euro RSCG Interactive, Amsterdam
Phil Bourne, KLP Euro RSCG, London
Matt Cumming, Euro RSCG Partnership, Sydney
John Dahlin, Euro RSCG Tatham Partners, Salt Lake City
Vincent Digonnet, Euro RSCG Partnership Asia Pacific, Singapore
Paul D'Inverno, Bounty Euro RSCG, London
Olivier Disle, BETC Euro RSCG, Paris
Matt Donovan, Euro RSCG Partnership, Sydney
Jay Durante, Euro RSCG MVBMS, New York
Jim Durfee, Euro RSCG MVBMS, New York
Mercedes Erra, BETC Euro RSCG, Paris
Gary Epstein, Euro RSCG Tatham Partners, Chicago
Mercedes Erra, BETC, Euro RSCG, Paris
Iain Ferguson, Euro RSCG Worldwide, New York
Glen Flaherty, Euro RSCG Wnek Gosper, London
Sander Flaum, Robert A. Becker Euro RSCG, New York
George Gallate, Euro RSCG Worldwide, New York
Israel Garber, Euro RSCG MVBMS, New York
Denis Glennon, Euro RSCG Tatham Partners, Chicago
Jerome Guilbert, BETC Euro RSCG, Paris
Romain Hatchuel, Euro RSCG Worldwide, New York
Don Hogle, Euro RSCG MVBMS, New York
Marianne Hurstel, BETC Euro RSCG, Paris
Michael Kantrow, Euro RSCG MVBMS, New York
Aron Katz, Euro RSCG Partnership, Sydney
Marcus Kemp, Euro RSCG MVBMS, New York
Cynthia Kenety, Euro RSCG MVBMS, New York
Pierre Lecosse, Euro RSCG Europe, Paris
John Leonard, Euro RSCG Tatham Partners, Chicago
Mason Lin, Euro RSCG Partnership, Beijing
Suzanne Lord, Euro RSCG Tatham Partners, Chicago
Ira Matathia, Euro RSCG MVBMS Partners, New York
Fergus McCallum, KLP Euro RSCG, London
Sean McCarthy, Euro RSCG MVBMS, New York
Dan McLoughlin, Euro RSCG MVBMS Partners, New York
Tom Meloth, Euro RSCG MVBMS, New York
Luca Menato, Euro RSCG Circle, London
Don Middleberg, Euro RSCG Middleberg

Tom Moult, The Moult Agency, Sydney
Julie Ng, Euro RSCG Partnership, Hong Kong
Joe O'Neill, Euro RSCG MVBMS, New York
Kuan Kuan Ong, Euro RSCG Partnership, Beijing
Trish O'Reilly, Euro RSCG MVBMS, New York
Daniel Pankraz, Euro RSCG Partnership, Sydney
Chris Pinnington, Euro RSCG Wnek Gosper, London
Ishan Raina, Euro RSCG India, Mumbai
Juan Rocamora, Euro RSCG Southern Europe, Madrid
Rich Roth, Euro RSCG MVBMS, New York
Sid Rothberg, Euro RSCG MVBMS, New York
Eugene Seow, Euro RSCG Partnership Asia Pacific, Singapore
Phil Silvestri, Euro RSCG MVBMS, New York
Suman Srivastava, Euro RSCG India, Mumbai
Annette Stover, Euro RSCG Worldwide, New York
Marty Susz, Euro RSCG MVBMS, New York
Charlie Tarzian, Euro RSCG Circle, New York
Joanne Tilove, Euro RSCG MVBMS, New York
Michelle Verloop, Euro RSCG Worldwide, San Francisco
Dominique Verot, Carillo Pastore Euro RSCG, São Paulo
Beth Waxman, Euro RSCG MVBMS, New York
Mark Wnek, Euro RSCG Wnek Gosper, London

Thanks to our clients for allowing us to share their Creative Business Ideas—and to the other companies (that we'd someday like to have as clients) whose stories helped illustrate the power of Creative Business Ideas.

Thanks to Airié Stuart and the team at John Wiley & Sons, Emily Conway, Jessie Noyes, and Michelle Patterson for their support.

And finally, a special thank you to Andrew Jaffe who initiated my writing this book and who graciously served as a juror on our second annual Creative Business Ideas Awards.

NOTES

INTRODUCTION

1. Brian D. Biro, *Beyond Success: The 15 Secrets to Effective Leadership and Life Based on Legendary Coach John Wooden's Pyramid of Success* (New York: Perigee Books, 1997).

CHAPTER 1

1. Wendy Law-Yone, *Company Information: A Model Investigation* (Washington, DC: Washington Researchers, 1980), pp. 29–32.
2. Alice Z. Cuneo, Raymond Serafin, "Agency of the Year: With Saturn, Riney Rings Up a Winner, But Integrated Marketing Programs Work for More Clients Than GM Unit," *Advertising Age*, April 14, 1993.
3. Marie Brenner, *Going Hollywood: An Insider's Look at Power and Pretense in the Movie Business* (New York: Delacorte Press, 1978), p. 123.
4. Lorraine Spurge, *MCI: Failure Is Not an Option—How MCI Invented Competition in Telecommunications* (Encino, CA: Spurge Ink!, 1998).
5. Patricia Sellers, Joyce E. Davis (Reporter Associate), "Do You Need Your Ad Agency," *Fortune*, November 15, 1993.

CHAPTER 2

1. Langdon Winner, *The Whale and the Reactor: A Search for Limits in an Age of High Technology* (Chicago: University of Chicago Press, 1986), p. 45.
2. Naomi Klein, *No Logo: Taking Aim at the Brand Bullies* (New York: Picador, 2000), p. 31.
3. George Plimpton, ed., *Writers at Work, the Paris Review Interviews, Ninth Series* (New York: Viking Penguin, 1992).
4. Volvo Cars of North America, *Forty Years of Selling Volvo* (Surrey: Brooklands Books, 1995); "Volvo Cars 1927–1999," Volvo Car Corporation Public Relations and Public Affairs, Sweden.
5. Information in the Disney case study was drawn from the following sources: "Disney Timeline," *Daily Variety*, June 26, 1998; Jay Carke, "Disney World Celebrates 100 Years of Magic," *Miami Herald*, October 9, 2001; Bill Capodagli and Lynn Jackson, *The Disney Way: Harnessing the Management Secrets of Disney in Your Company* (New York: McGraw-Hill, 1999).
6. Akio Morita, with Edwin M. Reingold and Mitsuko Shimomura, *Made in Japan: Akio Morita and Sony* (New York: E.P. Dutton, 1986).
7. Langdon Winner, *Autonomous Technology* (Cambridge: MIT Press, 1977), p. 24.

CHAPTER 3

1. Jesse Kornbluth, "Robin Williams's Change of Life," *New York*, November 22, 1995, p. 40
2. B. Joseph Pine II and James H. Gilmore, *The Experience Economy: Work Is Theatre & Every Business a Stage* (Cambridge: Harvard Business School Press, 1999).
3. Warren G. Bennis, citation from www.brainyquote.com.
4. Oliver Wendell Holmes Sr., citation from *Investor's Business Daily*, March 5, 2001.
5. John Nathan, *SONY: The Private Life* (Boston: Houghton Mifflin Company, 1999), p. 155.
6. Akio Morita, with Edwin M. Reingold and Mitsuko Shimomura, *Made in Japan: Akio Morita and Sony* (New York: E.P. Dutton, 1986), p. 81.
7. Richard Branson, *Losing My Virginity: How I've Survived, Had Fun, and Made a Fortune Doing Business My Way* (New York: Three Rivers Press, 1998).
8. Betsy Morris, Lisa Munoz (Reporter Associate), Patricia Neering (Research), "Overcoming Dyslexia," *Fortune*, May 13, 2002.
9. Richard Branson, *Losing My Virginity: How I've Survived, Had Fun, and Made a Fortune Doing Business My Way* (New York: Three Rivers Press, 1998), p. 59.
10. Ibid., p. 152.
11. Information about Virgin cited from www.virgin.com.
12. Andrew Culf, "Thou Shalt Have a New Moral Code: Royalty and MPs Are Regarded as Setting Poor Example but Mother Teresa Seen as Ideal Person to Point Way Through Moral Maze," *Guardian*, October 10, 1994.
13. Quotes from Bill Taylor throughout this chapter are drawn from an interview conducted by Euro RSCG Worldwide in February 2002.

CHAPTER 4
1. Information in the MCI case study was drawn from Lorraine Spurge, *MCI: Failure Is Not an Option—How MCI Invented Competition in Telecommunications* (Encino, CA: Spurge Ink!, 1998), pp. 139–142, 156, 169.
2. Langdon Winner, *The Whale and the Reactor: A Search for Limits in an Age of High Technology* (Chicago: University of Chicago Press, 1986), p. 45.
3. Frederic Raphael, *Somerset Maugham* (Maynooth: Cardinal Press, 1989), p. 49.
4. Bill Capodagli and Lynn Jackson, *The Disney Way: Harnessing the Management Secrets of Disney in Your Company* (New York: McGraw-Hill, 1999), pp. 9–10.
5. Quotes from Bill Taylor throughout this chapter are drawn from an interview conducted by Euro RSCG Worldwide in February 2002.
6. Walter Lippmann, citation from www.ibiblio.com.
7. Information about Benetton cited from www.benetton.com.
8. Eric J. Lyman, "The True Colors of Toscani," *Ad Age Global,* September 1, 2001.
9. Andrew Tuck, "Interview: Luciano Benetton—True Colours," *The Independent,* June 23, 2001.
10. "Car Board," *AutoWeek,* April 13, 1998.

CHAPTER 5
1. Pierre Teilhard de Chardin, *The Phenomenon of Man* (New York: Harper Perennial, 1976).
2. Information throughout the Perdue case study was drawn from the following sources: Wendy Law-Yone, *Company Information: A Model Investigation* (Washington DC: Washington Researchers, 1980); "Forbes 500 Largest Private Companies," *Forbes,* October 2001; www.perdue.com.
3. Wendy Law-Yone, *Company Information: A Model Investigation* (Washington DC: Washington Researchers, 1980), p. 31.
4. "Forbes 500 Largest Private Companies," *Forbes,* October 2001.
5. Information for the Intel case study was drawn from the following sources: Tobi Elkin, "Co-Op Crossroads Inside Intel: A Decade Old Campaign's Long Road from Nerdville to Geek Chic," *Advertising Age,* November 15, 1999; "Intel Corporation: Branding Ingredient," prepared by Leslie Kimerling under the supervision of Associate Professor Kevin Lane Keller (now at the Amos Tuck School of Business, Dartmouth College) for a Stanford University Graduate School of Business class [with the cooperation of Intel and assistance by Dennis Carter, Sally Fundakowski and Karen Alter], December 1994; Andrew S. Grove, *Only the Paranoid Survive: How to Exploit the Crisis Points that Challenge Every Company* (New York: Currency, a division of Doubleday, 1996).
6. Tobi Elkin, "Co-Op Crossroads Inside Intel: A Decade Old Campaign's Long Road from Nerdville to Geek Chic," *Advertising Age,* November 15, 1999.
7. Andrew S. Grove, *Only the Paranoid Survive: How to Exploit the Crisis Points That Challenge Every Company.* (New York: Currency, a division of Doubleday, 1996), p. 151.
8. Joshua L. Kwan, "Robet Noyce: The Genius Behind Intel," *San Jose Mercury News,* June 20, 2001.
9. Information for the Nasdaq case study was drawn from the following sources: "New Nasdaq MarketSite Opens Formally in Times Square," *PR Newswire,* January 3, 2000; www.nasdaq.com and the Nasdaq Stock Market, Inc.

CHAPTER 6
1. Theodore Levitt, "Marketing Myopia," *Harvard Business Review,* September–October 1975.
2. Hiawatha Bray, "Wang to Be Sold to Gentronics in $2b Cash Deal," *The Boston Globe,* May 5, 1999.
3. Information for the Starbucks case study was drawn from the following sources: Howard Schultz and Dori Jones Yang, *Pour Your Heart into It* (New York: Hyperion, 1997); www.starbucks.com.
4. Howard Schultz and Dori Jones Yang, *Pour Your Heart into It* (New York: Hyperion, 1997), p. 200.
5. Information about Yahoo! cited from www.yahoo.com.
6. Marshall McLuhan, *Understanding Media* (Cambridge: MIT Press, 1994), p. 167.

7. Marjorie Williams, Bruce Brown, Ralph Gaillard Jr., "MTV as Pathfinder for Entertainment," *Washington Post,* December 13, 1989.

8. Information for the MTV case study was drawn from the following sources: Tom McGrath, *MTV: The Making of a Revolution* (Philadelphia: Running Press Book Publishers, 1996); Jack Banks, *Monopoly Television: MTV's Quest to Control the Music* (Boulder, CO: Westview Press, a division of HarperCollins, 1996).

9. Information in the Hallmark case study was drawn from: Sharon King, "Floribunda! The Business of Blooms Consolidates: A Mixed Bouquet of Acquisitions Has Built U.S.A. Floral Products," *New York Times,* July 28, 1998.

10. Information for the MCI case study was drawn from: Lorraine Spurge, *MCI: Failure Is Not an Option—How MCI Invented Competition in Telecommunications* (Encino, CA: Spurge Ink!, 1998), pp. 174–176.

11. Information for the Guinness case study was drawn from the following sources: "End of Irish Boom in Sight?" *BBC News,* August 9, 2001; www.tradepartners.gov.uk.

12. Information on Ireland cited from www.bookreporter.com/authors/au-mccourt-frank.asp.

13. Information about Guinness cited from: www.witnness.com.

14. Information on Guinness cited from BBC Radio 1 website (www.bbc.co.uk/radio1/artist_area/wilt/).

15. Information on MTV and *The Osbournes* was drawn from: Gary Levin, "MTV Re-Enlists the Osbournes," *USA Today,* May 30, 2002; Marc Peyser, "Newsmakers," *Newsweek,* June 10, 2002.

16. Suzanne Kapner, "A Testy Branson Flirts with the Market Again," *New York Times,* May 26, 2002.

17. Steven Erlanger, "An American Coffee House (or 4) in Vienna," *New York Times,* June 1, 2002.

CHAPTER 7

1. Erich Joachimsthaler, David A. Aaker, "Building Brands Without Mass Media," *Harvard Business Review,* January/February 1997.

2. Samuel Beckett citation from www.ipv.pt/millenium/Ireland_esf4.htm.

3. Information from the Guggenheim case study is drawn from Krens's presentation to Euro RSCG Worldwide, December 2000.

4. Information from the Guggenheim case study was drawn from the following sources: Mark Honigsbaum, "Saturday Review: McGuggenheim? Motorbikes and Armani—Is This Any Way to Run a Great Gallery?" *Guardian,* January 27, 2001; Clare Henry, "The Modern Art of Survival: Thomas Krens, Director of New York's Guggenheim Museum, Has a Dream," *Financial Times,* February 24, 2001; Antony Thorncroft, "The Art of Making Money: The Guggenheim Museum Is Going Global," *Financial Times,* June 6, 1998; Douglas C. McGill, "Guggenheim Names a New Director," *New York Times,* January 13, 1988; Kim Bradley, "The Deal of the Century: Opening of the Guggenheim Museum Bilbao, Spain," *Art in America,* July 1997; Silvia Sansoni, "Multinational Museums," *Forbes,* May 18, 1998; Paul Lieberman, "Museum's Maverick Showman," *Los Angeles Times,* October 20, 2000; Frederick M. Winship, "Mellon Millions to Aid Reeling Arts Groups," United Press International, December 11, 2001; www.guggenheimlasvegas.org.

5. Information regarding the Guggenheim case study was drawn from Charles Osgood (Anchor), Martha Teicher (Reporter), "The Artful Lodger; Thomas Krens Directs Guggenheim into the 21st Century with the Guggenheim Bilbao," *Sunday Morning,* CBS-TV, November 1, 1998.

6. Ibid.

7. Clare Henry, "The Modern Art of Survival: Thomas Krens, Director of New York's Guggenheim Museum, Has a Dream," *Financial Times* (London), February 24, 2001.

8. Information regarding the building of the bridge at Madero Este in Buenos Aires was drawn from an interview with Jorge Heymann, president and creative director of Heymann/Bengoa/Berbari, October 2001.

9. Paul Angyal, "Nothing Zooms Like a Moped: Fast and Cheap—Western Distributor Hopes for a Comeback," *National Post,* January 26, 2001.

CHAPTER 8

1. Rick Lyman, "Moviegoers Are Flocking to Forget Their Troubles," *New York Times,* June 21, 2002.

2. Michael J. Wolf, *The Entertainment Economy: How Mega-Media Forces Are Transforming Our Lives* (New York: Times Books, Random House, 1999), pp. 75–76.

3. Information in the Disney case study was drawn from the following sources: Written and reported by Rebecca Ascher-Walsh, Ty Burr, Betty Cortina, Steve Daley, Andrew Essex, Daniel Fierman, Jeff Gordinier, David Hochman, Jeff Jensen, Tricia Johnson, Dave Karger, Allyssa Lee, Leslie Marable, Chris Nashawaty, Joe Neumaier, Brian M. Raftery, Joshua Rich, Erin Richter, Lisa Schwarzbaum, Jessica Shaw, Tom Sinclair, Benjamin Svetky, and Chris Willman, "The Nineties," *Entertainment Weekly,* September 24, 1999; Greg Hernandez, "Under His Spell: Fans Line Up Early for First Crack at 'Harry Potter' Video," *Daily News of Los Angeles,* May 29, 2002; " 'The Lion King' Classic Book from Disney Publishing's Mouse Works Picked as No. 1 Best Selling Children's Book of 1994 by USA Today," *Business Wire,* February 13, 1995; Michael McCarthy, Fara Warner, "Mane Attraction: Marketers, Disney Put $100 Million on Nose of Lion King," *Brandweek,* March 21, 1994; Barry Singer, "Theater: Just Two Animated Characters, Indeed," *New York Times,* October 4, 1998; Patti Hartigan, "Broadway's New 'King': In the Circle of Cultural Life, Disney's Animated Hit Is Raising Hopes for a New King of Musical Theater," *Boston Globe,* November 9, 1997; Evan Henerson, " 'King' of the World? Disney May Be Just That Much Closer with Its New Musical," *Daily News of Los Angeles,* October 15, 2000; "Disney's Animal Kingdom at Walt Disney World Resort Dedicated Tuesday in African-Themed Spectacle," *PR Newswire,* April 28, 1998; www.disney.go.com/disneytheatrical/lionking/awards.html.

4. Barry Singer, "Theater: Just Two Animated Characters, Indeed," *New York Times,* October 4, 1998.

5. Information for the Crayola case study was drawn from the following sources: www.crayola.com; www.binney-smith.com; www.wackyuses.com.

6. Information in the Nokia Game case study was drawn from the following sources: "Nokia Game Kicks Off on November 4: The All-Media Adventure Expands to 28 Countries in Europe and the Middle East," Business Wire, September 2001; "Nokia Game Players Complete Geneva's Final Assignment: Final Played by 25,000 Players in 28 Countries on November 23," M2 PRESSWIRE, November 26, 2001; "Nokia and Euro RSCG Worldwide Win Gold Lion Direct for Nokia Game at 2002 International Advertising Festival in Cannes," PR Newswire, June 24, 2002.

7. Information in the Project Greenlight case study was drawn from the following sources: www.projectgreenlight.com; Hayley Kaufman, "An Emerging Writer and Reluctant Star," *Boston Globe,* March 17, 2002; "LivePlanet on Track in Effort to Integrate Media in Entertainment and Technology," *Business Wire,* June 4, 2001; Mark Caro, "The Reel Reality: Pete Jones Won a Screenwriting Contest. His Prize? Being Filmed by HBO While He's Filming," *Chicago Tribune,* July 15, 2001; Kenneth Turan, "Movie Review: Drama in the Filmmaking, Not the Film," *Los Angeles Times,* March 22, 2002; Caryn James, "TV Weekend: Novice Directors, Be Careful What You Pray For," *New York Times,* November 30, 2001.

8. Kenneth Turan, "Movie Review: Drama in the Filmmaking, Not the Film," *Los Angeles Times,* March 22, 2002.

9. "LivePlanet on Track in Effort to Integrate Media in Entertainment and Technology," *Business Wire,* June 4, 2001.

10. Information in the Edwin Schlossberg case study was drawn from the following sources: "From the Publisher: A Conversation with Edwin Schlossberg, Author of *Interactive Excellence: Defining and Developing New Standards for the Twenty-First Century,*" Amazon.com; www.esidesign.com.

CHAPTER 9

1. Quotes from Bill Taylor throughout this chapter are drawn from an interview conducted by Euro RSCG in February 2002.

2. Tom Kelley with Jonathon Littman, *The Art of Innovation: Lessons in Creativity from IDEO, America's Leading Design Firm* (New York: Currency Books, Doubleday, 2001), p. 69.

3. Ibid., p. 71.

4. Information pertaining to IDEO's shopping cart project for *Nightline* was taken from *The Art of Innovation*, pp. 6–13.

5. Ibid., p. 56.

6. Charles Brower citation from www.wilcherish.com/cardshop/quotes/brower1.htm.

7. Presentation by Tom Kelley at Euro RSCG Worldwide 100-Day Meeting in Las Vegas, November 16, 2001.

8. *The Art of Innovation,* pp. 121–126.

9. Ibid., p. 123.

10. Ibid., p. 124.

11. Ibid., p. 146.

12. William Irwin Thompson, *At the Edge of History* (New York: Harper & Row, 1971), p. 178.

CREDITS

PHOTO CREDITS

Perdue, p. 22. Perdue is a registered trademark of Perdue Farms Inc.

Sony Walkman, p. 35. Copyright © Richard Pasley/Stock Boston LLC. Walkman is a registered trademark of Sony Corporation.

Virgin, p. 42. Getty Images. Virgin logo is a registered trademark of Virgin Enterprises Limited.

Virgin Atlantic Airways, p. 45. Getty Images. Virgin Atlantic is a registered trademark of Virgin Enterprises Limited.

Benetton Fabrica Features, p. 55. Copyright © Stefano Beggiato for Fabrica. Reproduced with permission of Benetton Group.

Volvo for life, p. 60. Copyright © Craig Cameron Olsen. Copyright © 2000–2002, Volvo Car Corporation, Volvo Cars of North America LLC or their related companies. Used with permission.

Revolvolution, p. 65. Copyright © Chris Bailey. Copyright © 2000–2002, Volvo Car Corporation, Volvo Cars of North America LLC or their related companies. Used with permission.

Intel, p. 80. Reproduced with permission of Intel Corporation.

Intel BunnyPeople, p. 82. BunnyPeople™ character is a trademark of Intel Corporation. Reproduced with permission of Intel Corporation.

Intel Bicycle Reflector, p. 85. Reproduced with permission of Intel Corporation.

Nasdaq, p. 89. Copyright © Alex Farnsworth/The Image Works.

RATP, p. 96. Copyright © Sébastien Meunier.

Starbucks, p. 100. Copyright © Vincent Dewitt/Stock Boston.

Yahoo!, p. 106. Copyright © 1999 Yahoo! Inc. All rights reserved.

MTV, p. 107. Copyright © Jan Butchofsky-Houser/Corbis. MTV is a registered trademark of MTV Networks.

Hallmark Flowers, p. 112. Hallmark is a registered trademark of Hallmark Licensings, Inc.

Hallmark Flowers, p. 117. Reproduced with the permission of Hallmark Cards, Inc.

1-800-COLLECT, p. 119. 1-800-COLLECT is a registered trademark of MCI.

Guggenheim New York, p. 141. Photograph by David Heald. Copyright © Solomon R. Guggenheim Foundation, New York.

Guggenheim Bilbao, p. 145. Copyright © Margaret Ross/Stock Boston.

The Art of the Motorcycle, p. 147. Photograph by Ellen Labenski. Copyright © Solomon R. Guggenheim Foundation, New York.

Puerto Madero, Buenos Aires, p. 153. Copyright © Michael Dwyer/Stock Boston.

Lion King, p. 161. Copyright © Michael Newman/Photo Edit, Inc.

Crayola Crayons, p. 163. Reproduced with the permission of Binney & Smith Inc., maker of Crayola products. Copyright © Network Productions/The Image Works.

Room Service, p. 175. Copyright © Petter Karlberg.

Project Greenlight, p. 178. Project Greenlight is a registered trademark of Project Greenlight and Greenlight Marks.

ESI Macomber Farm, p. 181. Copyright © 1982, Donald Dietz. Reproduced with permission of ESI Design.

IDEO, Palto Alto, p. 202. Copyright © Roberto Carra. Reproduced with permission of IDEO.

Fuel North America, Euro RSCG MVBMS Partners, p. 203. Copyright © Ruggero Vanni, IMAGELEAP, Inc.

BETC Euro RSCG Paris, p. 205. Copyright © Hervé Abbadie.

BETC Euro RSCG Paris, p. 206. Copyright © Hervé Abbadie.

CraveroLanis Euro RSCG Buenos Aires, p. 207. Reproduced with the permission of Apertura and Target Magazines.

TEXT CREDITS

Chapters 1, 2, 4 and 9. VOLVO, VOLVO FOR LIFE and the VOLVO logo are registered trademarks of Volvo Trademark Holding AB. REVOLVOLUTION is a trademark of Volvo Trademark Holding AB.

Chapters 1 and 5. Wendy Law-Yone, *Company Information: A Model Investigation* (Washington, D.C.: Washington Researchers, 1980).

Chapters 2 and 3. Akio Morita with Edwin M. Reingold and Mitsuko Shimomura, *Made in Japan: Akio Morita and Sony* (New York: E.P. Dutton, 1986). Reprinted with the permission of E. P. Dutton Penguin Putnam Inc.

Chapters 2 and 4. Bill Capodagli and Lynn Jackson, *The Disney Way: Harnessing the Management Secrets of Disney in Your Company* (New York: McGraw-Hill, 1999). Copyright © 1999 by the Center for Quality Leadership. Reprinted with the permission of The McGraw-Hill Companies.

Chapters 2, 4 and 8. This book makes reference to various Disney copyrighted characters, trademarks, marks and registered marks owned by The Walt Disney Company and Disney Enterprises, Inc., and are used by permission.

Chapter 3. "Overcoming Dyslexia," *Fortune,* May 13, 2002. Reprinted by permission.

Chapter 3. John Nathan, SONY: *The Private Life* (Boston: Houghton Mifflin Company, 1999). Copyright © 1999 by John Nathan. Reprinted with the permission of Houghton Mifflin Company. All rights reserved.

Chapter 4. "The True Colors of Toscani," *Ad Age Global,* September 1, 2001. Reprinted with permission from the September 2001 issue of Ad Age Global. Copyright © Crain Communications Inc., 2001.

Chapter 5. "Intel Corporation: Branding Ingredient," prepared by Leslie Kimerling under the supervision of Associate Professor Kevin Lane Keller (now at the Amos Tuck School of Business, Dartmouth College) for a Stanford University Graduate School of Business class [with the cooperation of Intel and assistance by Dennis Carter, Sally Fundakowski and Karen Alter], December 1994. Reprinted with the permission of Associate Professor Kevin Lane Keller, Amos Tuck School of Business, Dartmouth College.

Chapter 5. Andrew S. Grove, *Only the Paranoid Survive: How to Exploit the Crisis Points that Challenge Every Company.* (New York: Currency (a division of Doubleday), 1996). Reprinted with the permission of Doubleday, a division of Random House, Inc.

Chapter 6. Tom McGrath, *MTV: The Making of a Revolution* (Philadelphia: Running Press Book Publishers, 1996). Copyright © 1996 by Tom McGrath, published by Running Press Book Publishers, Philadelphia and London.

Chapter 6. Jack Banks, *Monopoly Television: MTV's Quest to Control the Music* (Boulder, CO: Westview Press, A Division of HarperCollins, 1996). Copyright © 1996 by Westview Press. Reprinted by permission of Westview Press, a member of Perseus Books, LLC.

Chapter 6. "Sing a Song of Seeing; Rock Videos Are Firing Up a Musical Revolution," *Time,* December 26, 1983. Copyright © 1983 by Time, Inc. Reprinted by permission.

Chapter 7. "Multinational Museums," *Forbes,* May 18, 1998. Used with permission from Forbes.

Chapter 7. "The Artful Lodger; Thomas Krens Directs Guggenheim into the 21st Century with the Guggenheim Bilbao," Sunday Morning, November 1, 1998. Used with permission of CBS News/*Sunday Morning.*

Chapter 7. Information from the Guggenheim case study used with permission of Thomas Krens, Director, The Solomon R. Guggenheim Foundation.

Chapter 8. Michael J. Wolf, *The Entertainment Economy: How Mega-Media Forces Are Transforming Our Lives* (New York: Times Books (Random House), 1999). Copyright © 1999 by Michael J. Wolf. Reprinted with the permission of Times Books, a division of Random House, Inc.

Chapter 8. "Theater; Just Two Animated Characters, Indeed," *The New York Times,* October 4, 1998. Copyright © 1998 by The New York Times Company. Reprinted by permission.

Chapter 9. Tom Kelley with Jonathon Littman, *The Art of Innovation: Lessons in Creativity from IDEO, America's Leading Design Firm.* (New York: Currency Books, Doubleday, 2001). Reprinted with the permission of Doubleday, a division of Random House, Inc.

Index

Absolut Reality, 93
Ad agencies:
  business focus of, 176–177, 212
  clients of (see Clients, of ad agencies)
  as creative thinkers, 26
  cross-discipline, 209–210, 219
  partnerships with, 183, 184, 220
  single-client, 204, 208–209
Ad campaigns:
  Dean's Milk Chug, 130–132
  Friends and Family (MCI), 12, 50
  Intel Inside®, 22, 80–86
  I Want My MTV, 110
  Nokia Game, 169–173
  1-800-COLLECT (MCI), 118–120
  Orange One (Hutchison), 120–123
  for Paris metro (RATP), 93, 208
  Perdue, 72–77
  for Puerto Madero (Buenos Aires), 150–155
  Red X (Intel), 78–80
  Revolvolution (Volvo), 61–70, 208
  Rock the Vote, 111
  Room Service TV series, 174–176
  Survivors (Volvo), 60–61, 192
  United Colors of Benetton, 54–56
  Witness (Guinness), 123–128, 172
Advertising:
  business market as target for, 50
  co-op, 80–81
  demise of, 157, 160, 177, 218
  entertainment value in, 160
  function of, 74
  going beyond, 149, 174, 176, 220
  interactive, 83, 138
  local, 204
  as marketing vehicle, 119
  role of, 74
  on television, 66, 81, 105, 110, 126, 129, 137–138
  ubiquity of, 16
Affleck, Ben, 177, 178

Ailes, Roger, 12
Alliances:
  with agencies, 183, 184
  as marketing strategy, 168
  with nontraditional partners, 179, 218–219
Alternative knowledge, value of, 29
Amazon.com, 203
America Online, 66
Andreesen, Marc, 201
A Nous Paris (newspaper), 96
AOL Time Warner building, design of, 180
Architecture:
  effect on company culture, 201–208, 210, 219
  interactive design in, 180
  promotional role of, 140, 142, 151–155
Armani, Giorgio, 147
The Art of Innovation (Kelley), 186
The Art of the Motorcycle exhibit, 146, 147

Beerda, Sicco, 170
Benetton, 54–57
Benetton, Luciano, 56–57
Berger, Ron, 10, 27, 88, 89
BETC Euro RSCG, 93, 94, 205–208
Bezos, Jeff, 203
Bienert, Phil, 69
Bikker Euro RSCG, 170
Bilbao (Spain):
  Guggenheim Museum in, 145–146
  as tourist destination, 149
  transformation of, 152–153
Billiken, 165–169, 208
Binney & Smith, 163–165
Black Rocket, 104–105
The Body Shop, 139
Boender, Marco, 170
Bohlin, Nils, 20
Bourne, Phil, 125, 214
Brainstorming, in creative process, 186, 188, 192

Brand:
  building, 75, 76, 79, 85, 139,
    160–162
  in business strategy, 29, 56, 219
  as CBI component, 30–31, 44,
    147
  commodity as, 21, 24, 50, 74, 80,
    86–87
  consumer connection to, 170,
    172, 176
  consumer participation in,
    165–169
  defining, 39, 150
  differentiating, 129–131, 167
  extending, 113–118
  in Five Points process, 196
  "glocal," 205
  importance of, 15–16, 217
  nontraditional product as, 140,
    142, 153
  rejuvenating, 123–128, 165, 166,
    184
  virtual entity as, 87–90
Brand ambassadors:
  customers as, 111
  employees as, 100–101
Brand awareness:
  building, 150
  cross-border, 172
  nontraditional media for, 66,
    84–85
Brand equity, 106, 164
Brand experience:
  as CBI component, 30–31
  creating, 24
  defining, 163
  Disneyland as, 20–21
  as entertainment, 172, 179,
    219–220
  Hallmark as, 115, 164–165
  interactive game as, 170
  The Lion King as, 160–162
  Starbucks as, 100–102
  television series as vehicle for,
    174–176
Brand image, 34, 163
Brand loyalty, 102, 167
Brand team, 94–96

Branson, Richard:
  business interests of, 41–45
  future prospects of, 134–135
  as renegade, 38–39
Bravo cable television network, 70
British Motor Corporation, 2–3
Buenos Aires (Argentina):
  advertising work in, 148–149,
    207
  creating landmark for, 18–19, 31,
    150–154, 213
Business, nature of, 102–103, 221
Business category:
  level of knowledge about, 165,
    190
  recognizing, 91–92, 97, 111, 118,
    219
  reinventing, 187–188
  reviving, 155–157
  revolutionizing, 130–132,
    176–177
Business model:
  developing, 96
  old versus new, 211, 219
Business strategy:
  agency role in, 212
  brand in, 29, 56
  creative thinking in, 8, 14, 20,
    24, 25, 44, 67, 143, 189
  developing, 103
  repositioning in, 156
  shifting, 131, 167
Business utility vehicles (BUVs),
    156, 157

Cadbury, 139–140
Calatrava, Santiago, 154, 213
Carey, Wally, Jr., 10
Carter, Dennis, 77–81, 86
CEOs:
  as company spokespersons, 76, 77
  creativity and, 33–38, 45–47,
    82–83
  dyslexia among, 40
Chambers, John, 40–41
Change:
  CBI role of, 32
  in company culture, 68

Chiarello, Stacy, 10
Clients, of ad agencies:
   involvement level of, 194,
      215–216
   relationship with, 116, 208–215,
      220, 221
   role of, 7, 51, 191
   understanding business of,
      102–103, 165, 190
Collaboration:
   agency-client, 116, 220, 221
   with consumers, 166–169
   creativity through, 126, 183–184
   importance of, 71–72, 97
Colors magazine, 55
Commodities, as brands, 21, 24, 50,
   74, 80, 86–87
Communication, as CBI component, 30, 44
Company culture:
   actions and attitudes in, 102
   creativity in, 49, 51–54, 57, 68,
      199
   employee respect in, 100–101
   physical space as effect on,
      201–208, 210, 219
Company structure:
   creative thinking in, 184–185
   cross-discipline approach to,
      209–210
   nonhierarchical, 190, 191, 199,
      201, 204, 205, 208, 219
Competitions:
   Creative Business Idea awards,
      57–59, 92, 138, 165, 208
   International Advertising Festival,
      59, 138, 172
   Project Greenlight, 177–178
Consulting firms, 183, 184
Consumers:
   as brand ambassadors, 111
   brand participation by, 165–169
   connecting with, 169–172, 176
   redefining relationship with, 179,
      219
   understanding, 102–103
   versus users, 95
Consumer trends, 132

Co-op advertising, 80–81
CraveroLanis Euro RSCG, 166,
   207–208
Crayola, 163–165, 173
Creative Business Ideas (CBIs):
   awards for, 57–59, 92, 138, 165,
      208
   brand relationship to, 113, 118,
      147
   change as force in, 32
   components of, 30–31, 44
   courage required for, 31, 217
   creation of, 196–197
   for customer experience, 42
   defined, 30
   environment for, 53, 68, 213–215
   examples of, 18–24, 97
   introduction of, 58
   need for, 17, 26
   as ongoing process, 69
   origin of concept, 27–28
   on small scale, 134
   thought process for, 24, 41
   versus traditional commercials,
      137
Creative leap:
   to business strategy, 24, 25
   CEO as instigator of, 33, 46
   as nonlinear, 31
   sources for, 111
   springboard for, 192
   timing of, 210
Creative thinking:
   as business strategy, 8, 14, 20, 44,
      67, 189, 218, 220
   by children, 168–169
   through collaboration, 126,
      183–184
   in company structure, 184–185,
      219
   domain of, 25, 181–182
   dyslexia and, 39–40
   failure and, 148
   as intellectual capital, 217
   by necessity, 140
   nonlinear, 18, 24
   process for, 186–188, 195–197,
      201

to redefine business, 157
starting with, 103
targeted, 190–191, 195
from teams, 184–185, 203, 211
Creativity:
  business role of, 31, 33–38,
    45–47, 139, 143, 221
  in company culture, 49, 51–54,
    57
  demand for, 17, 29
  nature of, 4, 185–186
  on television, 137–138
Cumming, Matt, 121
Customer experience. *See also* Brand
    experience
  creating, 42, 44
  as entertainment, 159, 162

Dahlin, John, 214
Dahlin Smith White, 79
Damon, Matt, 177, 178
Dean Foods, 130–132
Discipline, need for, 190, 192, 195,
    197, 199, 220
Disney, Walt, 21, 53
Disney Company, 160–162
Disneyland, 20–21, 53
Distribution channel, changing, 131,
    132
Donoghue, John, 119
Door-to-door selling, 122–123
Dot-com phenomenon, 189
Dreyer, Bill, 40
Durante, Jay, 63–64
Durfee, Jim, 215
Dyslexia, 39–40

Edwin Schlossberg Incorporated
    (ESI), 180
Eisner, Michael, 53, 162
Ellis Island museum, interactive
    exhibit at, 181
Employee recognition programs,
    51–52, 57–59
Employees:
  brand building role of,
    100–101
  empowerment of, 57, 201

Empowerment:
  of consumers, 196
  of employees, 57, 201
Engellau, Gunnar, 20, 38
Entertainment:
  brand experience as, 115,
    162–165, 172, 175, 176,
    219–220
  integrated media in, 179
  U.S. focus on, 159–160
The Entertainment Economy (Wolf),
    159
Euro RSCG Corporate, 93
Euro RSCG Five Points™ process,
    195–197
Euro RSCG India, 155
Euro RSCG Manille, 133
Euro RSCG MVBMS, 27, 164
Euro RSCG Partnership (Sydney),
    120
Euro RSCG Söderberg Arbman,
    173
Euro RSCG Tatham Partners, 79,
    130
Euro RSCG Worldwide:
  creative thinking at, 26–28
  Intel relationship with, 81
  origins of, 13–14
  reward program at, 58–59
  structure of, 195

Fabrica, 55–57
Facilitators, 95
Fast Company magazine, 37
Fear:
  as creative inhibitor, 199–200,
    217, 218
  as motivator, 200–201
Films, as brand experience,
    177–178. *See also specific films*
Filo, David, 104
Flaherty, Glen, 215
Friends and Family campaign
    (MCI), 12, 50
Fuel North America, 204–205, 208

Gallate, George, 81
Gehry, Frank, 146

Globalization:
  of brands, 205
  community aspect of, 172
  customization for, 83
  via Internet, 177
Good Will Hunting (film), 177
Green Giant, 132–135
Grove, Andy:
  ability to recognize creativity, 78,
    82, 83
  business strategy of, 85–86, 200
  office size of, 203
Guerrilla marketing, 126
Guggenheim Bilbao, 145–146
Guggenheim Museums, 140–148
Guinness, 123–128
Gwathmey Siegel & Associates
    Architects, 143

Hall, Joyce C., 112
Hallmark Cards:
  as brand, 113–117
  CEO of, 27
  Crayola brand and, 163–165, 173
  origins of, 112
Hallmark Entertainment, 165
Hallmark Flowers, 112, 115–117
Hart, Peter, 12
Hatchuel, Romain, 59, 138
HBO, 177, 178
HCM, 9
Hero Puch, 155–157
Heymann, Jorge, 148–155
Heymann/Bengoa/Berbari, 18
Hockaday, Irvine O., Jr.:
  as ad agency partner, 184
  brand leadership by, 112, 113
  as visionary, 27, 215
Holland, Brian, 88, 89
Horbury, Peter, 61
Huffstetler, Jim, 116, 117
Human-i Euro RSCG, 170
Hutchison Telecommunications,
    120–123

Ibuka, Masura, 23
IDEO:
  creative team process at, 186–189
  office space of, 202–203

Information sharing, 5, 189–195,
    199, 214
Innovation. *See* Creative thinking
Inside the Actors Studio (TV pro-
    gram), 70
Intel:
  ad agency relationship with,
    81–82
  brand awareness of, 83–86
  BunnyPeople campaign,
    82–83
  Computer Inside™ campaign,
    78–80
  fear factor at, 200
  Intel Inside® campaign, 22, 80–81
  Red X campaign, 78, 79
Interactivity:
  in advertising, 83, 138
  as brand experience, 170
  in design of spaces, 180–182
  in marketing, 70
International Advertising Festival,
    58, 59, 138, 148, 172
Internet:
  as business facilitator, 83
  communities created on, 177
  as marketing medium, 66–67, 69,
    126, 168, 169, 171–172
  marketplace impact of, 112
  navigating, 103–106

Katz, Aron, 214
Kelley, Tom, 186–189, 202, 203
KLP Euro RSCG, 123, 125
Knowledge:
  alternative, 29
  sharing of, 189–195, 199, 214
Krens, Thomas, 14, 140–148

Lack, John, 108, 109
Leadership. *See also* CEOs
  creativity recognized by, 33–38,
    46–47, 51
  as integral to CBIs, 148, 218
LeMarre, Jim, 4
Lin, Mason, 84
The Lion King (film), 160–162
LivePlanet, 179
Losing My Virginity (Branson), 39

Made in Japan (Morita), 36
Malaremastarna (Swedish Association of Painting Contractors), 173–176
Marketing:
  via advertising, 119
  awards for, 138
  entertainment value in, 160
  via films, 177–178
  via Internet, 66–67, 69, 126, 168, 169, 171–172
  product tie-ins in, 161
MarketSite, 89
Massachusetts Society for the Prevention of Cruelty to Animals, interactive exhibit by, 180–181
Massey, Wright, 101
Mass media:
  business market as target for, 50
  European versus U.S., 138–139
  going beyond, 84–85, 140, 168
  as traditional approach, 150
McCabe, Ed, 7, 72, 75
McCarthy, Sean, 66
MCI:
  advertising for, 11–12, 50
  creative culture at, 49–52
  new business categories for, 118–120
  trust-based agency relationship, 213
Media planning, 138
Merchandising, via *The Lion King,* 161
Messer, Thomas, 142
Messner, Tom, 10, 11, 51
Messner Vetere Berger Carey, 10–12
Messner Vetere Berger McNamee Schmetterer (MVBMS):
  flat structure at, 52, 201
  with Hallmark, 115, 116
  with MCI, 118
  origin of, 13
  Volvo as client of, 213
  war rooms at, 193
Mills Panoram Soundies, 108
Miramax Films, 177
Mistakes, dealing with, 199–200, 217

Moore, Chris, 177, 179
Morita, Akio, 23, 36–38
Moult, Tom, 214
MTV, 106–111, 134
Multimedia:
  as entertainment breakthrough, 179, 220
  in marketing strategy, 171, 175

Narrowcasting, 108
Nasdaq, 87–90
National Association of Securities Dealers (NASD), 87
Nesmith, Michael, 108
Netscape, 201
Newman, Jane, 197
Ney, Ed, 9
Nickelodeon, 108
Nokia, 169–172
Nonlinear thinking:
  in business domain, 25, 218
  in creativity, 18, 24, 31
  in dyslexia, 40, 41
  in MTV development, 109
Noyce, Robert, 86

Ogilvy & Mather, 9
Ohga, Norio, 36
Olsson, Hans-Olov, 63, 64, 68
100-Day Meeting, 27
Only the Paranoid Survive (Grove), 85
Orange One campaign (Hutchison), 120–123
Osbourne, Ozzy, 134

Pankraz, Daniel, 213
Paris metro. *See* RATP
Passion, role of, 4, 37, 38, 76, 102, 221
Peggy Guggenheim Museum, 143–144
Pentagram design firm, 149, 155
Perdue, Frank:
  advertising by, 74–77
  brand establishment by, 21–22, 73–74
  as early agency client, 6–7, 72–73
  passion of, 38

Perdue chicken:
   brand experience of, 30–31, 87
   origin of, 73
   pricing by, 75
Pesky, Alain, 72
Physical space, cultural effect of,
   201–208, 210, 219
Pittman, Bob, 109, 110
Plana, Eduardo, 149
The Pocket Calculator Game Book
   (Schlossberg), 179
Pour Your Heart into It (Schultz),
   99
Pouzilhac, Havas Alain de, 14
Price, Timothy, 119
Product:
   in brand tie-ins, 161
   as CBI component, 30, 44, 151
   design of, 186
   versus entertainment, 220
   improvement of, 16
   reinventing category for, 187–188
   repositioning of, 156
Project Greenlight, 177–179
Project management team, 116
Prosumer, defined, 196
Puerto Madero (Buenos Aires),
   150–155, 207

RATP (Regie Autonome des Transports Parisiens):
   agency evaluation of, 93–94
   problems with, 92
   transformation of, 95–97
   trust-based agency relationship,
   213
   users of, 94–95
Record industry, 109–111
Regina, 194–195
Renegade, role of, 38–39
Research:
   online, 67
   role of, 31
Reuters headquarters, 149
Revolvolution ad campaign, 61–70,
   208
Risk taking, 199, 217
Rock the Vote, 111

Roddick, Anita, 139
Room Service TV series, 174–176

Salzman, Marian, 197
Scali, Sam, 7, 72
Scali McCabe Sloves, 6, 8, 72, 74,
   108
Schlossberg, Edwin, 179–182
Schultz, Howard, 98–101, 135
Scopitone, 108
Securities and Exchange Commis-
   sion (SEC), 87
Seibert, Fred, 109
Select Comfort, 128–130
Shareholder value, 100
Shaywitz, Sally, 40
Sloves, Marvin, 5, 6, 72
Social activism, brand building via,
   139
Soho Guggenheim, 144, 148
Sony Betamax, 38
Sony Walkman, 23–24, 31, 35–38
Sony Wonder Technology Lab,
   180
Starbucks, 98–102, 135
Stolen Summer (film), 178
Strategic planning, 24, 197–199
Student magazine, 39, 41
Survivors campaign (Volvo), 60–61,
   192
Sutherland, Donald, 19, 60
Swatch, 139
Swedish Association of Painting
   Contractors (Malaremastarna),
   173–176

Taylor, Bill:
   on ad agency relationship, 212
   on creativity, 37
   on fear, 200–201
   on fresh perspectives, 53–54, 184
   on leadership and innovation, 46
Taylor, Jerry, 49, 199
Teams:
   brand, 94–96
   clients as members of, 191
   creative thinking from, 184–185,
   203, 211, 220

physical environment for, 202–203
project management, 116
work process of, 186–187
Technology, brand building role of,
    103, 105, 106
Television:
    as advertising medium, 66, 81,
        105, 110, 126, 129, 137–138
    as brand experience, 174–176
    interactive ads on, 83
    MTV role in, 106–111, 134
Thriller video, impact of, 111
Toscani, Oliviero, 55–57
Trust, role of, 5, 81, 213–215

Unique selling proposition, 16, 211,
    220
United Colors of Benetton, 54–56

Values, in brand identity, 114, 165
Van Liemt, Joost, 170
Vetere, Barry, 10, 51, 113, 115
Virgin Group:
    brand image of, 41–45
    future of, 134
    as unconventional, 38–39
Volvo cars:
    brand image of, 19–20, 59–61
    customer profile for, 4–5

dedicated agency for, 204
Revolvolution campaign,
    61–70
Survivors campaign, 191–192
trust-based agency relationship,
    213

Wang Laboratories, 91
Warner Amex, 108
War rooms:
    in company culture, 193, 201,
        204
    function of, 12
    knowledge applied in, 192–195
    origin of, 189–190
    physical space for, 190–191,
        203
    in planning, 199
Webcasting, 83
White, Jon, 79
Whitehead, Graham, 3, 89
Windows of knowledge, 12, 190,
    191, 193, 194
Witness ad campaign, 123–128,
    172

Yahoo!®, 103–106
Yang, Jerry, 104
Young & Rubicam, 9

About the Author

Bob Schmetterer is Chairman and CEO of Euro RSCG Worldwide. Under his leadership, Euro RSCG Worldwide has grown from the ninth to the fifth-largest marketing communications company in the world, with 233 offices in 75 countries, and ranks in the top 10 in Advertising, Marketing Services, Healthcare, and Interactive.

Throughout his career, Bob has been recognized as an industry innovator and leader as well as an enthusiastic and vocal proponent of change, innovation, and creativity in the business environment. He speaks frequently on consumer market dynamics and communication technology, the relationships between advertising and entertainment, and inspiring and rewarding new kinds of thinking. *Advertising Age* called Bob a "creative visionary with a clear view of the future of our business," and *Business Week* has profiled him as a "mover and shaker" in digital marketing.

Bob's vision and belief that those in the advertising industry are best equipped to think creatively about communications has been integral in developing Euro RSCG Worldwide's Creative Business Ideas™—concepts that, through groundbreaking thinking, transform regular business into unique and irresistible consumer experiences. He believes the benefits are great for companies that can instill the magic of creativity into the very fabric and nature of their business. This kind of innovative thinking has led to brilliant campaigns for such clients as Intel, Peugeot, Air France, Orange, Abbey National, MCI, Danone Group, Reckitt Benckiser, Volvo and Yahoo!

He was among the first to recognize the impact that the Internet would have on advertising and to encourage clients and colleagues to start thinking about integrated, media-neutral campaigns. In addition, he sits on the board of directors of Havas and is active in several other organizations, including the Foundation Board of the International Institute for Management Development (IMD), the New York Chapter of AAAA, the advisory board of @d Tech, and the steering committee of the ANA/AAA new media organization, CASIE. He has been the keynote speaker at numerous events and conferences, including the Cannes Lions International Advertising Festival, the AAAA-ANA Conference, the Jupiter Global Online Advertising Forum, and the Yahoo! National Sales Conference.

Earlier in his career, Bob was Chief Operating Officer of Scali McCabe Sloves, Chief Executive Officer of HCM Worldwide, and a founding partner of Messner Vetere Berger McNamee Schmetterer Euro RSCG.